Building English Skills

Red Level

Building English Skills   Purple Level

Building English Skills   Yellow Level

Building English Skills   Blue Level

Building English Skills   Orange Level

Building English Skills   Green Level

Building English Skills   Red Level

Building English Skills

Red Level

Prepared by the Staff of
The Writing Improvement Project

McDougal, Littell & Company
Evanston, Illinois

Staff of THE WRITING IMPROVEMENT PROJECT

J. A. Christensen, East High School, Salt Lake City, Utah

Kathleen L. Bell, Lincoln Junior High School, Mount Prospect, Illinois

Donna Rae Blackall, Chairperson, English Department, Miner Junior High School, Arlington Heights, Illinois

Eric L. Kraft, Writer and Editor, Stow, Massachusetts

Joy Littell, Editorial Director. McDougal, Littell & Company

M. Rachel McKay, Writer and Editor, Chicago, Illinois

William A. Seabright, Director of Design, McDougal, Littell & Company

Project Assistant: Peggy Jo Schleker

For their cooperation in the development of the sections on grammar, usage, and mechanics, grateful acknowledgment is made to:

Thomas Clark Pollock, Professor of English Emeritus of New York University, and Past President of the National Council of Teachers of English

Robert W. Rounds, Professor of English Emeritus, State University of New York College at Oneonta.

ISBN: 0–88343–450–4

Copyright © 1978 by McDougal, Littell & Company
Box 1667, Evanston, Illinois 60204
All rights reserved. Printed in the United States of America

The twelve sections on grammar, usage, and mechanics
contain, in revised form, some materials that
appeared originally in *The Macmillan English
Series, Grade 7,* by Thomas Clark Pollock et al.,
copyright © 1963, 1960, 1954 by The Macmillan Company.
Used by arrangement.

Contents

The page numbers for the Grammar and Usage sections (the second half of this book) appear in red.

The Table of Contents for

Grammar, Usage, and Mechanics

begins on the next page.

Grammar, Usage, and Mechanics

Chapter 1

The Story of Our Language

There are more than half a million words in the English language. Where did they all come from? We could give a quick answer to that question by saying that most of the words in English were "borrowed" from other languages. There is more to the story than that, however. To tell the whole story we have to begin in prehistoric times.

Part 1   The History of Our Language

The First Words

We are not sure who spoke the first words. We are not sure where they were spoken. We are not sure when they were spoken. We don't even know what they were. In trying to determine how words started, people have come up with some interesting ideas. One idea is that prehistoric people made noises that became words. If you lift something heavy, you might say "uh." If you are cold, you might say "brrr." If you are hot, you might say "whew." If someone gives you a cold drink, you might say "ahhh." People in prehistoric times probably made noises like these, too.

Uh, brrr, whew, and *ahh* are not quite words, but they could be used as words. Suppose you really used *ahhh* to mean "a cold drink." Suppose you really used *uh* to mean "a hard job" or "something heavy." Then *ahhh* and *uh* would be real words.

Another idea is that prehistoric people imitated the sounds they heard around them. These sounds could have become names for things. A saber-toothed tiger might have been called something like "grrr." Thunder might have been called "boom" or "crash."

Either of these ideas about the first words may be right. Both ideas may be right. Both ideas may be wrong. No one knows. It all happened so long ago that the beginning of our story will always be a mystery. All we know is that at some time, somewhere, someone began using sounds as words.

Exercise   The First Words

Suppose that the first words did come from sounds that prehistoric people made, or sounds that they heard around them. If you had been one of these early speakers, what might you have called each of the following things?

wind	burning twigs
pain	a dog
an owl	a cat
applause	happiness
a stream	sadness

The Beginnings of Different Languages

As time passed, the people who had invented language began to scatter in different directions. This scattering did not happen all at once. It took hundreds or thousands of years. People traveled in tribes looking for places where the hunting was good. Some tribes were driven away by others. Other tribes explored and settled in new areas.

As these tribes scattered, they took their language with them. In new places there were new animals and plants to talk about. There were new dangers and new tasks to talk about. As a result of new experiences, the language began to change. As the tribes grew far apart, their languages became very different from each other.

How do we know that all this happened? Linguists—people who study language—saw that some languages are related. They could see that some words in one language are like some words in another. For instance, they could see that English and German are related, so they began some language detective work. The clues told the linguists that English and German both come from an earlier language. They called this earlier language West Germanic.

Clues showed that other languages were related, also. French, Italian, Spanish, and Portuguese all seemed to be related. All of these languages came from Latin, the language spoken by the ancient Romans.

From the clues, linguists could draw "family trees" for these languages.

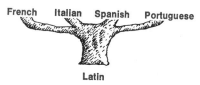

English German   French Italian Spanish Portuguese

West Germanic   Latin

Linguists had many more clues to work with, however. They could see that Latin and West Germanic were related to each other, too. Both must have come from still another language that had been spoken long ago. Linguists found additional languages that seemed related to West Germanic and Latin. All these languages seemed to have had one ancient ancestor. They had all come from one prehistoric language.

What was this language? Who spoke it? Where did the people live? The detective work went on. Linguists continued to study the words of Latin, West Germanic, and other ancient languages. They looked for words that these languages had in common. They found words for animals and plants that are found only in certain areas. For instance, they found that these languages had words for "bear" and "wolf" but not for "tiger" or "camel." From clues like these, some linguists decided that the prehistoric language had begun somewhere in northern Europe. While this conclusion may not be quite right, it seems like a good guess.

Linguists call the prehistoric language Indo-European. It was the language of the tribes that had scattered over India and Europe such a long time ago.

Native English Words

About A.D. 500, three tribes of people were living in northern Europe. They were the Angles, the Saxons, and the Jutes. They spoke one of the West Germanic languages. Linguists call their language Anglo-Saxon. We can think of Anglo-Saxon as the beginning of the English we speak today. In fact, some words used in Anglo-Saxon are still used in English today. We can call them native English words.

4

At the beginning of this chapter we said that most English words have been borrowed from other languages. The rest are native English words. Of the half million words in English, only about 15 percent are native English words. These important words are the simple, basic words of English. We couldn't do without them. They are words like *the*, *get*, *there*, *is*, and *of*. They are also words for basic ideas, such as *fire*, *word*, and *life*.

Let's look at the "top ten" English words. These words are used more often than any others:

the   of   and   a   to   in   is   you   that   it

If you read a hundred-word paragraph written in English, it is a good chance that more than twenty words will be from the "top ten." All the words in the "top ten" are native English words.

Exercise   Anglo-Saxon Words

The Anglo-Saxon words in English have changed as time has passed. But some of them haven't changed very much. Try to match the English words in the left column with the Anglo-Saxon words in the right column.

bridge	weg
day	daeg
eight	neaht
fish	hwil
gnat	gnaet
guest	scyrte
night	scell
seven	brycg
shell	thencean
shirt	thynne
thin	seofon
think	eatha
way	fisc
while	giest

The Beginning of Word Borrowing

The Anglo-Saxons were not alone in northern Europe. At that time the Romans ruled most of Europe, which included the Anglo-Saxons. The Roman language was Latin. The Anglo-Saxons took (linguists like to say "borrowed") many useful words from the Roman rulers. They used these words as their own, and we still use many of them today. Some of these words are *wine, kettle, cheese,* and *cup.*

Sometimes the Anglo-Saxons borrowed words even when they didn't need them. They borrowed the Latin word *strada* (which became *street*) even though they already had the words *weg* (which became *way*) and *rad* (which became *road*). The Anglo-Saxons seemed to think that "the more words the better." The English language has continued to borrow words ever since.

The Anglo-Saxon Invasion of England

The people who lived in Britain were called the Celts. The Romans ruled Britain, too, but everywhere the Roman Empire was in trouble. A tribe called the Goths was attacking near Rome itself. In about A.D. 450 the Romans left Britain so that they could better defend Rome.

The Anglo-Saxons had been making raids on Britain from northern Europe for some time. Now that the Romans were gone, the Anglo-Saxons invaded in force. It took a long time to conquer the Celts, but after a hundred years, the Anglo-Saxons took over.

The Arrival of the Norse

The Anglo-Saxons stayed in power for a little more than 300 years, but it was not a quiet time. The Norse people, from Denmark and Scandinavia, raided Anglaland (as Britain was called under the Anglo-Saxons) from the north. These Norse

people, called Vikings, finally invaded and conquered about half of England.

Their language was not too different from Anglo-Saxon. The Anglo-Saxons borrowed words as eagerly from the Norse as they had from the Romans. They borrowed *they, them, sky, law, take,* and hundreds of other words.

The Norman Conquest of England

Meanwhile, in France, the Normans were growing strong. They had been Norsemen themselves, long before, and had settled on the north coast of France. In 1066 they conquered England.

The Norman conquest set off a flood of French words into English. Today we use French words for food (*dinner, supper, jelly, cream*) and for many other everyday things (*curtain, money, dance, surprise, flower*). Borrowing went on at a faster pace than ever before.

Modern English

Linguists call the English spoken before the Norman Conquest **Old English.** The English spoken from about 1100 to 1500

Detail of *Bayeux Tapestry* depicting the Norman Conquest of A.D. 1066.

is called **Middle English.** The English spoken since 1500 is called **Modern English.** The story doesn't end when modern English appears, however. English is still growing. We still borrow as eagerly as the Anglo-Saxons did, and we even make up new words. In the second part of this chapter you will learn some of the ways that new words are added to the language today.

Before we leave the ancient history of English words behind, let's look at how far one Indo-European word has come. Linguists believe that Indo-European had the word *wedi*, meaning "to see." This word found its way into Greek, but it changed a bit. The *w* was dropped, for one thing. From *wedi*, Greek formed *ideia* and *eidolon* ("shape").

English borrowed both Greek words. From *ideia* we got *idea*, *ideal*, and similar words. From *eidolon* we got *idol*, *idolize*, *kaleidoscope*, and others.

In Latin, *wedi* became *video* and *visus*. From these words, English got *video*, *visible*, *invisible*, *visual*, *supervise*, *visit*, and many more words.

The Anglo-Saxons made *wītan* and *wīse* from wedi. From the Anglo-Saxon words we have *wit*, *witty*, *witness*, *wise*, *wisdom*, and more.

In an old form of German, *wedi* became *wisan* and *witan*. These words made their way into Old French. There they were changed, and then English borrowed the changed words from

the French. We have them now in *disguise* and *guide* and in other words.

Thus from the one Indo-European word, *wedi*, more than a hundred English words came into being. The chart below shows more of *wedi*'s family. Can you see how the idea of "seeing" is contained in the meaning of each of the modern English words that came from *wedi*?

Indo-European

wedi

Greek	Latin	Anglo-Saxon	Old High German
ideia	video	witan	wisan
eidolon	visus	wise	witan

English

idea	video	wit	disguise
ideal	evident	witty	guide
idealism	evidence	witness	guidance
idol	envy	wise	
	survey	wisdom	
	clairvoyant		
	view		
	review		
	visible		
	invisible		
	vision		
	television		
	visual		
	supervise		
	advise		
	visit		
	vista		

Part 2 How New Words Are Added to Our Language

You have seen that some—but not many—words in modern English came quite directly from Indo-European through Anglo-Saxon. Many more were borrowed from other languages. We have said that the story didn't end in 1500, however. English is still alive and growing. In this chapter you will learn six ways in which new words are being added to our language:

1. Borrowing words

2. Putting two words together

3. Using part of another word

4. Making a word from initials

5. Using the name of a person or place

6. Imitating a sound

Borrowing Words

English is still borrowing words from many other languages, and the number of borrowed words is huge. On pages 12 and 13 is a list of English words and the different languages they came from.

American Indian

French

Spanish

Dutch

German

Some English Words Borrowed from Other Languages

American Indian

Trees, Plants, Fruits	hickory	pecan	sequoia	squash

Animals	chipmunk	moose	muskrat	opossum
	raccoon	skunk	woodchuck	

Fish	muskellunge	porgy

Food	hominy	pone	succotash

Amerindian Culture	totem	papoose	squaw	makinaw
	moccasin	tomahawk	wampum	

French

Plants and Animals	caribou	gopher	pumpkin

Food	jambalaya	chowder	a la mode

Geography	bayou	butte	chute	crevasse
	levee	prairie	rapids	

Furniture and Building	bureau	depot	shanty

Exploration and Travel	carry-all	portage	toboggan

Coinage	cent	dime	mill

Miscellaneous	apache	picayune	Cajun	rotisserie
	lacrosse	(Indian) brave		

Spanish

Plants and Animals	alfalfa	yucca	armadillo	bronco
	burro	barracuda	cockroach	coyote
	mustang	palomino	pinto	

Some English Words Borrowed from Other Languages

Spanish (continued)

Ranch Life	buckaroo	chaparral	corral	hacienda
	lariat	lasso	ranch	rodeo
	stampede	wrangler		
Food	chile	frijole	enchilada	
	taco	tamale	tortilla	
Clothing	chaps	poncho	sombrero	
Geography	canyon	key	mesa	sierra
Building	adobe	cafeteria	patio	plaza
Law	calaboose	desperado	hoosegow	vigilantes
Miscellaneous	fiesta	filibuster	hombre	loco
	marina	pronto	tornado	bonanza

Dutch

Food	cole slaw	cookie	cruller	waffle
Transportation	caboose	sleigh		
Social Classification	boss	patroon	Yankee	
Miscellaneous	Santa Claus	snoop	stoop ("porch")	

German

Food	bratwurst	sauerbraten	dunk	sauerkraut
	hamburger	delicatessen	noodle	frankfurter
	liverwurst	pumpernickel	pretzel	zwieback
Education	semester	seminar		
Miscellaneous	bum	fresh ("impudent")		loafer
	ouch	phooey		

Exercises Word Borrowing

A. Following is a list of English words connected with cooking. Can you guess where each word came from? A dictionary will give you the answers.

succotash	beef	orange
lemonade	soup	smorgasbord
barbecue	chow mein	spaghetti
biscuit	olive	

B. Following is a list of English words that name places where people live. Can you guess where each word came from? A dictionary will give you the answers.

apartment	igloo	trailer
condominium	palace	shack
house	castle	mansion
tent	cottage	hut
tepee	cabin	villa

Putting Two Words Together

Two words put together to make a new word are called a **compound word.**

watch	+	dog	=	watchdog
ant	+	eater	=	anteater
half	+	back	=	halfback
motor	+	cycle	=	motorcycle

English has many compound words. New ones are being made all the time. The words *inside, outdoors,* and *overtake* have been in English for a long time. *Downtown* and *hardware* are newer. *Liftoff, input,* and *letdown* are very new.

If you put two words together and drop some of the letters, you will have a **blend.** The word *motel* is a blend of *motor* and *hotel. Brunch* is a blend of *breakfast* and *lunch.*

Compounds and Blends

A. Each word is a compound or a blend. Tell what each word means. Tell what two words it is made from.

handbag	boatel	laundromat
outfield	airline	dugout
smog	airport	lunchroom
squiggle	motorcycle	houseboat

B. Try making some new blends of your own. What would you call an animal that was a cross between an elephant and a hippopotamus? An elepotamus? A hippophant?

What would you call a cross between an antelope and a buffalo?

What would you call a cafeteria that served only soup?

What would you call a laugh that was half giggle and half snicker?

What would you call a gadget that did the work of a snap and a zipper?

Using Part of Another Word

People who speak English like to shorten long words. We shorten *omnibus* to *bus*, *hamburger* to *burger*, and *frankfurter* to *frank*. Each time we do, we add another word to the language. Using just part of a long word is called **clipping.**

Clipping

Here are the long forms of some English words. The clipped forms of these words are more familiar. Can you give the clipped form for each?

fanatic	gymnasium	luncheon
taximeter cabriolet	telephone	omnibus
superintendent	automobile	

Making a Word from Initials

Single words made from the first initials of a group of words are called **acronyms.** Most acronyms are new to English. Like clipped words, acronyms show that we like short ways to say things. For example, we would rather say NASA than National Aeronautics and Space Administration. Some acronyms, like NASA, are pronounced as words. Others, like CB (for Citizens' Band radio), are pronounced as separate letters.

Using the Name of a Person or Place

The Earl of Sandwich lived long ago in England. Legend says that he was a fanatic about playing cards. He didn't even want to stop playing long enough to eat a meal, so he invented a quick meal. He put some meat between two slices of bread. Then he could hold his meal in one hand and play cards with the other. His invention caught on, and today it bears his name. We call it a sandwich.

J. L. McAdam was a Scottish inventor. He invented a surface made of gravel for roads. Today we call this surface "macadam." Many other words in English have come from names of interesting persons or places.

Exercises Acronyms and Words from Names

A. Tell what acronym is used as a short form of each of the following names:

United Nations International Children's Emergency Fund

Cooperative for American Remittances to Europe

Federal Bureau of Investigation

Congress of Racial Equality

Organization of Petroleum Exporting Countries

Sequoya ◆ Bloomer ◆ Pasteur

Diesel ◆ Boycott ◆ Pompadour

Fahrenheit ◆ Sandwich ◆ Zeppelin

B. Louis Pasteur invented a way to kill germs in milk. What do we call milk that has been treated in this way?

J. T. Brudnell, the Earl of Cardigan, wore a sweater that was open in front. What do we call that kind of sweater?

A man named A. Sax invented musical instruments. One of them bears his name. Which one?

General A. E. Burnside wore whiskers on his cheeks in front of his ears. What do we call such whiskers now?

James Watt was a Scottish engineer and inventor. What measure of electrical power is named after him?

Rudolf Diesel invented an engine. What do we call that engine?

On Guy Fawkes Day in England, people carry straw figures of Guy Fawkes through the streets. These figures are called guys. How do we use that word?

The Frisbie Pie Company packs their pies in metal tins. The bakers used to throw these tins around for fun at lunchtime. What do we call a plastic disc that sails like a pie tin?

Imitating a Sound

At the beginning of this chapter we mentioned two ideas about how language began. One was that people imitated sounds in nature. Words that imitate actual sounds are called **echoic words.** They echo actual sounds. Think of *murmur, whisper, roar,* and *croak.* These are echoic words.

Exercises   Echoic Words

A. Think of echoic words that describe or name each of the following things:

the noise a chicken makes
what a glass does if you drop it

the sound of a running horse
the sound of a car coming to a sudden stop
the sound of a bell
what a door does if the wind blows it shut
the sound that your stomach makes when you're hungry
the noise a fly makes

B. Think of at least five more echoic words.

Chapter 2

Building Your Vocabulary

In Chapter 1 you saw that the vocabulary of English—that is, the number of words that are used in the language—has been growing since the language was born. You saw, too, that it is still growing. With so many words available, English is a powerful tool for communicating with people. We can use it to say or write anything we want. But like any other tool, learning to use it well takes understanding and practice.

Each of us uses only a small part of the vocabulary of English from day to day. The words a person uses are called a person's *working vocabulary*. Your working vocabulary has grown as you have grown older because you have "picked up" words that you have heard or read. Maybe you have also made a deliberate effort to add words to your working vocabulary.

Why should you try to add words to your working vocabulary? You have things to say, and words are the only way to say them. You have seen a movie and want to tell a friend what you thought about it. You have spent your vacation backpacking in the mountains and want to tell how it felt. You have watched a building being torn down and want to describe what happened. The better your working vocabulary, the better you can say what you have to say and the better you will be understood.

In this chapter you will learn how to make your working vocabulary larger by building on the vocabulary you already use. You will learn how to use a dictionary to add to your vocabulary, and you will learn how to use words to say exactly what you mean.

Part 1 Base Words

In Chapter 1, you saw that words or parts of words can sometimes be put together to make new words. The words *hangup* and *smog* were made this way.

Another way to make a new word is to add a beginning or an ending to a word. What base word was used to make the words in the following list?

> breaker
> breakable
> unbreakable

The word, of course, is *break*. The endings *-er* and *-able* were added to it. The beginning *un-* was also added.

In *breaker, breakable,* and *unbreakable,* the **base word** is *break*. You can think of the other words as "growing from" the root word *break*. In each of the other words *break* has had a beginning or ending added to it.

Exercise Root Words

Copy each of the following words on a sheet of paper. Find the base word in each. Write the base word after each word.

illegal	preheat
unable	player
instantly	infection
horizontal	miscalculate
prankster	helpful
patriotism	helpless
indigestion	unbeatable
misfire	dangerous
nonfattening	superbowl
useful	poisonous

Part 2 Prefixes

A **prefix** is a word part added at the beginning of a word. The word part *un-* is a prefix in *untie* and *uncertain*. When a prefix is added to a word, it changes the meaning of the word. It creates a new word. If *un-* is added to *certain*, a new word is made: *uncertain*. *Certain* is the base word in *uncertain*. *Un-* is the prefix.

Prefix   Base Word

un   +   certain   =   uncertain

Following are nine prefixes that are used frequently in English. Each one has one or two clear meanings. If you learn these nine prefixes and their meanings, you will have made a start toward understanding thousands of English words.

Nine Frequently Used Prefixes

mis- This prefix always means "wrong." To *misplace* something is to place it in the wrong spot. To *misspell* a word is to give the wrong spelling.

non- The meaning is always "not." A *nonswimmer* is a person who cannot swim. A *nonhuman* creature is not human.

pre- The prefix *pre-* always means "before." A *prefix* is attached before a base word. A *preview* is a view of something before other people see it.

un- This prefix may have one of two meanings. It may mean "not." A person who is *unsettled* is not settled. It may also mean "the opposite of." The opposite of *tie* is *untie*.

dis- The meaning may be "the opposite of" or "away." The opposite of *charge* is *discharge*. To *displace* something is to move it away from where it was.

sub- This prefix may mean "under" or "less than." Something *subsurface* is under a surface. A *subteen* is a person less than thirteen years old. Another name for a subteen is *preteen*.

super- The prefix *super-* may mean "above" or "more than." The *superstructure* of a ship is the part built above the deck. A *supertanker* is more than an ordinary tanker. A *superstar* is more popular and more successful than some other star.

re- This prefix may mean "back" or "again." If the factory *recalls* your car, it calls it back to repair something that is wrong. If you *restart* a car, you start it again.

in- This prefix may also be spelled *im-, ir-,* or *il-*. It may mean "not." Something *informal* is not formal. Something *improper* is not proper. Something *irregular* is not regular. Something *illegal* is not legal.

This prefix may also mean "in." *Input* is something put into a computer. To *imprison* a person is to put him or her in prison.

As you are reading, you may come across a word that looks as if it has a prefix but really doesn't. For example, you can see at once that the letters *dis-* are not a prefix in *dish*. It may be harder to tell that *mis-* is not a prefix in *mister*.

How can you tell when a group of letters is a prefix and when it is not? Try to decide whether the word makes sense when you think of the meaning of the prefix. You know that *mis-* means "wrong." Does "wrong ter" make sense? No. Then *mis-* is not a prefix in *mister*.

Exercises   Prefixes

A.   Half the words in the following list have prefixes. Half do not. On a sheet of paper, list only the words with prefixes. Circle the prefixes.

misery	mismanage	disconnect	dishcloth
none	nonsense	rental	renew
preschool	pressure	inhuman	industry
uncertain	united	impatient	imitate

B.   Use any of the prefixes in the list on the left with any of the base words in the list on the right. Make as many new words as you can. For example, from *place* you can make *misplace, displace* and *replace*. Check a dictionary to make sure you have made actual words.

mis-	regular
non-	locate
pre-	conscious
un-	load
dis-	human
sub-	deal
super-	heat
re-	order
in-	charge
ir-	direct

c. 1. If a deed is something a person does, what is a *misdeed?*

2. If something *flammable* is something that burns easily, what is something *nonflammable?*

3. If a person sitting on a horse is *horsed*, what has happened to a person who is *unhorsed?*

4. If a person who is calm and collected is *composed*, what is a *discomposed* person like?

5. If *cognition* is an awareness of things when they happen, what is *precognition?*

6. If a *continent* is a large land mass, what is a *subcontinent?*

7. If *sonic* speed is the speed of sound, what is *supersonic* speed?

8. If *imburse* is an old English word that meant "to pay," what does *reimburse* mean?

9. If something *palpable* is something you can touch, what is something *impalpable?*

10. If *legible* handwriting is handwriting that is clear enough to read, what is *illegible* handwriting?

Part 3 Suffixes

A **suffix** is a word part added at the end of a word. The word part *-able* is a suffix in *breakable* and *enjoyable.* Like a prefix, a suffix changes the meaning of a word.

Following are seven suffixes that are used often in English. Most of these suffixes have one clear meaning.

Seven Frequently Used Suffixes

-er (or **-or**) "a person or thing that does something"
(A *helper* helps, and a *heater* heats. A *reflector* reflects.)

-fold "so many times as much"
(*Tenfold* is ten times as much.)

-ward "in the direction of"
(*Homeward* is in the direction of home.)

-less "without"
(A *worthless* thing is without worth.)

-able (or **-ible**) "can be" or "having this quality"
(A *bendable* thing can be bent; a *reasonable* person has the quality of reason.)

-ful "full of" or "having"
(A *useful* thing has a use.)

-ous "full of" or "having"
(A *dangerous* mission has danger in it.)

When a suffix is added to some base words, a letter is changed or dropped or doubled.

penny	+ less	=	penniless
operate	+ or	=	operator
run	+ er	=	runner

Exercises   Suffixes

A. Copy the following words on a sheet of paper. After each word write the base word and the suffix that was added.

refrigerator	twofold
westward	careless
curable	beautiful
furious	horrible
thriller	poisonous
windward	fashionable
toothless	luckless

B. Put the following base words and suffixes together. Check the spelling in a dictionary.

excuse + able   fame + ous
plenty + ful   bake + er
mercy + less   create + or
move + able   plan + er
space + ous   swim + er
fancy + ful   slice + er

Part 4   Using the Dictionary To Build Word Power

A good dictionary is the best source of information about words. It will answer your questions about the meanings and the spellings of words.

Alphabetical Order

The words in a dictionary are arranged in alphabetical order. Words that begin with *a* are listed before words that begin with *b*, and so on.

If two words have the same first letter, they are alphabetized by the second letter. If the second letters are alike, the words are alphabetized by the third letter. The following sets of words are in alphabetical order.

able   design   knock   send
about   detail   knot   senior
above   detect   know   sense

Exercise   Alphabetical Order

Following are six groups of ten words each. Arrange each group of words in alphabetical order.

1	2	3
pumpkin	clarinet	carburetor
pickle	guitar	gearbox
cabbage	bass	gear
lettuce	bassoon	gearshift
taco	trumpet	piston
tamale	trombone	muffler
knish	saxophone	radiator
spaghetti	glockenspiel	fan
doughnut	tuba	fanbelt
hamburger	flute	windshield

4	5	6
football	run	newscast
baseball	sprint	television
soccer	dash	theater
tennis	hop	movie
badminton	skip	telephone
golf	lope	newspaper
billiards	trot	radio
handball	walk	announcer
stickball	gallop	broadcast
kickball	jump	telegraph

Opening the Dictionary at the Right Place

You will be able to find words more quickly if you learn to open the dictionary at the right spot. If you open a dictionary in the middle, you will probably find yourself in the L's or the M's. That means that you will find words beginning with A through L in the first half of the dictionary. You will find words beginning with M through Z in the second half.

A good way to find your way around in the dictionary is to try to open it to a particular letter. Practice until you are good at it.

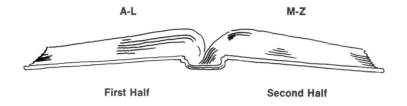

A-L   M-Z

First Half   Second Half

Exercise   Opening the Dictionary at the Right Place

Divide a sheet of paper into two columns. Label the first column First Half. Label the right column Second Half. Copy each of the following words into the correct column.

beach	water	eel	umbrella
surf	underwater	shell	radio
dive	crab	boardwalk	surfboard
jellyfish	fish	seagull	cloud
sunburn	tuna	blanket	wind

Guide Words

At the top of each page in most dictionaries you will find **guide words.** The guide word at the top of the left-hand page is the first word on that page. The guide word at the top of the right-hand page is the last word on that page. The other words on the page will fall between these two guide words in alphabetical order.

Let the guide words help you when you are looking for a word. As you flip pages in search of your word, watch the guide words. First look for guide words with the same first letter as the word you are looking for. When you have reached the pages having the right first letter, begin looking at the following letters of the word. Remember that your word will probably not be a guide word. You will have to watch for guide words that come before or after your word in alphabetical order.

often because one is forced to or has agreed to b) the money returned
kick·ball (-bôl') *n.* a children's game similar to baseball, but using a large ball that is kicked rather than batted
kick·er (-ər) *n.* **1.** one that kicks **2.** [Slang] *a)* a surprise ending *b)* a hidden difficulty
kick·off (-ôf') *n.* ☆**1.** *Football* a place kick from the forty-yard line of the kicking team, that puts the ball into play at the beginning of each half or after a touchdown or field goal ☆**2.** a beginning of a campaign, drive, etc.
kick·shaw (kik'shô') *n.* [< Fr. *quelque chose*, something] **1.** a fancy food or dish; delicacy **2.** a trinket; trifle; gewgaw Also **kick'shaws'** (-shôz')
☆**kick·stand** (kik'stand') *n.* a short metal bar fastened to a bicycle or motorcycle: when kicked down it holds the stationary cycle upright
kid (kid) *n.* [prob. < Anglo-N.] **1.** a young goat **2.** its flesh, used as food **3.** leather from the skin of young goats, used for gloves, shoes, etc. **4.** [Colloq.] a child or young person —*adj.* **1.** made of kidskin ☆**2.** [Colloq.] younger [my *kid* sister] —*vt., vi.* **kid'ded, kid'ding** [Colloq.] to deceive, fool, or tease playfully —☆**no kidding!** [Colloq.] I can hardly believe it!: an exclamation of doubt or surprise —**kid'der** *n.* —**kid'like', kid'dish** *adj.*
Kidd (kid), Captain (**William**) 1645?-1701; Brit. privateer & pirate, born in Scotland: hanged
kid·dy, kid·die (kid'ē) *n., pl.* **-dies** [dim. of KID] [Colloq.] a child
kid gloves soft, smooth gloves made of kidskin —☆**handle with kid gloves** [Colloq.] to treat with care, tact, etc.
kid·nap (-nap') *vt.* **-napped'** or **-naped', -nap'ping** or **-nap'ing** [KID + dial. *nap*, NAB] **1.** to steal (a child) **2.** to seize and hold (a person) against his will, by force or trickery, often in order to get a ransom —**kid'nap'per, kid'nap'er** *n.*

the last of or all of (a bottle of liquor, etc.) —*vi.* **1.** to destroy life **2.** to be killed [plants that *kill* easily] —*n.* **1.** an act of killing **2.** an animal or animals killed **3.** an enemy plane, ship, etc. destroyed —**in at the kill** **1.** present when the hunted animal is killed **2.** present at the end of some action
☆**kill²** (kil) *n.* [< Du. < MDu. *kille*] a stream channel; creek: used esp. in place names
☆**kill·deer** (kil'dir') *n., pl.* **-deers', -deer':** see PLURAL, II, D, 1 [echoic of its cry] a small, N. American bird of the plover family, with a high, piercing cry: also **kill'dee'** (-dē')
kill·er (kil'ər) *n.* **1.** a person, animal, or thing that kills, esp. habitually **2.** *same as* KILLER WHALE
killer whale any of several fierce, grayish to black, small whales that hunt in large packs and prey on large fish, seals, and other whales
☆**kil·li·fish** (kil'ē fish') *n., pl.* **-fish', -fish'es:** see FISH [< KILL² + -IE + FISH] any of several minnowlike freshwater fishes used in mosquito control and as bait: also **kil'lie** (-ē), *pl.* **-lies**

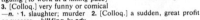
KILLER WHALE (to 25 ft. long)

kill·ing (kil'iŋ) *adj.* **1.** causing death; deadly **2.** exhausting; fatiguing [to work at a *killing* pace] **3.** [Colloq.] very funny or comical —*n.* ˙**1.** slaughter; murder **2.** [Colloq.] a sudden, great profit or success —**kill'ing·ly** *adv.*
kill-joy (-joi') *n.* a person who destroys or lessens other people's enjoyment: also **kill'joy'**
kiln (kil, kiln) *n.* [< OE. *cylne* < L. *culina*, cookstove] a furnace or oven for drying, burning, or baking something, as bricks, pottery, or grain —*vt.* to dry, burn, or bake in a kiln

Exercise Guide Words

Copy the following sets of imaginary guide words onto a sheet of paper. Leave five lines between each set of guide words.

stop	1	supper
cart	2	crate
splash	3	splinter
drive	4	duty
fan	5	fern

List each of the following words under the correct set of guide words.

cash	super	sudden	catcher
splatter	superstar	dusty	drum
strikeout	fan	stride	story
drop	fanbelt	fast	fasten
cave	crash	splint	summer

The Many Meanings of Words

Most words in English have more than one meaning. When you look up a word to find its meaning, you must be sure to find the right meaning for what you are reading. Look at the dictionary entry for *frame*. There you will find many definitions for this one word.

\text{Dictionary Entry for } \underline{\text{Frame}}

frame (fram) **vt. framed, fram′ing** [prob. < ON. *frami*, profit, benefit; some senses < OE. *framian*, to be helpful] **1.** to shape or form according to a pattern; design [to *frame* a constitution] **2.** to put together the parts of; construct **3.** to put into words; compose; devise [to *frame* an excuse] **4.** to adjust; adapt [a tax *framed* to benefit a few] **5.** to enclose (a picture, mirror, etc.) in a border ☆**6.** [Colloq.] to set up false evidence, testimony, etc. beforehand so as to make (an innocent person) appear guilty —**n. 1.** *a)* formerly, anything made of parts fitted together according to a design *b)* body structure in general; build [a man with a broad *frame*] **2.** the basic structure or skeleton around which something is built [the *frame* of a house] **3.** the framework supporting the chassis of a motor vehicle **4.** the supporting case or border into which a window, door, etc. is set **5.** a border, often ornamental, in which a picture, mirror, etc. is enclosed **6.** [*pl.*] the framework for a pair of eyeglasses **7.** any of certain machines built in or on a framework **8.** the way that anything is constructed or put together; form [the *frame* of a charter] **9.** setting or background circumstances **10.** mood; temper [a bad *frame* of mind] **11.** an established order or system [the *frame* of government] ☆**12.** [Colloq.] the act of framing (sense 6) ☆**13.** [Colloq.] *Baseball* an inning **14.** *Bowling,* etc. any of the divisions of a game, in which all ten pins are set up anew ☆**15.** *Motion Pictures* each of the small exposures composing a strip of film **16.** *Pool same as* RACK[1] (*n.* 2) ☆**17.** *TV* a single scanning by the electron beam of the scene being transmitted —**adj.** having a wooden framework, usually covered with boards [a *frame* house] —**fram′er n.**

In each of the following sentences the word *frame* is used with a different meaning.

That building is made of glass with a steel *frame*.
I'm going to put that picture in a simple *frame*.

The jury wouldn't believe that Louie had been *framed*.
I had a strike in the first *frame*.
Weekends put me in a happy *frame* of mind.

Exercise   The Many Meanings of Words

Number a sheet of paper from 1 through 10. Use the dictionary entry for *frame* to write a definition for *frame* as it is used in each of the following sentences.

1. My car's body is rusty, but the frame is solid.
2. Moriarity tried to frame me by sending that letter, Mr. Holmes.
3. She has bowled a strike in every frame.
4. These row houses have brick fronts and wooden frames.
5. This picture would look best in a wooden frame.
6. I think I'll get metal frames for my next pair of glasses.
7. He's usually in a horrible frame of mind on Monday mornings.
8. We spent all afternoon trying to frame a set of by-laws for the club.
9. Cold air is getting in between the window and the frame.
10. An animated cartoon is drawn one frame at a time.

Part 5   Gaining Precision in the Use of Words

Earlier in this chapter, we said that the English language requires understanding and practice before it can be used well. This is especially true of the words that make up the vocabulary of English because there is such a huge number of words to choose from. No two are exactly alike in meaning. Most have more than one meaning. In order to say exactly what you mean, you have to choose the best words to express your ideas. The closer you come to choosing the best way to say what you have in mind, the better you will be understood.

Synonyms

Words that are very close to each other in meaning are called **synonyms**. Following is a list of synonyms for *break*.

> **break:** smash, crash, crush, shatter, crack, split, fracture, splinter

All these words have meanings that are like *break*, but they are not exactly like *break*. If you drop a glass, you might say that it broke or shattered. But you aren't likely to say that it

Sox Trounce Yanks

GIANTS CLOBBER PHILLIES

Pirates Blitz Braves

crushed or split. Neither *crushed* nor *split* has a meaning that fits a broken glass. If you try to drive a large nail into thin wood, the wood may crack or split or splinter. But it won't smash or shatter.

The word *break* can also be used in another way. A person can break a world's record in track, for instance. Suppose the new record is much better than the old one. The newspaper headlines may say "Marathon Record Shattered." The word *break* doesn't seem strong enough to describe a spectacular new record. The word *shatter* seems stronger.

In the sports pages of a newspaper you can find dozens of synonyms for the word *beat*. Look at the headlines below.

Which games would you say were close? Which were run-aways? Even though *trounce, clobber, nip, top, down,* and *blitz* all mean "beat" in these headlines, you can see that there are differences among them.

Brewers Top Blue Jays

Orioles Nip Mariners

ASTROS DOWN CUBS

If you are going to describe something, take time to think about the words you will use. Have you picked the word that best describes what you have in mind, or is there a synonym that comes closer to what you mean? Does a squirrel just *run*? Or does it *scamper*? Does wind just *blow* in a storm? Or does it *howl*? Is a hockey player *angry* over a referee's call? Or is he *furious*?

Exercises   Using Synonyms

A. Following is a list of synonyms for *beat*. These might be used in sports headlines. Following the list of synonyms is a list of baseball scores. Write a headline for each game. Choose a word that fits the score.

thrash	clobber	slaughter
edge	smash	hammer
pound	top	trounce
blast	nip	crush

Red Sox 10, Yankees 1   Yankees 2, Red Sox 1
Giants 6, Phillies 4   Phillies 5, Giants 0
Orioles 12, Mariners 2   Mariners 3, Orioles 2
Brewers 1, Blue Jays 0   Blue Jays 5, Brewers 4
Astros 8, Cubs 1   Cubs 6, Astros 0

B. Choose the better word for each sentence.

1. With the bases loaded and two out, Mitchell hit a towering home run. The crowd broke out in a (shout, cheer.)

2. I was so (tired, exhausted) that I couldn't lift my feet.

3. What's the matter with you? You seem a little (angry, furious) this morning.

4. The movie was (funny, hilarious), but it wasn't (funny, hilarious).

5. She's usually a very (glad, cheerful) person.

6. I need some (help, aid) with this math problem.

7. Use some glue to (unite, join) those two pieces of wood.

8. Help me (lift, elevate) this box.

9. Be careful not to break that expensive (old, antique) armchair.

10. Somehow he manages to (smile, smirk) even when things go wrong.

C. List as many synonyms as you can for each of the italicized words in the following phrases.

a *quick* walk

a *strange* dream

a *cute* smile

a *great* show

a *big* shark

a *quiet* spot

a *good* time

a *bad* job

a *happy* person

D. Choose two of the synonyms you listed for each phrase in Exercise C. Explain how they are different. For example, explain how a *quiet* spot is different from a *peaceful* spot.

Antonyms

Words that are opposite or nearly opposite to each other in meaning are called **antonyms.** The words *happy* and *sad* are antonyms. *Large* and *small* are antonyms, and so are *heavy* and *light*.

Antonyms can be useful when you want to compare things. You might say that a new gym is so large that it makes the old one seem small. A little exaggeration may be more effective. You might say that the new gym is so *huge* that it makes the old one seem *tiny*.

37

Exercises   Using Antonyms

A. Write an antonym for each of the following words.

quiet	healthy	long	deep
strong	careful	easy	bright
simple	young	fast	early
straight	far	honest	useful

B. Compare your antonyms for the words in Exercise A with the antonyms listed by others in your class. Did all of you choose the same antonyms? Can you explain why there are differences?

Review Exercises   Putting Your Vocabulary Skills Together

A. Write the base word for each of the following words. After the base word write any prefix or suffix.

immovable	matchless	fielder
mismatch	renewable	unallowable
supermarket	inexcusable	resealable

B. Arrange each group of words in alphabetical order.

1	2	3	4
octopus	carpenter	blue	January
squid	boxes	lavender	February
shark	lawyer	red	March
stingray	doctor	purple	April
whale	plumber	pink	May
dolphin	electrician	puce	June
jellyfish	welder	orange	July
barracuda	painter	olive	August
tuna	sculptor	yellow	September
flounder	writer	brown	October

C. Following are ten pairs of dictionary guide words. List two words that would appear on each page.

1. doormat	double	6. question	quit
2. hide	high school	7. rhinoceros	ribbon
3. mummy	mush	8. seven	shackles
4. parsley	partridge	9. skeleton	skull
5. pickle	pig	10. soft	solar

D. Write a definition for the word *place* as it is used in each of the following sentences. Use a dictionary for help.

1. Come over to my *place* after dinner.

2. In the first *place* I don't feel like going to the movies tonight, and in the second *place* I don't have any money.

3. I finished in fourth *place*.

4. Don't bend the page down; use a bookmark to keep your *place*.

5. Will you save my *place* for me while I get some popcorn?

6. That first album earned her a *place* in musical history.

7. I'm sure I know her, but I just can't *place* her.

8. Julio lives over on Jefferson *Place*.

9. Here we have a *place* for everything, and everything is in its *place*.

10. We need a *place* to hold our next meeting.

E. Complete each sentence with a synonym for the italicized word.

1. The soup isn't just *hot*; it's _____ .

2. The soil isn't really *wet*; it's just _____ .

3. Tom didn't just *say* he was best; he _____ it.

4. That show wasn't just *bad*; it was _____ .

5. It wasn't just a *storm*; it was a _____ .

6. That joke isn't just *old*; it's _____ .

Chapter 3

Using the Senses

"There were some days compounded completely of odor, nothing but the world blowing in one nostril and out the other. Some days were days of hearing every trump and trill of the universe. Some days were good for tasting and some for touching. And some days were good for all the senses at once." —Ray Bradbury

Have you ever felt this way? Have you ever felt completely tuned in to the world around you? Your senses can provide a richer life for you because they can help you come alive to your world. If your senses are sharp, they can also help you learn more about your world.

One way to sharpen your senses is to practice using them. Get a little notebook and write down what you see or hear or touch or taste or smell. Try to write down something every day. Writing down your impressions will help to make you more alive to your senses. It will also provide a wonderful storehouse of ideas for your writing.

The following pages will help you to practice using each one of your senses.

Part 1   The Sense of Sight

You can see everything around you, but do you ever really stop to look at something? Do you examine something carefully so that you can describe it precisely enough to help someone to see exactly what you saw?

Study the picture on the opposite page. Take time to examine everything carefully. Pretend you are in this park and this is what you are seeing. Then write some sentences that answer the following questions. Use the list of Sight Words on pages 54–56 to make your descriptions more vivid. Include color words in your description.

1. What kind of day is it?
2. Describe the color, the shape, and the appearance of the ground, the trees, the bushes.
3. Seeing a goat is a surprise. Describe the color, the shape, and the appearance of the goat. What is it tied with? Is it friendly?
4. Describe the bench behind the goat. Is it comfortable?
5. Is anyone else in the park?
6. Is it a city park? How do you know?

Exercise   Using "Sight" Words in Your Writing

Choose three of the following things, or some of your own, and write some sentences describing them. Try to describe them as vividly as you want your reader to see them.

a garden	your house	a busy street
a lake	your yard	an amusement park
a woods	your room	a shopping center
a field	your pet	a snowstorm

Part 2 The Sense of Hearing

Most of us hear well enough, but we don't listen. We are surrounded with so many sounds all the time that they all run together. We hear the sounds merely as noise.

The picture on the opposite page shows part of an amusement park. Study the picture. Think about each separate sound you might hear if you were there. Then write some sentences that answer the following questions. Use the list of Hearing Words on page 57 to help the reader hear what you hear.

1. What kind of music is playing? Who or what is playing it? How does it sound?

2. What separate sounds do you hear when you are walking with the people on the ground?

3. Describe the sounds you might hear in the various shops under the round center canopy.

4. You are up in the air in the bucket on the left side of the picture. What sounds do you hear? How do the sounds change when the bucket sweeps low to the ground?

5. Might you hear animals somewhere in the park? a roller coaster? Describe the sounds.

6. Do the children sound different from the adults? Describe the speech sounds.

7. You walk into the woods at the top of the picture. How do the sounds change?

Exercise Using "Hearing" Words in Your Writing

Here are nine sounds you are familiar with. Try to hear the sounds in your mind. Write a sentence or two about each sound. Describe it as vividly as you can.

a motorcycle	a dog barking	roller skating
rain on the roof	firecrackers	a thunderstorm
a whistle	a bird	sawing wood

Part 3   The Sense of Touch

You react more immediately to your sense of touch than to any of your other senses. Your brain records an immediate response if you touch something hot or sharp, for example, so that your finger immediately pulls away. You know at once how it feels to be cold or wet or dizzy or in pain.

However, describing how things feel can often be difficult, especially when you want your reader to experience the same feeling you experienced. A good way to handle the problem is to compare something with something else. For example:

> The old stuccoed walls felt like rough sandpaper.

In the picture on the opposite page, notice how many things are related to the sense of touch. Answer the following questions about the picture by using new and interesting comparisons to describe how you think the various things feel. Use the Touch Words on page 58 to help you think.

1. What would the round prickly burrs on the plant feel like if you touched them?
2. How sharp are the long thorns?
3. What do the bare stems feel like?
4. What do the roots feel like?
5. If you touched the boy's hair, how would it feel?
6. How would his jacket feel? His socks?

Exercise   Using "Touch" Words in Your Writing

Choose five of the following things, or some of your own, and write some sentences describing how each thing feels. Try to avoid tired, overused comparisons. Strive for fresh, new comparisons so your reader won't lose interest.

a peach	a new tennis ball	a balloon
a pillow	a plastic bag	riding a bike
a blister	a feather	swimming on a hot day

Part 4   The Sense of Taste

Is the way food tastes important to you, or do you eat anything just because you're hungry? Have you ever seen something you would like to taste but are afraid to? Is there anything you refuse to eat even though you have never tasted it?

Look at the Taste Words on page 58. Try to think of a specific food or drink for each of the words. Share your answers with the class. Do you disagree with any of the answers? If so, can you explain why?

Study the picture on the opposite page. What is happening in the picture? Can you remember what this fruit tastes like? Answer the following questions, being as precise and interesting as possible.

1. In order to peel the orange, you first bit a hole in the skin. Describe how that bite tasted.

2. You then opened your orange, sectioned it, and ate it. Describe how it tasted.

3. You were still hungry, so you ate a bag of potato chips. Describe how they tasted.

4. You finished up with a candy bar. How did your particular candy bar taste? Were there nuts in it? What part of the candy bar tasted best to you? Describe that taste.

Exercise   Using "Taste" Words in Your Writing

You have probably tasted the following foods or drinks. If not, substitute some of your own. Write a sentence about each one. Describe the taste as vividly as you can. Review the Taste Words on page 58.

milk	spinach	French fries
popcorn	soft-boiled eggs	cookies
buttered toast	cake	marshmallows

Part 5   The Sense of Smell

You don't usually think much about your sense of smell unless you smell something unusually good or something particularly unpleasant. In other words, you are aware of strong odors, but you are not sensitive to delicate ones. You probably need to make a conscious effort to be more aware of smells and to train your nose to identify them.

Study the picture on the following page. A traveling circus has come to the outskirts of a small town and practically everyone has come out to help raise the main tent. Study the Smell Words on page 59, and then answer the following questions:

1. Everyone seems dressed for cool weather. How does the air smell when it is chilly outside?
2. Trucks are driving about, bringing hay for feeding and bedding the animals. Describe the different smells of the hay and the trucks.
3. The circus people are preparing the different foods sold at a circus. Describe the smells of the various foods.
4. It is early in the morning, and breakfast is being prepared for the circus people. Describe the smells of breakfast cooking.
5. As you walk around the circus grounds, you notice many other smells. Choose two faint, or delicate smells and describe them.

Exercise   Using "Smell" Words in Your Writing

Write a sentence describing the smell of the following things. Review the Smell Words on page 59 and take enough time to remember exactly how each of the things smells before you describe it.

a dill pickle	wood burning	a drugstore
a hamburger	gasoline	a garage
chocolate cake	rain	your favorite smell

Part 6　Using All of the Senses

The world around you involves all of your senses working together. Now that you have worked with each of your senses separately to sharpen each one, you are probably more aware of your sensory powers. You are ready to make them work harder for you.

Study the picture on the opposite page. Pretend you are there, lying on a rock, completely relaxed. In fact, close your eyes and actually be there in your imagination. Breathe the air. Feel the warmth of the sun on you. Let your senses take over in this beautiful place. When you feel you are really lying here, open your eyes and answer the following questions:

1. Describe what you see around you. Describe things in the distance, things near you, and things really close to you.

2. Describe what you hear. Can you hear the water? any birds? Do the trees make sounds? Can you hear human voices? Are there any other sounds?

3. Describe what you can touch or feel. How does the sun feel on you? The rock you are lying on? What can you touch around you? How does the fresh air make you feel?

4. The smells here are probably delicate. Try to identify them. Describe how the air smells. Can you smell the water? How does the book smell? Are there any plants near you that have a pleasant or an unpleasant smell? Does a sunny place on the rock smell different from a shady place?

Exercise　All of the Senses Working Together

Read over all the sentences you have written about the picture. Select the best ideas and write a paragraph about your experience that includes all of your senses working together. Revise any sentences or ideas that you need to in order to write a good paragraph. Choose strong, descriptive words. Try to make the reader feel that he or she is right there with you.

A List of Sight Words

Colors

red

pink
salmon
rose
coral
raspberry
strawberry
cherry
crimson
cardinal
vermillion
ruby
garnet
wine
maroon
burgundy

blue

sky
sapphire
azure
porcelain
turquoise
aqua
aquamarine
violet
peacock
cobalt

royal
navy
steel

yellow

beige
buff
peach
apricot
butter
buttercup
lemon
canary
chrome
gold
topaz
ochre
sulphur
mustard
butterscotch
orange
tangerine
persimmon

green

celery
mint
apple
lime
kelly

emerald
olive
pistachio
chartreuse

white

snow
milky
marble
cream
ivory
oyster
pearl
silver
platinum

purple

lavender
lilac
orchid
mauve
plum
mulberry
magenta

black

jet
ebony
licorice

gray

ashen
dove
steel

brown

sandy
almond
amber
tawny
hazel
cinnamon
nutmeg
chocolate
coffee
copper
rust
ginger
bronze
walnut
mahogany

colorless
rainbow

A List of Sight Words

Movements

fast

hurry
run
scamper
skip
scramble
dart
spring
spin
sprint
stride
streak
propel
trot
gallop
drive
dash
bolt
careen
rush
race
zoom
zip
ram
speed
chase
hurl
swat
flick

whisk
rip
shove
swerve
smash
drop
plummet
bounce
dive
swoop
plunge
swing
fly
sail

slow

creep
crawl
plod
slouch
lumber
tiptoe
bend
amble
saunter
loiter
stray
slink
stalk
edge
sneak

stagger
lope
canter
waddle
drag
sway
soar
lift
drift
droop
heave

Shapes

flat
round
domed
curved
wavy
globular
scalloped
ruffled
frilled
crimped
crinkled
flared
oval
conical
cylindrical
tubular
hollow

rotund
chubby
portly
fat
swollen
lumpy
clustered
padded
tufted
topheavy
pendulous
jutting
irregular
proportioned
angular
triangular
rectangular
hexagonal
octagonal
square
pyramidical
tapering
branching
twiggy
split
broken
spindly
skinny
thin
wiry
shapely
winged
shapeless

A List of Sight Words

Appearance

dotted
freckled
spotted
blotched
wrinkled
patterned
mottled
flowery
striped
bright
clear
shiny
glowing
glossy
shimmering
fluid
sparkling
iridescent
glassy
flashy
glazed
sheer
transparent
translucent
opaque
muddy
grimy
young
drab
dingy
dull

dark
dismal
rotted
old
used
worn
untidy
shabby
messy
cheap
ugly
ramshackle
tired
exhausted
arid
awkward
crooked
loose
curved
straight
orderly
formal
crisp
pretty
heavy
flat
stout
wide
rigid
narrow
overloaded
congested
cluttered

crowded
jammed
packed
bruised
tied
stretched
tall
erect
lean
slender
supple
lithe
lively
muscular
sturdy
robust
hardy
strong
healthy
frail
fragile
pale
sickly
small
tiny
miniature
timid
shy
nervous
frightened
wild
bold
dramatic

tantalizing
irresistible
energetic
animated
perky
arrogant
imposing
regal
stately
elegant
large
huge
immense
massive
gigantic
showy
decorative
dazzling
opulent
jeweled
lavish
exotic
radiant
fiery
blazing
fresh
clean
scrubbed
tidy
handsome
pleasant
calm
serene

A List of Hearing Words

Loud Sounds

crash
thud
bump
thump
boom
thunder
bang
smash
explode
roar
scream
screech
shout
yell
whistle
whine
squawk
bark
bawl
bray
bluster
rage
blare
rumble
grate
slam
clap
stomp
stamp
noise
discord

jangle
rasp
clash
clamor
tumult
riot
racket
brawl
bedlam
pandemonium
hubbub
blatant
deafening
raucous
earsplitting
piercing
rowdy
disorderly

Soft Sounds

sigh
murmur
whisper
whir
rustle
twitter
patter
hum
mutter
snap
hiss

crackle
bleat
peep
buzz
zing
gurgle
swish
rush
chime
tinkle
clink
hush
still
speechless
mute
faint
inaudible
melody
resonance
harmony
musical

Speech Sounds

stutter
stammer
giggle
guffaw
laugh
sing
yell
scream

screech
snort
bellow
growl
chatter
murmur
whisper
whimper
talk
speak
drawl

A List of Touch Words

cool	slippery	silky	gritty
cold	spongy	satiny	sandy
icy	mushy	velvety	rough
lukewarm	oily	smooth	sharp
tepid	waxy	soft	thick
warm	fleshy	woolly	pulpy
hot	rubbery	furry	dry
steamy	tough	feathery	dull
sticky	crisp	fuzzy	thin
damp	elastic	hairy	fragile
wet	leathery	prickly	tender

A List of Taste Words

oily	sugary	tangy	gingery
buttery	crisp	unripe	hot
salty	ripe	raw	burnt
bitter	bland	alkaline	overripe
bittersweet	tasteless	medicinal	spoiled
sweet	sour	fishy	rotten
hearty	vinegary	spicy	
mellow	fruity	peppery	

A List of Smell Words

sweet	odorous	acrid	stagnant
scented	pungent	burnt	mouldy
fragrant	tempting	gaseous	musty
aromatic	spicy	reeking	mildewed
perfumed	savory	putrid	damp
heady	sharp	rotten	dank
fresh	gamy	spoiled	stench
balmy	fishy	sour	
earthy	briny	rancid	
piney	acidy	sickly	

Chapter 4

Writing Paragraphs

When you like a story or a book you are reading, you probably don't think about the way it is written. However, the way it is written is usually the key to the success of the story. A good writer works hard to make a story interesting to the reader.

An important element in good writing is learning how to organize your ideas so that a reader can understand what you are trying to say. The basic tool for organizing ideas in writing is the paragraph. This chapter will introduce you to some of the ways in which paragraphs can help you to organize your ideas.

Part 1 Defining the Paragraph

A paragraph is a group of sentences that work together to explain or support a central idea. Here is an example of a well organized paragraph.

> My mother always came to meet me. She knew it was I, for no one else pushed the bell so hard. Grownups were usually not so urgent; they would thumb once lightly, stand and wait, tumbling hats in their hands. I would climb the stairs, and even before I had gained half of them, she would appear at the landing. She would wait, and as I hopped level with her, would touch my cheek or run her hand over my forehead, and if she found sweat, would march me to the bathroom and swab my face with a clean-smelling washcloth.—WILLIAM MELVIN KELLEY

The first sentence tells you what the mother did. It is the central idea of the paragraph. The rest of the sentences work together to describe the meeting.

Here is another example of how sentences work together to support a central idea.

> If today's camper is not the rough-it type, he or she can travel with a deluxe cabin on wheels that includes a kitchen sink, an innerspring mattress, a refrigerator, a closet with full-length mirror, a wall-to-wall carpet, and a TV set. There are now thousands of campsites where these vehicles can be plugged into a source of electricity and a sewage system. However, many camp vehicles have completely independent electrical systems. The driver can pull up under the trees beside a lake deep in the wilderness and spend a night as comfortably as in his or her own home.—OLIVE S. NILES

All of the sentences in this paragraph tell you about the conveniences of modern camping. Once again, the paragraph is well organized because all of the sentences work together. However, if Ms. Niles had written in the following manner, all of the sentences would not work together. Can you find the sentences that do not belong here?

If today's camper is not the rough-it type, he or she can travel with a deluxe cabin on wheels that includes a kitchen sink, an innerspring mattress, a refrigerator, a closet with full-length mirror, a wall-to-wall carpet, and a TV set. Danger and hardship were the hourly companions of America's earliest campers, the wilderness explorers. There are now thousands of campsites where vehicles can be plugged into a source of electricity and a sewage system. However, many camp vehicles have completely independent electrical systems. The driver can pull up under the trees beside a lake deep in the wilderness and spend a night as comfortably as in his or her own home. He knows that if he doesn't return when expected, some Forest Ranger or police officer will be out looking for him.

The two sentences, "Danger and hardship were the hourly companions of America's earliest campers, the wilderness explorers" and "He knows that if he doesn't return when expected, some Forest Ranger or police officer will be out looking for him," do not tell you about the conveniences of modern camping facilities. Therefore, they do not work with the rest of the sentences to support the central idea, and the paragraph is not well organized.

In order to be sure that all your paragraphs are well organized from now on, check to make certain that all of the sentences work together to support the central idea.

Exercise   Sentences That Work Together

Here are ten lists of sentences. In each list, there are one or more sentences that do not work together to support a central idea. In each list, pick out the sentences that do work together. Explain why the other sentence or sentences do not belong in the list.

1. a. Gerbils are small, furry animals about five inches long.
   b. They are actually members of the rodent family.
   c. My friend down the street has three white mice.
   d. Female gerbils may have as many as four babies every four weeks.

2. a. My sister and brother built a tree house in our old oak tree.
   b. They used leftover lumber from the garage Dad had built.
   c. There are more girls than boys on this block.
   d. Mr. Kane gave them a box of shingles and some nails.

3. a. The pitcher plant is a meat eater.
   b. Crawling insects are trapped in its hollow leaves.
   c. When the insects die, the plant absorbs them as food.
   d. Many interesting books have been written about plants.

4. a. My sister Marie is eleven years old.
   b. Whenever my sister practices the trumpet, I get a headache.
   c. Sometimes I'm convinced that she has lost her sense of hearing.
   d. Each tortured note is louder than the other one.

5. a. There are many myths about catching fish.
   b. One of them says, "Wind from the east, fish bite least."
   c. I spent last summer fishing in Colorado.
   d. Actually, fish don't know the direction of the wind.

6. a. I know a family that celebrates Christmas in July.
   b. Our family celebrates Christmas in December.
   c. The family claims that July is the only time everyone is free.
   d. Everyone in the family schedules vacations in July.

7. a. Have you ever wondered why birds sing?
   b. Some of their songs are warnings.
   c. Birds also sing to call the flock together.
   d. There is an oriole nest in our walnut tree.

8. a. The earth is over 70 percent water.
   b. Shell collecting can be profitable as well as interesting.
   c. Some shells are extremely rare, and sell for fancy prices.
   d. One perfect specimen was sold for more than a thousand dollars.
   e. Some shops specialize in rare shells.

9. a. Many seagoing words are part of our everyday talk.
   b. *Shipshape* means anything that is clean and neat.
   c. Sir Francis Drake was a pirate as well as a sea captain.
   d. *Paddle your own canoe* means do your own job.
   e. A small-ship weather warning was just issued.

10. a. The car skidded on the slippery pavement, and into a street light.
    b. Fortunately, the driver was not injured.
    c. Driving a car can be dangerous.
    d. He claimed that wearing a seat belt had saved his life.
    e. The driver paid for the damaged street light.

Part 2   The Topic Sentence

To make sure that all sentences in a paragraph are working together, each paragraph should have a *topic sentence*. The topic sentence is usually the first sentence in a paragraph. It tells what the paragraph is going to be about by stating the central idea of the paragraph.

There are two important reasons for using topic sentences:

1. The topic sentence helps you, the writer, to keep track of your ideas. By making certain that your sentences refer back to the topic sentence, you will not make the mistake of bringing in ideas that do not relate to each other. All your sentences will work together.

2. The topic sentence helps the reader. It acts as a guide by stating what the paragraph is going to be about.

Let's look at two examples of topic sentences.

Example 1

Jimmy Piersall had a hard time as a kid.

After reading this topic sentence, the reader expects the rest of the paragraph to explain why Jimmy Piersall had a hard time as a kid. Study the following paragraph to see if all of the sentences work together to explain this idea.

Jimmy Piersall had a hard time as a kid. He had a brother almost twenty years older than he was. His brother died before Jimmy ever really knew him, so Jimmy was brought up as an only child. His father had been an orphan. He had been brought up in an orphan's home and had to fight for everything he got. He loved Jimmy as much as any father could love his son. Jim's dad was very strict and hard on him, however. Jimmy grew up worrying all the time about what his father would think of what he did. He worried if his father would like it or not.

In this paragraph, the sentences all work together to explain the idea set forth in the topic sentence. The paragraph is well organized and interesting.

Example 2

When the war was over, Lieutenant Audie Murphy was flown home as a hero.

Study the following paragraph to see if all the sentences work together as well as they did in the preceding paragraph.

> *When the war was over, Lieutenant Audie Murphy was flown home as a hero.* It was a long flight home. After his arrival in the United States, he was interviewed an average of five times a day. He was the most decorated soldier of World War II. His twenty-three decorations included the Medal of Honor, the Bronze Star, three Purple Hearts, the Legion of Merit, the Silver Star, and the Distinguished Service Cross. The French Government also awarded him the Legion of Honor and the Croix de Guerre. Today, Audie is married and has two sons.

In this paragraph, the writer has lost track of the main idea in two different places. The sentences, "It was a long flight home" and "Today, Audie is married and has two sons," have nothing to do with the idea of Lieutenant Audie Murphy as a hero.

Exercise   Studying Paragraphs

In some of the following paragraphs, all of the sentences work to support the main idea of the topic sentence. In some of the other paragraphs, however, the writer has lost track of his or her ideas, and the sentences do not work together. In each paragraph, the topic sentence is the first sentence. Study each paragraph and decide whether all the sentences in each paragraph work together to support the main idea of the topic sentence. When sentences stray away from the main idea, try to explain why they don't belong in the paragraph.

1

> Reverence for animal life may be as old as humanity. The early hunters took only as much game as was needed. Nothing was wasted. If they returned the blood to the earth and the bones to the water, new animals would appear. This attitude lives on in our growing and quite rational concern that the earth's limited resources should not be needlessly squandered.

2

The thing I liked best about the house was the old back stairs that ran from the kitchen to the second-story bedrooms. Those steps held all the joys and sorrows of my childhood. On those steps, I explored the unknown, the future, and the dreams of childhood. I saw the green willow trees of China newly bathed in rain. I smelled the spices of India and saw the riches of Persia. On those steps I held the power of a god. The house was my grandmother's and it was as old as she was.

3

In 1920 women in America won the right to vote, bringing to a close a movement that began in 1848. At that time, women had few rights of any kind. In most states they could not own property. They were discouraged from going to college. It was very difficult for a woman to become a doctor or a lawyer, and in no state did women have the right to vote. In 1848, a group of women led by Elizabeth Cady Stanton and Lucretia Mott met in Seneca Falls, New York. There they drew up a list of rights they believed women should have.

4

Thomas Jefferson and Alexander Hamilton did not get along. They were both handsome, intelligent men. The tall, red-headed Virginian had little use for the ideas of the smaller, dark-complexioned former lawyer from New York. The two disagreed on the idea of democracy. Jefferson was in favor of it, Hamilton against it. They disagreed, too, on which group the national government should favor—farmers, or those who owned factories and businesses. Hamilton was killed in a duel.

5

When I was in my boyhood, the year was divided into times. There was a time when you played marbles. Everybody had a large bag of marbles. There was a time when you built carts out of wooden boxes. There was a time when you made parachutes out of a handkerchief and some string and stone. There was a time when you played "soccer." Every boy did it. Girls did not play marbles. It was like the trees coming into green. There was something that clicked, and the gears shifted, and we all got up in the morning and put marbles in our pockets because that was the day everybody started to play marbles.

6

Some advertising may be dangerous because it promotes the use of products that could be hazardous to health. The best illustration of such advertising concerns what is known as the "smoking and health" problem. The American Cancer Society, the U.S. Public Health Service, the American Public Health Association, and the Surgeon General of the United States, among others, have reported smoking to be a major cause of lung cancer and other diseases. Yet cigarette sellers and advertisers have not limited a profitable source of income, despite the dangers to which consumers may be exposed if they continue to smoke.

7

On the drive or at a roundup, home base for the cowboy was a circle with the chuck wagon at its center. The radius of the circle was short—no farther than a man felt like walking after supper to roll out his bedding. The chuck wagon itself served as a general store on wheels, crammed full of everything from bedrolls to spare bullets. At mealtimes, on the ground next to the wagon, gathered the rough, sweaty crew that for more than one cowboy was the closest approximation to a family he might have during his working life.

Part 3 Writing Topic Sentences

At the beginning of this chapter, we said that a good writer works hard to make a story interesting for the reader. If the first sentence in a paragraph is dull or unimaginative, the reader may not want to read the rest of the paragraph. Therefore, a topic sentence must not only give the reader an idea of what a paragraph is going to be about, it must also be interesting enough to make the reader want to continue reading. It must catch the reader's attention.

Suppose a writer were to begin a paragraph with the following topic sentence:

> This paragraph is going to tell you how early human beings hunted for food.

The sentence certainly makes it clear enough what the paragraph is going to be about, but it is not at all interesting. The writer might also have written, *"Early human beings had to hunt for their food."* Again, the sentence clearly states what the paragraph will be about, but unfortunately the sentence is still dull.

Suppose, however, the writer had written, *"For the hunt, early human beings depended more on guile than weapons."* Your first reaction might be, "What? You mean, the cave people didn't really depend on weapons in their hunt for food? Then how did they get their food? What did they use their weapons for?" The writer has caught your attention so that you want to learn more about what he has to say.

> For the hunt, early human beings depended more on guile than weapons. They set snares and traps and used disguises to get within stabbing distance of their prey. If they came to America as early as some archeologists believe, their first stone implements were primarily for butchering, skin dressing, and woodworking.—HAROLD COY

Let's look at another example. Suppose someone writes, *"There are both good and bad sides to news reporting."* The sentence is fairly clear, and fairly interesting. However, it does create some problems. For example, does the writer mean there have *always* been good and bad sides to news reporting? If so, he is going to have a difficult time explaining the whole history of good and bad news reporting in one short paragraph. Does he mean that the reporting of *all news* has been good or bad? If so, he will again have a difficult time explaining all this in one short paragraph. His topic sentence fails to be clear and interesting because the reader has the feeling that the writer will not be able to cover all the material in one paragraph.

Suppose, however, the writer had written, *"Recently we have seen good and bad press coverage of public events."* Now the sentence is interesting—and clear. You know what the paragraph is going to tell about the good and bad reporting of *recent public events.* Your interest is aroused. You know clearly what the paragraph is going to be about, and you know that the writer will be able to cover his material adequately— as the following paragraph shows.

> Recently we have seen good and bad press coverage of public events. When President John F. Kennedy was assassinated in 1963, the general coverage by television, radio, and newspapers was excellent and complete. But the confusion caused by the many newspapermen present two days later, when accused assassin Lee Harvey Oswald was being transferred from one jail to another, was partially responsible for Oswald's being shot by a member of the surrounding crowd. In addition, the press coverage about Oswald's actions, and the many background stories about him, have raised the question of whether he could have received a fair trial, had he lived.—DAVID J. GOLDMAN

In writing, remember the following about the topic sentence:

1. It helps you, the writer, by keeping you on the track.

2. It makes certain that all the ideas in a paragraph relate to each other.

3. It acts as a guide by giving the reader an idea of what the paragraph is going to be about.

4. It should be clearly stated.

5. It should be interesting enough to catch the reader's attention.

6. It should let the reader know that you can cover the material adequately in the paragraph.

Exercises   Working with Topic Sentences

A. Here is a list of topic sentences. Some of them are interesting as they stand, but others need a fresh approach. Decide which sentences are interesting, and which are not. Rewrite the sentences that seem dull and make them interesting.

1. A certain feeling of intrigue and mystery filled me as I boarded a plane for the first time.

2. I think that one of the most interesting and fascinating topics a person could write about is the variety of individuals you see walking down a busy street.

3. My paragraph is going to be about the excitement of motocross racing.

4. I see the world like no one else through the lens of my camera.

5. I would really like to write about the fact that this city needs an all-purpose sports complex so that kids can have some place to go.

6. The crackling fireplace, the homemade apple cider, the gold, orange, red, and brown leaves strewn about our lawn remind me that autumn is my favorite season.

7. It would be worthwhile to write about the need for theaters to adjust their prices to the movie ratings.

8. Cities need to build and maintain bicycle trails so that people can use bikes more frequently as economical, healthy, and non-polluting transportation.

9. Campers and hikers should be more conscientious about keeping the wilderness clean and intact.

10. With mud splattered all over my face, and with my jersey sleeve torn away, I didn't need to be reminded that this was the toughest game of the season.

B. Here is a list of topic sentences. Some of them can be covered adequately in a well organized paragraph. Some of them cannot. Decide which sentences can be covered adequately, and why. Rewrite the other sentences so that they can be covered in a paragraph.

1. Conservation is everyone's responsibility.

2. The first day of school is always a new, exciting adventure.

3. My room has always been a safe place for me, my refuge, and my hide-away.

4. I was truly disappointed when I found out there really was no Santa Claus.

5. The winner of the Olympic decathlon deserves to be called "the world's greatest athlete."

6. Maintaining your individuality is not always an easy thing to do.

7. Converting from miles to kilometers isn't as difficult as it seems.

8. In my imagination, I can be who I want, be where I want, and do what I want.

9. I don't know what I would do without my best friend.

10. A trip to a museum can sometimes be a better learning experience than reading a history book.

C. A good topic sentence is clear and interesting. It helps to make all the other ideas in a paragraph work together. Here are five groups of sentences. Write a clear and interesting topic sentence for each group, making sure that the topic sentence makes all the other sentences work together.

1. a. Forests can be maintained or enlarged.

b. Trees can be harvested in such a way that new growth can replace trees that are cut for human use.

c. Soil erosion by wind and water can be largely prevented.

d. Exhausted, eroded land can be made usable again by the application of good conservation methods.

2. a. Bif, my old English sheepdog, goes almost everywhere with me.

b. He can run errands with me, romp through the yard with me, or just accompany me silently on a quiet walk.

c. Oftentimes his playfulness is replaced with calmness and he quietly takes his place in a corner while I do my homework, read, or watch TV.

3. a. Some sports events, like professional wrestling, even went through a period when matches were rehearsed to make them more "telegenic."

b. Every wrestling match featured "a hero and a villain."

c. It was terrible sportsmanship and worse sport.

d. To an unsophisticated video audience, it was exciting TV.

4. a. Color and texture of the fur or hair covering the body of the animal may help to make it beautiful.

b. Movement is another quality that contributes much to the beauty of an animal.

c. Some animals are graceful, others clumsy and awkward.

5. a. The long train ride to Grandma and Grandpa's house seemed almost unbearable, but I soon forgot the journey when I arrived at my destination.

b. Grandma, for instance, was dedicated to making me a special person in her house.

c. She filled my requests for a favorite meal, listened to continuous reports of my busy life back home, and allowed me a few liberties I didn't have at my house.

d. Grandpa was an accommodating, kind, and generous person, too.

e. He was always interested in what I did and what I thought, and we spent many hours sharing thoughts with each other.

Chapter 5

Ways of Developing Paragraphs

You know that a good paragraph must have a clear and interesting topic sentence. The topic sentence must set forth a central idea that can be adequately covered in a paragraph. All of the sentences in a paragraph must work together to support the central idea. This chapter will discuss three different ways of adding sentences to develop a paragraph:

1. Using specific details

2. Using examples

3. Using facts or figures

Part 1 Using Specific Details

Specific details are most often used in developing paragraphs that describe something. Suppose, for example, you have been asked to write a paragraph on the topic "My Favorite Month." Where would you start?

First of all, you have twelve months to choose from. Do you prefer swimming or ice skating? When is your favorite holiday? Do you like the fresh new smell of May, or the hustle and bustle of Christmas, when secrets abound and tempting smells fill the air? Perhaps a hot, lazy summer month appeals to you. Is it July, with parades and fireworks on the Fourth? Is it August, when your family goes on vacation?

When you have decided on your favorite month, jot down a list of details that you might include in your paragraph. Let's assume that you have decided to write about October. Your list of items might look like this:

crisp red apples	a new classroom
Halloween parties	football games
leaves turning red and gold	your birthday
carving a jack o' lantern	scrunching leaves beneath
the smell of burning leaves	your feet
chrysanthemums in bloom	goldenrod
cider and doughnuts	the first frost
the harvest moon	

As you go over your list, you find that some details work together better than others. Decide what you really want to say about October. Do you want to describe the way it appeals to your senses? Do you want to describe the events that take place? If you want to describe the appeal to your senses, select only those details that will work together. Your final list might look like this:

crisp red apples (taste)	the harvest moon (sight)
leaves turning red and	scrunching leaves beneath
gold (sight)	your feet (touch)

the smell of burning	cider and doughnuts (taste)
leaves (smell)	goldenrod (sight)
chrysanthemums in bloom	the first frost (all
(sight and smell)	the senses)

Your actual paragraph might look like this:

> When I think of October, all my senses come alive. The scrunch of fallen leaves beneath my feet makes me realize that the trees are getting ready for their long winter sleep. Right now they are dressed in red and gold, touched by the first frost. The smell of burning leaves signals an end to another summer. Purple chrysanthemums and yellow goldenrod brighten yards and fields with color. October is the taste of a crisp red apple, and cider and doughnuts. It is the sight of a harvest moon turning the world to red-gold as it glides above the horizon, and then to silver as it sails through the sky.

Notice how the topic sentence alerts the reader to what the paragraph is going to be about. The specific details from the list have been turned into interesting sentences that work together to describe the month of October.

Suppose you had decided to write about the *events* that take place during the month of October. Your list might look something like this:

Halloween parties	a new classroom
carving a jack o' lantern	football games
cider and doughnuts	your birthday

After you decide on a good topic sentence and arrange your specific details in sentences that work together in an interesting way, your final paragraph might look like this:

> October is a month filled with hustle and bustle. It is a time to find out if your new teacher is really as strict as your brother has told you. It is a time to make new friends. October is Friday night football games, the frightening glare of a jack o' lantern, and the excitement of the Halloween parade. It is the fun of a birthday party, with cider and doughnuts, lots of laughter, and old and new friends.

**Developing a Paragraph by Using
Specific Details**

Following is a list of topic sentences, each one of which may be expanded into a paragraph through the use of specific details. Choose two of the topic sentences that interest you. Then, using specific details, develop each of them into well written paragraphs. Remember that *you are describing what something looks like.* You will need to use your imagination to complete these paragraphs.

1. Margot was a frail girl who looked as if she had been lost in the rain for years.

2. Valion stood in the great jungle that covered the planet Venus.

3. Above, crouched on a rock, was a great golden cat, a cougar.

4. It was the day before Thanksgiving, and the snow had started falling early in the morning.

5. Juan was frail, and quite small for his age.

6. The sad-eyed dog remained alone at the edge of the clearing.

7. The night was unusually warm.

8. At thirteen, Harry Glover was as big as a college sophomore.

9. From the top of Graham Street, you can see clear across the valley.

10. It was the worst storm I had ever seen.

Part 2   Using Examples

Sometimes a topic sentence may be a general idea that can best be developed through the use of an example. Suppose that you are planning a paragraph based on your own experience with snakes. There are many things you could say about snakes, but one particular incident, or example, stands out in your mind. Here is a paragraph about one person's experience with snakes.

> Garter snakes are not good mothers. The day I discovered that my garter snake had unexpectedly given birth to thirty babies, I was sure I had a gold mine right there in my aquarium cage. I immediately made a mental list of friends who would be happy to pay a dollar apiece for their very own snake. Mother was enthusiastic about getting rid of them—once she stopped holding her head and moaning. She even promised to buy me a new football the day the last snake was sold. The next day, however, only twenty babies were left in the cage. The snake supply dwindled daily. By the time the little snakes would have been big enough to sell, Mother Garter Snake had gobbled every one for breakfast, lunch, and dinner.

The writer of this paragraph has used a very convincing example, indeed, of why "Garter snakes are not good mothers."

Exercise   Developing a Paragraph by Using Examples

Following is a list of topic sentences. Choose two of the topic sentences that interest you. Then, using specific examples, develop them into well written paragraphs.

1. Friday the thirteenth has always been unlucky for me.
2. The practical joke I tried to play really backfired.
3. My dog is convinced that he (or she) is a person.
4. Moving day was busy, and a little sad.
5. Debbie's first day of work at the Pizza Hut was almost her last.
6. It was the most exciting day of my life.
7. You can't always believe what you hear.
8. You never get something for nothing.
9. Some people just never grow up.
10. Sometimes you have to laugh at yourself.

Part 3 Using Facts or Figures

Developing a paragraph by using facts or figures is similar to developing a paragraph by using examples. The difference between the two is that in developing a paragraph by using examples, the writer usually uses just *one example*, in order to explain that example in greater detail. In developing a paragraph by using facts or figures, the writer chooses *several short, specific examples* to prove a point, or to make an idea clear, as in the following paragraph:

> The Twentieth Century has witnessed the important work of many black persons in the field of medical science. Dr. Daniel H. Williams pioneered in heart surgery at Provident Hospital in Chicago. Dr. William Hinton taught at Harvard University Medical School and directed a laboratory at the Massachusetts Department of Public Health. Dr. Charles Richard Drew was a pioneer in methods of preserving blood plasma. During World War II he was director of the American Red Cross blood donor project, and later he served as chief surgeon of Freedman's Hospital in Washington, D. C.
> —EARL SPANGLER

It is easy to see how this writer has developed his paragraph through the use of facts concerning Dr. Williams, Dr. Hinton, and Dr. Drew. All of the facts, of course, relate specifically to the idea in the topic sentence.

Let's look at another paragraph.

> America has become an urban society. Seventy years ago more people lived on farms or in rural areas. At that time about 40 percent, or two out of every five persons, lived in the country. Now only 25 percent, or one person in four, live there.—MARC ROSENBLUM

In this paragraph, the writer has used specific figures to prove the statement in the topic sentence.

Exercise Developing a Paragraph by Using Facts or Figures

Following is a list of topic sentences, each one of which may be expanded into a paragraph through the use of facts or figures. Choose two of the topic sentences that interest you. Then, using facts or figures, develop them into well written paragraphs.

1. We have a good basketball team in our school.
2. Today's students are good students.
3. _____ Restaurant has the best food in town.
4. Our school has good athletic facilities.
5. Watching too much TV is a waste of time.
6. My father is a kind, considerate person.
7. Reading a good book is an excellent form of entertainment.
8. Skateboarding can be dangerous.
9. Some hobbies can be expensive.
10. Our city has many beautiful parks.

Chapter 6

Kinds of Paragraphs

A writer always has to think about the best way to make a subject interesting to the reader. Not every topic should be handled in the same way, because the writing would soon become dull and lifeless. Just as there are several ways of developing a paragraph, there are also several *kinds* of paragraphs. This chapter will discuss three of those kinds:

1. Narrative

2. Descriptive

3. Explanatory

Part 1   The Narrative Paragraph

Of the different kinds of paragraphs, the narrative paragraph is the easiest to write. It is our most familiar and natural form of communication. It is the type of writing used by the storyteller who begins a story, "Once upon a time. . . ." It is the type of writing you use when you write a letter that begins, "You'll never guess what I did yesterday."

Something different or interesting happens to you on the way to school, and you want to tell a friend about it. You use narration. Your school basketball team just won an exciting game, and you want to tell your parents what happened. You use narration. A narrative paragraph, then, is a "what happened" paragraph.

Because the narrative paragraph tells what happened, it needs some kind of organization. Otherwise, the events may get all mixed up, and the reader will be confused. The kind of organization most often used in the narrative paragraph is that of *time sequence*. In using time sequence, the writer tells what happened *in the order that it happened*, as in the following example:

> Buster and I had been in the woods, and now we were plunging down the hill through the fast-falling dark to the carnival. I could see the tent and the flares and the gathering crowd. We stopped to rest, and Buster stood very straight and pointed down below, making a big sweep with his arm like an Indian chief in the movies.—RALPH ELLISON

Because the narrative paragraph is such an easy and natural way of writing, you may find that some narrative paragraphs do not have topic sentences. However, for now, you should try to write strong and interesting topic sentences and use a time sequence in your paragraphs.

You may also find that writing narrative paragraphs will be easier if you write about things that have happened to you personally. This type of writing is called *first-person narrative* because it is you, the writer, telling about something that happened to you, rather than about something that happened to someone else.

Read the following examples of first-person narrative. Notice that the writer has created strong topic sentences and narrated the events in an orderly time sequence.

1

I had just passed the old cedar tree that marks the start of Troublesome Hollow, when I heard a low, odd-sounding whine. I stopped and looked all around, and after a little searching I found what had made the noise. It was a pup of some sort, with a funny-shaped head and dark fur, and the most appealing blue eyes I had ever seen. I tried to pick it up, but the little thing was frightened and ran off a little way. I kept clicking my tongue and whistling and calling, but it would just crouch with its nostrils twitching wildly and run when I approached.—MITCHELL F. JAYNE

2

Mama was waiting for us when we got home. I put on my shoes and ran into the front room to show them to her. My father proudly explained how I'd won them. Mama turned on her player piano and I did my routine. She smiled. "My, oh, my! You're a real dancer now." She shook her head at my father. "You buy him shoes when you don't have money for food. I always knew you was smart."—SAMMY DAVIS, JR.

3

One evening my mother told me that thereafter I would have to do the shopping for food. She took me to the corner store to show me the way. I was proud; I felt like a grown-up. The next afternoon I looped the basket over my arm and went down the pavement toward the store. When I reached the corner, a gang of boys grabbed me, knocked me down, snatched the basket, took the money, and sent me running home in panic. That evening I told my mother what had happened, but she made no comment; she sat down at once, wrote another note, gave me more money, and sent me out to the grocery again. I crept down the steps and saw the same gang of boys playing down the street. I ran back into the house.—RICHARD WRIGHT

Using Details in the Narrative Paragraph

In the preceding chapter, you learned the importance of using specific details to make an experience come alive for the reader. In writing a narrative paragraph, using vivid details is particularly important in helping the reader to share your experience. Notice the use of details in the following paragraph.

I was the last contestant in the bubble gum contest at school, and I was determined to win. Constant practice had limbered my jaw and improved my blowing technique. I chewed the sugary wad of Blow Hard confidently until it arrived at the properly smooth texture. I inhaled deeply; then I blew. The bubble was the size of a marble—the size of an egg—the size of a baseball. When it finally burst, like a rubbery pink balloon, the class cheered. I was clearly the new bubble gum champ of Washington Junior High.

The carefully selected details not only make the experience interesting, but they also create a feeling of suspense for the reader.

Exercise   Writing First-Person Narrative Paragraphs

Following is a list of topic sentences. Choose two that interest you, or make up two of your own. Then, using your imagination or your personal experience (or a little of each), develop each sentence into a first-person narrative paragraph. Select the kinds of specific details that will help to make the experience come alive for the reader.

1. After I left school yesterday afternoon, things really began to go wrong.
2. It was our family's first experience on an airplane.

3. I finally decided to have my hair cut.

4. I walked along the road until I found a path through the woods.

5. It was the hardest job I ever had to do.

6. Because of what happened, I didn't get home until late.

7. That afternoon proved to me that I could really be somebody if I tried.

8. It was my first try at skiing, and I was really scared.

9. It was an unpleasant event that taught me never to fight again.

10. I didn't know until yesterday that Pete was a coward.

Part 2   The Descriptive Paragraph

It is not always easy to tell the difference between a narrative and a descriptive paragraph. A narrative paragraph, as you know, tells "what happened." A descriptive paragraph, on the other hand, does not have much action because the writer's main purpose is to paint a picture with words.

The descriptive paragraph appeals to our senses, particularly those of sight and sound, because they are usually the most highly developed of all our senses. These two kinds of descriptive paragraphs—sight description and sound description—are the ones you will study in this chapter. You may wish to review Chapter 3, Using the Senses, as you work with this section.

Using Specific Details

Imagine that you are describing a man walking down the street. To simply write, "The man walked down the street," does not paint much of a picture. Is he a young man? a middle-aged man? an old man? To say merely that he *walked* down the street is not very clear, either. There are many ways of walking.

In order to make your word-picture more exact, suppose you write, "The young man sauntered happily down the busy street." Now your picture becomes more exact, and also more interesting. However, in order to develop the picture more fully, you need to expand your paragraph with several more specific details.

> The young man sauntered happily down the busy street. His head was high; his chin was up; and his long arms swung in breezy arcs against the pockets of his new green sport jacket. The heels of his freshly polished black shoes made a loud, snapping "pop, pop" as he maneuvered his way through the hurrying crowd.

Now we can not only see this man clearly, we can almost feel the energy of his movements. The specific details have created an interesting, lively word-picture.

In order to stress the importance of specific details, let's select different ones to describe the same young man. Notice how the picture changes completely in the following paragraph.

> The young man shuffled sadly down the empty street. His head was low; his chin drooped against his chest; and his long, thin arms hung dejectedly against the frayed pockets of his faded green jacket. The soles of his battered, once-black shoes made a whispered "shush, shush" sound as he wandered through the lonely silence.

Of course, someone may say, "That's not a good word-picture because I don't know what the young man looks like." You must remember, however, that the paragraph must contain only what the topic sentence says it will contain. The topic sentence says the paragraph will describe the young man going down the street, not what he looks like.

Let's work on another description, one of sound. In this one, we are going to describe the sound of a bell. First, we must decide what kind of bell it is. Is it old? new? silver? brass? Second, where is the bell? Finally, what does it sound like?

The old brass bell hanging in the church steeple tolled softly. Its sad, mournful tone, made discordant by a crack in its rim, floated down gently about the assembled mourners. Then the sound echoed and re-echoed, once, twice, before it disappeared into the forest like the sound of a distant mourning dove.

Rewrite this paragraph, changing whatever details are necessary in order to change the description of the sound of the bell.

Following a Logical Order

In discussing the writing of the narrative paragraph, we said that the events should be told in a time sequence. That is the logical order in writing the narrative paragraph.

To make the ideas clear in the descriptive paragraph, you also need a logical order. For the descriptive paragraph, that order is usually a *space relationship*. By space relationship, we mean how the things you are describing are situated in relation to each other in the area or space you are describing.

To understand the idea of space relationship more clearly, let's look at the following paragraph. Notice how specific the writer is as he describes the room.

> All the living space for the family was in the one large room, about twelve feet wide and three times as long. Against the wall between the two doorways was the *pretil*, a bank of adobe bricks three feet high, three across, and two feet deep. In the center of the *pretil* was the main fire pit. Two smaller hollows, one on either side of the large one, made it a three-burner stove. On a row of pegs above the *pretil* hung the clay pans and other cooking utensils, bottom side out, the soot baked into the red clay. A low bench next to the *pretil*, also made of adobe, served as a table and shelf for the cups, pots, and plates.—ERNESTO GALARZA

In this paragraph, the writer has shown the relationship of the different things to each other through the use of specific *direc-*

tion words, such as "against the wall," "between the two doorways," "in the center," "one on either side," "above," and "next to." These words help the reader to see where all the things the writer is describing are placed in relation to each other.

There are times, of course, when it is not necessary to use space relationship words. That is when the writer describes things in a *natural order*. For example, reread the description of the young man going down the street. The description moves from his head, to his arms, to his feet. That is a natural order. If the description had moved from his head, to his feet, and back to his arms, the natural order would have been broken, and the description might have confused the reader.

Sustaining a Point of View

The topic sentence prepares the reader for a certain way of looking at what the writer is describing. In order to help the reader *feel*, as well as see, what you are describing, you must keep your point of view the same all through the paragraph. Remember the two entirely different impressions of the man walking down the street? The topic sentence of each of them presented the point of view, and the remainder of the paragraph sustained it. The same thing happened in the paragraphs on the sound of the bell.

If your topic sentence says, "The eerie old house smelled dank and strange; all of us were suddenly afraid," your reader expects you to describe a frightening or a depressing experience. If your topic sentence says, "The happy old house had once rocked with joyous laughter and seemed to welcome us inside," you have prepared your reader for a paragraph describing pleasant experiences.

The most important purpose in writing a descriptive paragraph is to create a single, unified impression in the mind of your reader.

Exercise   Writing Descriptive Paragraphs

Following is a list of topic sentences. Choose two sentences that interest you—one describing sight, and one describing sound. Then, using either your personal experience or your imagination, develop each sentence into a descriptive paragraph, using specific details, logical space relationships, and a sustained point of view. If none of these sentences interests you, make up some sentences of your own.

1. The pale moon rose eerily over the distant mountains.

2. My grandmother's garden was a splash of brilliant colors.

3. She was wearing the strangest costume I had ever seen.

4. The creature was obviously from another planet.

5. The gymnasium looked like the inside of some huge old barn.

6. The sound of Mike's motorcycle broke the early morning stillness.

7. The _____ is my favorite room in the house.

8. Baker Street is the most rundown street in town.

9. The sound of traffic was ear-splitting.

10. Holly loves to walk through the dry, autumn leaves.

11. The sound of music was everywhere.

12. The thunderstorm was like a brilliant fireworks display.

13. My neighborhood is blissfully quiet in the early morning.

14. The cheering section at the football game exploded in wild screams.

15. _____ is the most beautiful place I have ever seen.

Part 3 The Explanatory Paragraph

You will probably do more explanatory writing throughout your life than any other kind. As its name suggests, the explanatory paragraph *explains*. It does not tell a story. It does not paint a word-picture. Instead, it explains, as clearly as possible, *how* or *why*.

The "How" Paragraph

The "how" paragraph explains *how something is done*. Your friend Mary wants to know how to ride a skateboard. Your little brother wants to know how to play "Fishermen." Your friend Bill wants to know how to build a campfire. In order to explain how these things are done, you will need to give your instructions very clearly and in a logical order.

The logical arrangement of ideas in the "how" paragraph is *time sequence*, the same arrangement you used in writing the narrative paragraph. You explain what should be done first, what should be done next, and so on. As an example, let's look at a paragraph that explains how to make a tortilla.

> Dona Esther was already at the *comal*, making the fresh supply of tortillas for the day. She plucked small lumps, one by one, from the heap of corn dough she kept in a deep clay pot. She gave the lump a few squeezes to make a thick, round biscuit which she patted and pulled and clapped into a thin disk. The corncake grew larger and larger until it hung in loose ruffles around her hands. She spread her fingers wide to hold the thin, pale folds of dangling dough. As she clapped she gave her wrists a half turn, making the tortilla tilt between each tat-tat of her palms. On each twist the tortilla seemed to slip loose but she would clamp it gently for another tat-tat. When the tortilla was thin and round and utterly floppy, she laid it on the *comal*.—ERNESTO GALARZA

If a person can follow your instructions successfully, you know your explanation is clear. However, if you have to give further explanation, you know that your paragraph needs more work.

The "Why" Paragraph

The "why" paragraph gives reasons why something is believed to be so. It begins with an idea or an opinion, and is then expanded by giving the writer's reasons why he or she believes the idea or opinion is true. It may also give the reason why something happened. For example, "Why were you so late coming home from school?" "Why didn't you eat your lunch?" "I really enjoyed that new movie." Questions or statements like these ask for reasons.

The usual tendency in answering questions is to respond with something like this: "I couldn't get my locker open"; "I wasn't very hungry"; or "It was an exciting movie." Such answers are inadequate because they really haven't explained "why."

In order to be convincing, a "why" question requires adequate supporting details, such as "Why couldn't you get your locker open?" "Why weren't you hungry?" "Why was the movie exciting?" The answers to these questions will require even more supporting details. For example:

"Why couldn't you get your locker open?"
"Because Jim put gum in the lock."
"Why did he do that?"
"Because he was mad at me."
"Why was he mad?"
"Because I wouldn't let him borrow my bike."
"Why wouldn't you let him borrow your bike?"
"Because the last time he used it he had a flat tire and refused to fix it."
"And you didn't want anything to happen again?"
"That's right."

Now we understand "why." The supporting details have finally made the reason clear.

Organizing the supporting details in a "why" paragraph requires a different arrangement from those in a "how" paragraph. As you can see from the above dialogue, the supporting details of a "why" paragraph usually consist of several reasons that can't be placed in a specific time sequence. Therefore, you need a different kind of arrangement of details. The usual arrangement for a "why" paragraph is to place the least important ideas first, and to move toward the most important idea, as in the following example:

> Yataro was more fortunate than the motherless, fatherless, little sparrow searching for food in the snow. He had a father. He had a warm house. And he had a friend—his grandmother. She was very old and not strong, but she loved Yataro and took care of him. Yataro's father was too busy to pay much attention to him, but his grandmother was always there when he needed her.—HANAKO FUKUDA

The writer begins the paragraph with a topic sentence that raises the question, "Why was Yataro more fortunate than the sparrow?" The writer gives the reasons, moving from the least important to the most important:

1. Yataro had a father.

2. He had a warm house.

3. He had a grandmother who took care of him because his father was too busy to pay attention to him.

Let's look at another example. This one is a little more complicated because it asks two "why" questions.

> Every soul in the little fishing village at the foot of the mountain had learned to accept the fog. It was part of their life. They knew that for weeks on end they must live within

its circle. They made no pretense of liking it. Those who tilled their little plots of land hated it when it kept their hay from drying. The men who fished dreaded it, for it either kept them on shore altogether and cut down their meager earnings, or it made their hours on the sea more dangerous than ever.—JULIA L. SAUER

The first question is, "Why did the people in the village accept the fog?" The second is, "Why didn't they like the fog?" The writer gives specific answers to both questions— moving from the least important to the most important.

By breaking the paragraph down into separate parts, we can more clearly see the writer's method of arrangement.

Question 1: Why had the people learned to accept the fog?

Answer 1: It was part of their life.

Answer 2: For weeks on end, they had to live within the fog.

Question 2: Why didn't they like the fog?

Answer 1: It kept the farmers' hay from drying.

Answer 2: It kept the fishermen from going to sea, so they lost money.

Answer 3: It made fishing more dangerous if the fishermen decided to go to sea.

With this type of arrangement of supporting details in a "why" paragraph, the reader can easily follow the writer's reasoning.

Exercise Writing Explanatory Paragraphs

Following is a list of topic sentences. Some of them may be developed as "how" paragraphs, others as "why" paragraphs. Choose one of each kind of topic sentence and develop it into a well organized paragraph. If none of these topic sentences interests you, make up some sentences of your own.

1. It's easy to learn to play checkers.
2. Of all the jobs I can think of, I dislike _____ most.
3. The first think I ever cooked turned out awful.
4. Skateboarding is not as easy as it looks.
5. To make a pot, you first have to get some clay.
6. Hamsters require a lot of care.
7. My brother taught me how to load a camera.
8. Although *Gone with the Wind* is an old movie, it is still worth seeing.
9. A dog is the best pet a person can have.
10. I can't wait until I'm eighteen.
11. I learned the best way to barbecue hamburgers last summer.
12. I can hardly wait for school to start each year.
13. The salesperson showed me how to adjust our color TV.
14. The school day should be shorter/longer than it is.
15. _____ is a very good form of exercise.

Chapter 7

Writing the Composition

From your reading, and from your own experience in writing, you know it is not always possible to say everything you want to say in a single paragraph. Usually, it takes several paragraphs to explain an idea fully. This chapter will introduce you to some of the ways that paragraphs can be joined together to make a composition.

Part 1   What Is a Composition?

Just as the paragraph is a group of related sentences that "work together," the composition is *a group of related paragraphs* that "work together." You know that the paragraph usually begins with a topic sentence that tells what the paragraph is going to be about, as in the following example:

> *Tom slept more soundly that night than he had in a long time.* His dreams were of the new friend he had found. He dreamed of the deer and himself running over the green meadows and up the gentle slopes of the hills. He dreamed beautiful dreams like these until the morning when the sun came through his window and woke him.—JENNY DEBOUZEK

In a composition, the topic sentence is expanded into an *introductory paragraph.* This paragraph, like the topic sentence, tells the reader what the composition is going to be about.

Let's look at an example of a composition. Notice that the introductory paragraph consists of three sentences. These sentences tell the reader what the composition is going to be about.

ACHIEVEMENTS OF THE CHINESE-AMERICANS

Today the Chinese-Americans are highly respected persons who can enter any business or profession for which they are qualified. There are Chinese in all walks of life. They are engineers, judges, scientists, and pharmacists, as well as cooks, taxi drivers, barbers, and laborers.

Modern Chinese-Americans are active in politics. Some of them have served as mayors of cities, members of state legislatures and of the U.S. Congress. The role of today's Chinese woman is changing. In 1971, when the San Francisco City School Department tried to bus children out of Chinatown to other schools, the women protested so vigorously that they were featured on television and radio and written about in newspapers across the nation.

Some Chinese overcame earlier handicaps of prejudice and discrimination to become noted. One was Gim Gong Lue, who arrived in San Francisco in 1872 at the age of twelve. Like Luther Burbank, Lue was a genius at breeding new strains of fruits and flowers. He developed the Lue orange, which proved to be one of the finest commercial varieties.

The U.S. Department of Agriculture honored him with the Wilder Medal. Lee received little financial reward from the orange and died in poverty. His gift to the citrus fruit industry, however, was worth millions of dollars.

In 1957, two young Chinese-American physicists received the Nobel Prize in physics. At that time, Dr. Chen Ning Yang, a member of the Institute for Advanced Study at Princeton, was only thirty-four. His partner, Dr. Tsung Dao Lee, a professor of physics at Columbia University, was thirty. These two brilliant young men developed a new theory about the nuclear structure of the atom. Their theory led to a better understanding of the forces that govern our universe, and its application will benefit mankind.

The Chinese-Americans are a small minority. According to the 1970 census, there are 435,062 people in this group. Nevertheless, their achievements have enriched American life far out of proportion to their numbers.—DOROTHY AND JOSEPH DOWDELL

It is easy to see that this composition is made up of five paragraphs. The first paragraph is the topic or introductory paragraph and tells us what the rest of the composition is going to be about. The next four paragraphs work together to develop the ideas in the introductory paragraph. The last, or concluding, paragraph ends the composition by briefly summarizing the main ideas of the composition. You can also see that each of the six paragraphs begins with a clearly written and interesting topic sentence.

Part 2 Finding a Subject

"I don't have anything to write about" is the most common complaint of students when they are asked to write a composition. Unfortunately, students who complain in this manner are overlooking the most interesting subject in the world—themselves.

As a person, you are unique. There is no one else in the world just like you. Your own life, your own experiences, your own knowledge is different from that of any other person who has ever lived. Therefore, you have a wealth of material to write about that no one else has.

One of the most important things that writers must learn is that they must have something to say if they wish to write well. What one can write about best, of course, is what one is most familiar with. Now some student may ask, "But what about people who write history books?" or "What about people today who write stories about the Civil War or about life in Ancient Greece? They were never there." The answer to these questions is that those writers have studied their subjects until the material has become familiar to them. It has become part of their personal knowledge.

In order to write well, it is not always necessary for a writer to experience everything personally. What is necessary is that he or she study enough to be able to write about the subject with familiarity and understanding.

Look at the following example:

THE PYRAMID OF KHUFU

The most spectacular and famous of all Egyptian tombs is the Great Pyramid of Giza, built by the Pharaoh Khufu, who is also known by his Greek name, Cheops. Many pyramid tombs were built along the Nile by ancient Pharaohs—more than seventy we know—and many of great size. But Khufu's was by far the largest.

Khufu ruled about 4,500 years ago, in the beginning of the 4th Dynasty. Yet today, when the most complicated and sophisticated engineering feats are taken for granted, we marvel at this incredible structure and wonder that it was ever achieved. It still stands as the largest stone structure in the world. Its base covers thirteen acres. Two million, three hundred thousand blocks of stone were used, each weighing from two to thirteen tons.

It took 100,000 men more than twenty years to build Khufu's pyramid. And the toll of human lives must have been terrible. They worked in relentless heat, dirt, wind, and sand. The wheel had not been invented then, nor had the pulley.

Men cut the stone—nearly ten billion pounds—from quarries east of Giza, across the Nile. They loaded the enormous stones on barges, and men harnessed with ropes pulled the sledges to the river. When the waters rose and the flats were flooded, they moved the stones onto huge rafts and floated them across the wide valley. At the base of the hill on which the pyramid was being built, an immense ramp was constructed. Up this incline the stones were hauled. Then came the formidable task of lifting them into position. With the use of ropes and small graveled ramps, gangs of men managed to push and haul and lift them into place.

These thousands of men lived where they worked. Hence a small city had to be built to house them and to provide for all their needs. It is thought that they were allowed to go home, in shifts, to sow their crops. But on the whole, for twenty years or more this tremendous amount of manpower was spent on building a tomb in the desert.

Was Khufu ever buried in his magnificent tomb? No one knows. His burial chamber was empty when an entrance into the pyramid was found in modern times.—MILDRED MASTIN PACE

In writing this composition, the writer certainly did not have first-hand experience with the building of the Pyramid of Khufu. What she did was to study until the information became familiar to her. Only then could she write *as though she had had the experience.*

Exercise   Finding a Subject

To help you to think about your life, your experience, your knowledge as the subject for a composition, study the following list of subjects. After you have studied the list, make a list of five subjects of your own that you feel you could write about with familiarity and understanding. If any of the subjects listed here interests you, you may add it to your list. *Keep your list for a future assignment.*

1. Collecting rocks as a hobby
2. My dog's best trick
3. A happy moment with my grandmother
4. I had the craziest dream
5. Raising tropical fish
6. Water-skiing for fun
7. Japanese festivals
8. The night I fell out of bed
9. Cheerleading
10. Writing a poem
11. Sometimes I do the craziest things
12. Shadows
13. The life of a butterfly
14. Lunchtime at school
15. Growing apples
16. Van Gogh, the artist
17. A rainy-day pastime
18. When my father was a boy
19. Learning to play a musical instrument
20. What it means to be a (girl) (boy)

Part 3 Planning the Composition

Once you have decided on a *general subject* for your composition, there are several steps you must take to make certain that your composition will be interesting and understandable.

Narrowing the Subject

The first step is to *narrow the subject* so that the material can be covered adequately in your composition. To understand what "narrowing the subject" means, look at the following two examples of possible ideas for subjects:

1. A Friend Who Wasn't
2. Chinese Holidays

In the first example, the writer has chosen a subject from *personal experience*. In the second, the writer has chosen a subject from *personal knowledge*. The first subject suggests that the writer is going to tell us about an experience in which she discovered that a friend was not really a friend. Because the subject may be about one specific experience, or one specific friend, the writer can easily explain her "discovery" in a short composition. Therefore, the subject does not need to be narrowed any more.

The second example presents a different problem. Like all people throughout the world, the Chinese have many holidays. If the writer were to try to cover all of them, he or she would have to make the composition very long, or else give the reader such a small amount of information on each holiday that the reader would not learn very much about any of them. Therefore, this subject needs to be narrowed.

The writer who is familiar with Chinese holidays knows that the New Year is the most important of all of them. It would also be a good subject because it can be easily explained in a short composition.

Having narrowed that subject, we now have two *specific* subjects, each of which can be developed into a short composition.

1. A Friend Who Wasn't
2. The Chinese New Year

A. Each of the following subjects is too broad to be handled in a composition. Narrow each subject so it can be covered in a short composition.

1. Exercise	6. Vacations
2. Music	7. Birds
3. Animals	8. Sports
4. Television	9. American cities
5. School	10. Money

B. From the list of subjects you made in the previous exercise on page 105, choose one subject you would really like to write about. Study the subject carefully. Is it narrow enough so that you can easily cover it in a short composition? If not, narrow the subject so that you can write a clear and understandable composition on it. You may wish to check your final subject with your teacher.

Part 4   Writing the Introduction

After you have decided on the specific subject for your composition, your next step is to work on your opening paragraph. Because you want people to read your entire composition, you will want your introductory paragraph to catch your reader's attention. You will also want to give your reader a clear idea of what your composition is going to be about.

Read the following two introductory paragraphs:

1

Once in second grade, I had a friend named Lois. I liked her a lot because she had beautiful blonde hair and a new bicycle. She also got twenty-five cents a week for an allowance.

2

In this composition, I am going to tell you about the Chinese New Year. I have studied about this holiday ever since my father and mother took me to one in San Francisco. It was a lot of fun.

Both of these paragraphs give the reader an idea as to what the compositions are going to be about, but neither one of them is interesting. There is really nothing there to make the reader want to read any further. Now read these two paragraphs:

1

My braided brown hair and old red tricycle looked shabby compared with the long golden curls and shiny two-wheel bicycle of my friend. Lois also had a twenty-five cent allowance and long fingernails. I named all my dolls Lois. She was my ideal, everything I wanted to be.

2

To the Chinese in the United States, as well as elsewhere in the world, the most important festival of the year is that of the New Year. This holiday can fall anytime between January 21 and February 19. It is believed that the forces of Yang, warmth and light, are ready to overcome the forces of Yin, cold, dark winter.

These introductory paragraphs have certainly been improved. The writers have given the reader an idea of what the compositions are going to be about. They have chosen their words carefully and created interesting sentences to tempt their readers to read further.

Exercises   Working with Introductory Paragraphs

A. Following are ten introductory paragraphs. Some of them are well written; some of them are not. Study the paragraphs carefully; then decide which paragraphs are the best. In class discussion, give reasons for your decisions.

1

For the fifth year, Father Joe was spending his Christmas visiting the Indians. He kept the pinto moving briskly along, for he hoped to see his entire mission before nightfall. However, the horse could not make very rapid progress through the snow that lay about a foot deep on the plateau.

2

My composition is going to tell you about Eddie and his friend Horace Squiggle. Eddie was five years old when we moved next door to him. One day, soon after we came, I was reading on our back porch when I heard his high, shrill voice. He was always screaming like that.

3

Skeezix was a sorrel, although the pigment of his mouth showed signs that he might turn blue like his mother. He had one white stocking, a bald face, and several big fawn-like splotches. He had long legs, too, and long ears and a long, slender muzzle, but everything else was short. Especially his life.

4

Spring evening restlessness had pulled me outdoors as soon as the supper dishes were done. I watched from behind the trumpet-vine trellis while my older sister left the house with her date. Then, moodily, I ducked behind the garage and started up the alley toward the elementary school playground two blocks away. There were friends I could have gone to see, but tonight I preferred to be alone, and to enjoy the sorrow of being alone.

5

This is about when I was eight years old. I came home from school one Friday evening to have my father tell me that he was going to take me 'possum hunting. I was so thrilled I could hardly wait until night came. I had heard many stories about 'possum hunting, and I wondered if it would be as I expected.

6

I'd like to tell you about a memorable day in my life. When I awoke, I had no idea of the thrilling event that was to take place. It seemed that a usual morning passed with the duties of housework, but around noon I began to have a strange feeling in my bones.

7

We have a haunted telephone. Strangely and yet truthfully enough, it is haunted by mysterious and sometimes irritating phantoms.

8

The first step in building a house is to find somewhere to put it. We put ours in a big hole. The whole (pun) idea seemed silly to me, but who was I to try to change these foolish customs?

9

Have you ever thought how important doors are? I have, and in my composition I want to give you some of my ideas. But first, in order to approach this subject with an unbiased and open manner, we must first consider the two types of doors—those with doorknobs and those without. We shall begin by discussing that type known as the revolving door.

10

All the food and bedding had been loaded into the car. After last-minute checkings from each of our mothers, we started off on our one week's vacation in the pleasant and somewhat exciting atmosphere of Brighton.

B. Write the introductory paragraph for your own composition. Make it as clear and interesting as you can. When you have finished, you may wish to discuss the paragraph with your teacher or your classmates. Revise it where necessary.

Part 5   Planning the Body

Once you have written the introduction, you are ready to organize your ideas and begin writing the *body* of your composition. This is an important part of your composition because it is in the body that you explain the ideas you introduced in your opening paragraph.

Organizing the Ideas

Before you begin writing the body of the composition, you will want to make certain that you are going to include all the information necessary to explain your introductory paragraph. You will also want to make certain that your ideas are arranged in a logical order. Therefore, it is a good idea to make a list of the ideas you want to include in the body of your composition, like the following:

A FRIEND WHO WASN'T

INTRODUCTION: My braided brown hair and old red tricycle looked shabby compared with the long golden curls and shiny two-wheel bicycle of my friend. Lois also had a twenty-five cent allowance and long fingernails. I named all my dolls Lois. She was my ideal, everything I wanted to be.

1. I tagged after Lois but she often told me to go home.

2. I was sure I would make her think I was good enough to be her pal.

3. One day an incident happened that opened my eyes.

4. Lois became less of a friend.

5. She destroyed my dream castles.

THE CHINESE NEW YEAR

INTRODUCTION: To the Chinese in the United States, as well as elsewhere in the world, the most important festival of the year is that of the New Year. This holiday can fall anytime between January 21 and February 19. It is believed that the forces of Yang, warmth and light, are ready to overcome the forces of Yin, cold, dark winter.

1. Homes decorated with flowers and fruit

2. A time for a new beginning

3. The Dragon Dancers in the parade

4. The big New Year's parade

Since you have listed all the ideas you want to write about, you could, of course, begin writing the body of your composition now. However, the reader would have a difficult time following your ideas because they are not in logical order. Your next step, then, is to organize your ideas so that the reader can follow them easily.

After looking at the first list of ideas, you can see that the best way to organize the ideas is in *time sequence*, telling what happened first, then what happened next. The order of the ideas would look like this:

A FRIEND WHO WASN'T

INTRODUCTION:

1. I tagged after Lois but she often told me to go home.

2. One day an incident happened that opened my eyes.

3. I was sure I would make her think I was good enough to be her pal.

4. She destroyed my dream castles.

5. Lois became less of a friend.

The writer would begin with a general explanation of her "friendship" with Lois, and then explain, in time sequence, the specific incident that ended that "friendship."

In the second list, the ideas do not follow in chronological order because many of the events of the Chinese New Year occur at the same time. Therefore, the best method for organizing these ideas is from *the least important to the most important*. The order of the ideas would look like this:

THE CHINESE NEW YEAR

INTRODUCTION

1. A time for a new beginning

2. Homes decorated with flowers and fruit

3. The big New Year's parade

4. The Dragon Dancers in the parade

In both examples, the ideas are now arranged in an order that is easy for the reader to follow.

Exercises   Organizing Ideas

A. Following is a list of subjects with their supporting ideas. As you can see, the ideas are not organized in any logical manner. Decide which method of organization would be best for each list of supporting ideas. Then reorganize the lists.

1. The life cycle of the butterfly

a. The butterfly egg hatches into a caterpillar.

b. The adult butterfly emerges.

c. The butterfly begins life as an egg.

d. The caterpillar sheds its skin and goes into the pupa stage.

e. The pupa spins a silky cocoon.

2. My first fishing trip.

   a. Finally, I felt a nibble on my line.

   b. Dad woke me at dawn that morning.

   c. The fresh fish was the most delicious I'd ever eaten.

   d. At noon, we built a campfire to fry our catch.

   e. When I reeled in my line, the pike looked enormous.

   f. We fished silently on the lake for two hours.

3. Winter wonderland

   a. My friends and I decided to take a hike in the snow.

   b. Below us, we saw a deer drinking from a pool.

   c. We stood at the edge of the cliff and looked down.

   d. First, we climbed a cliff overlooking the valley.

   e. A falling rock startled the deer, and she bounded
into the woods.

4. Planning a bike hike

   a. Travel a reasonable distance each day.

   b. Why not get some friends together for a bike hike
this summer?

   c. First, plan your route; avoid major highways.

   d. Once you're on the road, share food and
chores equally.

   e. Prepare maps, showing sightseeing spots along
the way.

5. Why I was late for school

   a. My shoelace was broken, and I had to find another.

   b. Our car is being repaired so I had to walk.

   c. The alarm clock didn't go off this morning.

   d. I was nearly a block from home when I had to go
back for my homework.

   e. After I laced my shoe, Mom insisted that I
eat breakfast.

B. You should now have your introductory paragraph written. List the ideas you wish to include in the body of your composition; then arrange those ideas in a logical order.

Part 6 Writing the Body

Earlier in this chapter, we said that the body of your composition is important because it is in the body that you explain the ideas you introduced in your introductory paragraph. Now that you have your ideas arranged in order, your next step in writing the body is to fill in all the necessary details to explain the ideas on your list.

In adding the details, you must be sure that you do not add *too many* details or you will confuse your reader. You must also be sure that the details you include are specific and clear.

As examples of how the body of a composition explains the ideas in the introductory paragraph, let's continue with our compositions. Here is the introductory paragraph for "A Friend Who Wasn't."

> My braided brown hair and old red tricycle looked shabby compared with the long golden curls and shiny two-wheel bicycle of my friend. Lois also had a twenty-five cent allowance and long fingernails. I named my dolls Lois. She was my ideal, everything I wanted to be.

After the writer had listed the ideas for the body, we said that the paper would be best organized by giving a general explanation of the "friendship" with Lois. We would then explain, in *time sequence*, the specific incident that ended the "friendship." Notice how the writer has followed through in this organization and supplied specific details.

> Although Lois was only in the fifth grade, she always had boys tagging after her. *I tagged after her*, too, but she didn't like that half as much. *She often told me to go home*, but I thought this was because she had some work to do.

One day an incident happened that opened my eyes. We were walking to school and *I was sure I would make her think I was good enough to be her pal.* "I can spell Mississippi," I announced proudly.

"So what?" she said "Anyone can spell that!" It seemed as if *she had destroyed all my dream castles* with one blow. To my second-grade eyes it was a great and difficult accomplishment. No one else in my grade could spell it, and I had practiced for two weeks on it.

From that moment, *Lois became less important to me.* Her hair faded, and her bike became less shiny. What good was a twenty-five cent allowance if you had to do dishes and sweep the floor for it? What good were long fingernails? You couldn't even play baseball.

Here is the introductory paragraph for "The Chinese New Year."

> To the Chinese in the United States, as well as elsewhere in the world, the most important festival of all is that of the New Year. This holiday can fall anytime between January 21 and February 19. It is believed that the forces of Yang, warmth and light, are ready to overcome the forces of Yin, cold, dark winter.

For this composition, we said that the paper would be best organized by going *from the least important idea to the most important idea.* Notice how the writer has followed through with this method of organization and supplied the necessary details.

> However, the New Year is more than a welcome to spring. *It is a new beginning,* a time to make a fresh start. Before the holiday, housewives are busy giving their houses a thorough cleaning. Windows are washed and curtains cleaned; silver is polished and everything made spotless. If possible, each person gets new clothes. It is the season to celebrate with families and friends and to attend special banquets and reunions.
> *Flowering branches* of peaches, pears, almonds, or apri-

cots, as well as red paper hangings with good-luck inscriptions, *brighten the Chinese-American home.* Azalea and camellia plants and dishes of flowering narcissus and daffodil bulbs foretell spring. *Fruit arrangements* of oranges, kumquats, and tangerines, symbols of fertility, *add to the color.*

The highlight of the New Year is the big parade in Chinatown. Firecrackers to scare away evil demons burst while men strike cymbals, drums, and metal gongs. Decorated floats and performing bands go by. Groups of lion dancers perform. The lion's head is made of papier-mâché and is painted red, yellow, green, and orange. One dancer holds the head while others are inside the silk body.

A huge dragon nearly a block long breathes out fire and smoke. Dozens of dancers inside make him twist and writhe down the street. To the Chinese, the dragon is not a monster, but a kind supernatural being who has charge of the rainfall. In a country that grows rice and needs water, the gifts of rainfall and help from the dragon are most important. Because the dragon had power to rise from earth to heaven, which no man can do, he became the symbol of the Emperor. According to legend, the dragon awakens from a year's sleep and appears on earth at the New Year. Thus he is symbolized by dancers in the parade.

From these two examples, you can see how all the paragraphs in the two compositions help to explain the introductory paragraphs. By following a logical arrangement of ideas, the writer has made them clear enough for the reader to follow them easily. The specific details are well chosen and make both compositions interesting to read.

Exercise   Writing the Body of the Composition

Complete the writing of the body of your composition. Make sure your ideas follow the organization you set up in the preceding assignment. Also, be sure that all your paragraphs are related to the introductory paragraph. Try to make your specific details both meaningful and interesting.

When you have finished, reread what you have written. Revise where necessary.

Part 7 Writing the Ending

In addition to the introduction and the body, your composition should also have an ending. The ending may be a summary of what you have written. It may be a quotation from someone else that relates to your topic; or it may be a short, interesting statement that indicates "The End" to the reader. As an example, our composition on "A Friend Who Wasn't" might end with a single sentence that indicates how the writer felt after the experience with Lois:

With six words she had lost a true friend.

Our composition on "The Chinese New Year" might end with a longer statement such as this:

An old Chinese proverb says: "A phoenix begets a phoenix, a dragon begets a dragon." Therefore, one New Year begets another New Year. Perhaps the most important reason the Chinese celebrate the New Year is that by doing what custom says one should do, one will also live to "beget" the next New Year.

Because your ending is the last idea your reader will take from your composition, you will want to make it as clear, as important, and as interesting as your introductory paragraph.

Exercises Writing the End of the Composition

A. Write the ending to your composition. Be sure that it is interesting and relates to the rest of your paper. You may wish to discuss your ending with your teacher or your classmates.

B. Reread your entire paper. Revise it where necessary.

Chapter 8

Kinds of Compositions

Before you write, you must decide what your purpose is. Do you want to tell a story? Do you want to describe something? Do you want to explain something? In Chapter 7 you learned how to choose a topic and organize your ideas into a composition. In this chapter you will learn to write three different kinds of compositions:

1. Narrative

2. Descriptive

3. Explanatory

Although you will be writing these three different kinds of compositions, you will still use the basic skills you learned in Chapter 7.

1. Choose a topic you are familiar with—one from your own life, your own experiences, or your own knowledge.
2. Narrow your topic so that it can be easily explained in a short composition.
3. Write an introductory paragraph that will explain what your composition is going to be about in a way that will catch the reader's attention.
4. List the ideas you want to cover in your composition.
5. Arrange your ideas in a logical order.
6. Write the body of your composition, giving all the details necessary to explain your ideas.
7. Write an interesting ending to your composition.
8. Reread your composition, and revise it where necessary.

Part 1 The First-Person Narrative Composition

You may remember that when you studied the narrative paragraph, you learned that it told a story, that it was a "what happened" kind of paragraph. The same definition applies to the narrative composition. It tells "what happened." Just as the narrative paragraph is organized in a *time sequence*, telling what happened in the order it happened, the narrative composition uses the same kind of organization.

THE STORY OF WILLIAM BILLY GOAT

His name was William, and the dignified name fit him about as well as your right shoe fits your left foot. William was a very undignified goat. He had been spoiled in his youth as a star member of the Children's Petting Zoo. When the new Town Hall was built, the zoo closed down, and William was offered free to a good home. When my brother Jimmy and I pleaded with Dad, he reluctantly allowed us to adopt William.

Dad was soon to regret his decision. William (Billy for short) gobbled up everything in sight. Dad was in despair, but Jimmy and I were delighted. Billy plowed up the garden so that there wasn't any need of weeding it. We couldn't tell which stalks were weeds and which were plants. He cropped the grass so short that it didn't have any ambition to come up again, thus saving the lawn mower, and our backs. About once a day, Billy would walk through the sliding door into the living room with a bold expression on his bewhiskered face. He seemed to be saying, "Well, folks, I had a few minutes to spare, so I dropped in to pay you a little visit. What's to eat?"

There was one good feature about Billy, however. He was a fine watch goat. We would be awakened in the middle of the night by a startled yell, and we'd know that Billy was butting some surprised trespasser over the back fence.

But the reign of Billy was coming to an end. He sealed his own fate. One day Dad said to me, "Bob, I give you fair warning. If that goat gets into any more trouble, he goes. Look at this shoe. Nothing is left but the sole. I can't imagine why I ever let you keep him in the first place."

It was hot that day, and Dad decided to take a nap in the hammock that hung between two trees in the garden. I had been helping Mother in the house, and came out to cool off. As I stepped out of the door, I saw a horrible sight. There stood William Billy Goat, calmly munching the hammock ropes. I yelled a warning, but it was too late. With a heavy thud, Dad and the hammock struck the ground.

The next day, Dad gave William away to a farmer just outside of town.

In the introductory paragraph, the writer explains that the composition will be about an undignified goat named William.

The writer arouses the reader's interest by suggesting that William is in trouble because he is creating so many problems for the family. The writer then tells, in time sequence, exactly what William did.

1. He ate everything in sight.
2. He plowed up the garden.
3. He cropped the grass.
4. He walked into the living room.
5. He butted trespassers over the back fence.
6. He chewed up Dad's shoes.
7. He chewed the ropes on the hammock.

The writer ends the composition in one short sentence by telling the reader what happened to William as a result of his misdeeds.

Exercise Writing a First-Person Narrative Composition

Perhaps you have had a humorous experience with an animal. How did it begin? What happened? How was the problem or conflict finally solved? Decide on a good subject for a first-person narrative composition, and write it. It should be at least five paragraphs long. When you have finished your first draft, revise it so that it says exactly what you want it to say. Copy your final version in ink, and turn it in. If you can't think of a topic, the following list may give you an idea to get you started.

1. The day I became thirteen
2. What happened on the first day of school
3. How I made money last summer
4. The first time I ever spent a week away from home
5. My most dangerous experience
6. An exciting football game
7. Honesty is the best policy
8. Our last family reunion
9. The trouble with being a teen-ager
10. I've learned to appreciate the little things in life

Part 2 The Descriptive Composition

Just as the descriptive paragraph paints a word-picture by appealing to the senses, so does the descriptive composition. The writer chooses the details carefully and arranges them in order, usually in a *space relationship*, so that the reader has a mental picture of what is being described.

Study the following example of a descriptive composition.

THE PEACOCK THRONE

The Mogul Emperors of India were noted for their wealth and splendor, but they outdid themselves in the building of the magnificent "Peacock Throne." The throne was designed and built for the Shah of Jehan by a Frenchman named Austin and is said to have been valued at over thirty million dollars.

The Mogul's palace in Delhi was called the "Hall of Private Audiences," and in the center of this palace stood the famous throne. It had been named "The Peacock" because of the two great golden peacocks that stood behind it. Their tails were spread and were inlaid with sapphires, rubies, emeralds, pearls and other precious stones to imitate the colors of real peacocks. Between the two peacocks stood the life-size figure of a parrot which was said to have been carved from a single emerald.

The throne itself was six feet long by four feet wide. It stood on six huge feet which, with the body, were of solid gold inlaid with rubies, emeralds, and diamonds. One of these diamonds was believed to have been the famous Kohinoor, the Mountain of Light, which is now part of the Crown Jewels of England.

Above the throne hung a golden canopy supported by twelve pillars all covered with costly gems. A fringe of pearls decorated the border of the canopy. On each side of the throne stood an umbrella, one of the Indian emblems of royalty. Each umbrella was made of thick crimson velvet with costly pearls. The handles, each eight feet tall and two inches thick, were of solid gold.

In 1736, the Persian ruler, Nadir Shad, captured Delhi and stripped the jewels from the "Peacock Throne." The throne itself was then broken up and carried away. The ruins of the palace and a marble memorial tablet where once the throne stood are all that now mark the scenes of that faded beauty.

In the introductory paragraph, the writer tells you that the composition will be about the "Peacock Throne." He catches your attention by telling you that the throne was valued at over thirty million dollars. What could such a throne have been like?

In the body of the composition, the writer describes the throne by giving you specific details, such as "inlaid with sapphires, rubies, emeralds, pearls"; "six feet long by four feet wide"; "a golden canopy supported by twelve pillars all covered with costly gems." Space relationships are indicated with such words as 'in the center," "above," "between," "at each side," so that the reader has a clear picture of the throne.

The writer ends the composition in an interesting way, by telling you what finally happened to the magnificent throne.

Here is a different kind of descriptive composition, one that appeals to your senses. Details are arranged in a space relationship here also, to help your eyes move from one place to another.

HOME AGAIN

It was a shadowless day in June. The cows, great bulks of contentment, were grazing near the bars of a zigzag fence. As if on signal, they stopped their grazing, and wound in single file back up the cow path. Then they sprawled motionless in the shade of two giant maples. Their huge, liquid eyes squinted tight, then opened wide with rythms of safety and peace.

Near the house, the wild crabapple tree foamed with blossoms against the stainless sky. The blue half-shell of a robin's egg lay on the ground beneath, like a fragment of broken sky. Swallows, with a dab of glistening mud or a hyphen of straw in their beaks, swooped toward their purse-mouthed houses.

Sounds did not disturb the day. The rushing of the brook, the tinkle of cowbells—none of them disturbed my ear as on other days.

The air smelled of sunlight and grass. It smelled of towels on the line and nests of birds under the gabled roof. It smelled of warm earth and the cloth over rising bread. It smelled of tree sap and fresh green leaves. It smelled of wild roses on the stone wall and milk cans hanging in the well. It smelled of the coming of ripe apples and tasseled sweet corn.

Every detail of everything I looked at made me glad to be alive and back home again.

Here the writer has appealed not only to your sense of sight, but to your other senses as well. Careful use of details helps you "see" what the writer is describing. Details are chosen to support the mood of peace and contentment.

Exercise Writing a Descriptive Composition

You have seen two ways of developing a descriptive composition. Choose a topic that you are familiar with, and write a descriptive composition, including details that create a vivid picture in the mind of your reader. If you can't think of a subject, the following list may give you some ideas.

1. The first warm day in spring
2. A busy city street
3. A space ship from another planet
4. The gingerbread house from Hansel and Gretel
5. A parade
6. A cluttered room
7. An old fort or church
8. The first snowfall
9. Preparations for a holiday dinner
10. A wildly decorated van

Part 3 The Explanatory Composition

The explanatory composition, like the explanatory paragraph, explains. It tells *how something is done,* or *why something is so.*

The "How" Composition

The "how" composition is usually used to give instructions. It is usually organized in time sequence, explaining what is done first, what is done next, and so on. Could you make an appleface doll after reading the following explanatory composition?

HOW TO MAKE APPLEFACE DOLLS

I used to think that apples were strictly for eating until I learned how to make appleface dolls. Now my collection of small appleface personalities includes the likeness of a weathered New England sea captain, a haughty countess, and a lively leprechaun.

The first step in making an appleface doll is to pare the apple, and cut the outline of a nose. Carve away some of the apple near the outline so the nose will stand out. Next, use your paring knife to dig shallow eye sockets. Make a slit above each eye. As the apple dries and shrinks, the slits will turn into lifelike wrinkles. Put the finishing touches on your carving by sloping the forehead backward slightly, rounding the cheeks, and narrowing the chin. A straight cut for the mouth will change to a frown or a smile as the apple shrivels.

Finally, roll the apple head in lemon juice to keep it from getting dark, and hang it up to dry. You may tie a string to the stem, or push a wire or pipe cleaner through the apple and tie the string to that instead. Make sure the apple hangs free as it dries. Otherwise, it may rot or lose its shape.

Part of the fun of making appleface dolls is watching them dry. Imagine seeing small heads dangling around your room. The dolls all look like old people because when the apples dry the "skin" shrivels, the eyes squint, the lips pucker, and the wrinkles deepen into furrows. Soon each face develops a character of its own. Some look like grizzled pioneers, some like fierce pirates, and others like friendly grannies.

After the head has dried for about two weeks, use straight pins with colored plastic heads for eyes, and stick them in the eye sockets. Grains of rice may be used for teeth. Let your applehead dry for about three more weeks. Then use your imagination. Colorful yarn or fluffy cotton may be used for hair. Paints or cosmetics will give your appleface a more realistic appearance.

Shape the body with wire and pad it with tissue to form the body. Glue and strips of crêpe paper will hold the padding in place. Use scraps of old material to dress the doll. Pieces of black felt make a dashing pirate outfit; worn-out blue jeans may be used to garb a friendly old farmer.

So far, I've made eight appleface dolls. My mother says I'm the only boy in town whose collection of dolls is the "apple of his eye."

In the introductory paragraph, you learn what the composition is going to be about in a way that catches your attention. Then the writer gives you step-by-step instructions for making your own appleface dolls. The ending may have come as a surprise. You probably assumed that the composition was written by a girl.

The "Why" Composition

The "why" composition differs from the "how" composition in one important way: The explanation of why something is so does not always fall into a logical time sequence. You will probably find it easiest to organize your ideas from the *least important to the most important*.

The introductory paragraph should begin by stating a fact or opinion that you believe to be true. The body of the composition should explain *why* you believe your opinion or idea is true. You may develop your composition through facts or statistics, specific examples, or incidents or anecdotes. In the following composition, the writer uses anecdotes to explain why fathers are hard to bring up.

BRINGING UP FATHER

I have recently discovered that bringing up a father to be a grown-up, mature man is a hard, time-consuming job. Fathers seem to progress nicely until about the time we reach high school. Almost overnight, they become not only difficult, but impossible. My father is a perfect example. He has several bad habits that he hasn't outgrown—even though I've brought them to his attention a number of times.

At times, he fancies himself as an opera singer. These musical moods are usually heralded by ear-splitting arias echoing from the shower. Don't misunderstand me: I love music. But at 6:30 A.M.? There is a limit to one's patience. I shudder to think of how the neighbors must feel.

Then there's the matter of his table manners. As soon as he finishes his last mouthful of dinner, he asks, "What's for dessert?" Most of the time, the rest of the family hasn't even finished the main course. I've tried to reason with him, but he refuses to change.

Probably his worst fault is his behavior at costume parties. Father is usually a conservative dresser, but every Halloween, a strange change comes over him. Last Halloween, he and mother gave a party. Nearly everyone in the family was there, including my grandmother who is very prim and proper. Suddenly, a hairy savage, clad only in a leopard skin, bounded into the room. When someone suggested that it must be Father, Grandmother sniffed disdainfully, and said "Hmph! My son wouldn't dream of disgracing himself like that!" Was she surprised when she took a second look.

Aside from these bad habits, my father is really the greatest guy I know. He's a little immature right now, but I'm working on him. I'm sure that in a few years everyone will agree that he has been well trained.

The introduction establishes the humorous mood of the paragraph, and promises to tell you why fathers are hard to bring up. Using her own father as an example, the writer tells you several anecdotes that support her opening statement. She has gone from least important to most important by saving the most humorous incident for the last. The writer ends her composition by saying that in a few years she will have her father well trained.

Exercise Writing an Explanatory Composition

Write an explanatory composition, telling either "how" or "why." If you decide to write a "how" composition, give the instructions in clear, chronological order. If you choose to write a "why" composition, decide what method you could use to develop it best: facts and statistics, incidents and anecdotes, or specific examples. Be sure to limit your topic sufficiently. When you have finished your first draft, revise it. Copy your final version in ink, and turn it in. The following list of topics may give you some ideas.

1. How to avoid doing the dishes
2. Why I need a raise in my allowance
3. How to clean a fish
4. Television can be educational
5. Training a dog
6. Why a CB radio is useful
7. The secrets of playing a certain sport well
8. How to make or build something
9. Rules for playing a game
10. Ways of earning money

Chapter 9

Writing Letters

What is your favorite kind of mail to receive? Is it a postcard from a friend on a trip, an invitation, a letter from a far-away friend, or a reply from a business contacted? Whichever form of mail you most enjoy receiving, remember that in order to receive letters, you also need to write them.

This chapter will explain several kinds of social letters, each for a different occasion. It will also explain the specific forms for writing business letters, with examples of various kinds.

Part 1 Writing Friendly Letters

When you are writing a friendly letter, you should keep in mind these three basic guidelines:

1. You want the letter to be interesting.

2. You want to use the correct form.

3. You want the letter to have a neat appearance so it can be easily read.

Making the Letter Interesting

In a friendly letter, you are writing to someone you know very well—someone with whom you have shared many experiences and who wants to know what you are doing. Keep your language informal, as if you are actually speaking to the person. Share your feelings with the person, and use interesting and colorful language when you describe your experiences.

The information you include in your letter should be interesting both to you and to the person to whom you are writing, so the person will be anxious to reply to your letter. If you are

603 Bethel Avenue
Indianapolis, Indiana 47303
August 7, 1978

Dear Marlene,

It sounds as if you're really busy. I wish I could be there with you.

It's been raining all week here, so you can imagine how bored I've been. I wish you were still here visiting. We sure had fun, didn't we?

School will be starting soon, and yet it seems as if vacation has hardly begun.

Mom's calling me to clean my room, so I guess I'd better get busy. Say "hi" to everyone for me.

Always,
Laura

replying to a letter, answer any questions the person has asked, and make comments about the information the person has shared with you.

Compare the two letters below. Which is more interesting? The second letter is a much better example of how to make a friendly letter more interesting. Sometimes you may not have much to say, but the way you say it can make all the difference. Just remember to follow these guidelines:

1. Write as naturally as if you were speaking to the person.

603 Bethel Avenue
Indianapolis, Indiana 47303
August 7, 1978

Dear Marlene,

Your letter sure makes it sound as if you have a full schedule! Drill team tryouts sound pretty tough, but with your smile I'm sure the judges won't even notice if you trip. I sure hope you make it! And how do you manage to take both flute and guitar lessons and still have time to practice?

My school registration forms came in the mail yesterday. I guess vacation is quickly coming to an end. One good thing about school's starting is that I'll finally get some new clothes. Have you bought anything new yet? If you have, send a list and describe what you got.

Can't wait to hear from you again. Good luck in tryouts! Say "hi" to your family for me.

Always,
Laura

2. Write about things that are interesting both to you and to the person to whom you are writing.

3. Begin by answering the other person's questions or by commenting on his or her information.

4. Add plenty of details and use a variety of descriptive words.

5. Indent each paragraph and start a new paragraph for each new idea you talk about.

Following Correct Letter Form

Using the correct letter form helps you organize your letter. Each letter has five main parts:

Heading 230 Yellowstone Avenue
Billings, Montana 59102
May 18, 1978

Salutation

Dear Rick,

Body

Yours, Closing

Jerry Signature

The **heading** of a letter tells where you are and when you are writing. It should be written in the upper right-hand corner. The heading consists of three lines in the following order:

> house address and name of street
> city, state zip code
> month day, year

Notice the punctuation used in the heading. The following capitalization and punctuation rules apply:

1. Capitalize all proper names.

2. Place a comma between the name of the city and state.

3. Put the zip code after the state. No comma is needed to separate the state and the zip code.

4. Place a comma between the day and the year.

5. Do not abbreviate.

The **salutation** or greeting is the way you say "hello" to your friend. It can be as casual as you wish. Here are some suggestions:

Dear Mike,   *Greetings Holly,*

Hi Marcia,   *Howdy Friend,*

The salutation is written on the line below the heading and begins at the left margin. The first word and any other nouns are capitalized. Also, a comma follows the salutation in a friendly letter.

In the **body** of a friendly letter, you talk to your friend. If the letter is a good one, it will make your friend feel almost as though you were there in person. When your friend finishes the letter, he or she will feel like replying as soon as possible.

The **closing** is a simple way of saying "good-bye" to your friend. Some closings such as *Love, Sincerely, Always,* are common. Other closings are original and represent a close friendship or even the attitude of the letter, such as the following:

Your friend,   *Missing you,*

Still waiting,   *Anxiously,*

Capitalize only the first word of the closing and use a comma at the end of the closing. The closing should line up with the first line of the heading.

When you are writing a friendly letter to someone who will recognize you by your first name, use your first name as your signature. Otherwise, sign your full name. Skip a line after the closing and sign your name in line with the first word of the closing.

Giving the Letter a Neat Appearance

If you want your friend to enjoy reading your letter and to understand everything you have said, the appearance of your letter is important. In fact, it reflects a great deal about you as a person. If you are willing to take the time, your letter can show that you are a neat, well organized person who shows respect for the person to whom you are writing.

The best way to give your letter a neat appearance is to follow these guidelines:

1. **Stationery.** When writing to a close friend, you may wish to use a special, colorful, or humorous type of stationery. When writing to an adult, however, it is best to use plain white or cream colored stationery. The first stationery is casual and the second is formal.

2. **Margins.** Try to keep your margins straight and clear so the reader can follow what you are saying without reading up the side of the page or into the corner.

3. **Handwriting.** Use blue or black ink so that your writing can be read easily. Be careful of smudges and try your hardest not to cross out words that interrupt reading. Most important of all, use your best penmanship. This extra courtesy will make a big difference to the person reading the letter. You may even want to write a rough draft first and then copy it carefully onto your stationery.

Exercises   Writing Friendly Letters

A. Choose two of the following series of events. Expand each series into an interesting paragraph that could be used in a friendly letter. Include description and details.

1. We won our last basketball game. This game gave us a perfect record. A lot of people were at the game. I scored 10 points.

2. I got a ten-speed bike for my birthday. It looks good. I rode to the park for the day.

3. I cleaned my room yesterday and found an envelope of pictures that were taken when you visited last summer. They were funny. Do you want any of them?

4. Our class went on a field trip last week. We went to the newspaper office. The weather was good, but the bus was crowded. It was fun, though.

5. Our new cat got into trouble. It dug into Mom's plants, and it ate one of our goldfish. I hope Mom will let us keep the cat.

B. In your best handwriting, write the heading, salutation, closing, and signature for each of the following letters. Use the correct form, margins, punctuation, and capitalization. To show where the body of each letter should go, skip two lines and print the word *BODY*. Supply the date and use appropriate salutations and closings for the people involved.

1. From sara mason, camp tomahawk, raleigh, north carolina 27608, to her mother.

2. From terry orlanda, 114 north hermitage avenue, trenton, new jersey 08618, to his teacher, ms. barker.

3. From raul perez, 818 harrison street, boston, massachusetts 02118, to his sister maria.

4. From michelle noland, 1414 elmwood avenue, rochester, new york 14620, to her friend mary chris.

5. From jason bell, 1201 west leonard street, pensacola, florida 32501 to his band director, Mrs. griffith.

C. Write a friendly letter to one of your best friends. You may use one of the following situations, or you may write a letter you will actually mail to a friend. Use interest, form, and appearance as your guidelines.

1. You have received a letter from your friend. She has written about her experience at summer camp and about her diving lessons. She is also learning how to play the piano. She has asked you what you would like for your birthday.

In your reply, tell your friend what your suggestions are for a birthday gift and that you are taking guitar lessons.

2. Your friend has just written to tell you that he is on the school soccer team. He plays goalie and loves it, even though practice is hard. He is also one of the sports writers for the school newspaper.

In your reply, tell your friend that next month you will be trying out for the basketball team, that you are presently practicing your shooting, and that you are running two miles every day. You have just been chosen as one of the yearbook photographers.

3. You have received a long letter from your friend who moved away last summer. She has told you all about the new

school she attends. The school has an indoor pool and a swimming team for the boys and for the girls. The classrooms are carpeted, and the décor is very modern. She has made several new friends with whom she goes roller skating, shopping, and cycling. She has almost finished reading *The Lord of the Rings*, the set of books you gave her.

In your letter of reply, you are excited about all of your friend's experiences. You tell her about your school schedule, that you are Student Council vice-president, and that you have a babysitting job every Thursday after school.

Part 2 Writing Social Notes

Social notes are used for special occasions, such as inviting someone to a party, thanking someone for a present, or accepting an invitation. Social notes have the same form as a friendly letter except they are much shorter. Sometimes only the date is used in the heading instead of your whole address.

The social notes you will use most frequently are the following:

1. Thank-you notes

2. Bread-and-butter notes

3. Notes of invitation, acceptance, and regret

The Thank-You Note

The purpose of the thank-you note is, of course, to tell the person receiving the note how much you appreciated his or her kindness or thoughtfulness. You may not particularly like a gift that was given to you, but you can still sincerely thank the person for thinking of you. Write a note as soon as possible after receiving a gift.

2723 Midtown Court
Palo Alto, California 94303
March 14, 1978

Dear Ginnie,

The photo album you sent for my birthday was just what I needed. Can you believe that I already have it half full?

Mom let me invite some friends for a sleep-over Saturday night to celebrate. It was great fun, but as usual, we didn't get any sleep. My friend Andrea took pictures, and I promise to send you some. They are unbelievably funny.

I also got a new radio, three albums, a new pair of jeans, and a Rocky poster. It was a great birthday.

Thank you again for the gift.

Always,
Julie

The Bread-and-Butter Note

Another form of thank-you note is called a "bread-and-butter" note. You would write this kind of note when you have stayed overnight at someone's house. Bread-and-butter notes should also be written as soon as possible after the event.

626 North Quentin Road
Palatine, Illinois 60067
May 5, 1982

Dear Aunt Lorraine and Uncle Bill,

    Visiting with you on your ranch was really a great experience. I love to ride horses and seldom get the chance to ride around here. I learned so much about caring for and training horses, too.

    For a city boy, working on a ranch isn't quite as easy as it looks on T.V. I'm really glad I had the opportunity to learn so much. I only hope that I worked hard enough and didn't eat too much. Riding surely increases my appetite, and your cooking is delicious.

    Mom and Dad say I've grown taller and stronger. I guess Arizona agrees with me. Thanks again for the wonderful time.

          Love,
          Jeff

Exercise Writing Thank-You and Bread-and-Butter Notes

Write one thank-you note and one bread-and-butter note. You may choose from the following list or use a real experience.

1. A note thanking your uncle for helping you build your mini-bike.

2. A note thanking your friend's parents for letting you spend the weekend.

3. A note thanking your best friend for the surprise party he or she gave for you.

4. A note thanking your parent's business partner for the free tickets to a football or baseball game.

5. A note thanking your grandparents for letting you visit for two weeks.

6. A note thanking your aunt and uncle for taking you to a large attraction, such as an amusement park.

Notes of Invitation, Acceptance, and Regret

Invitations should be written carefully to make sure that all details are included. Even printed invitations that can be bought in the store do not always include all of the information you might need to give. State the following information clearly in your invitation:

1. Type of activity

2. Purpose of activity

3. Where the activity will be held

4. The day, date, and the time of the activity

5. How the person should reply to you

If you invite an out-of-town guest, include helpful transportation schedules and suggestions.

> 705 Forbes Avenue
> Pittsburgh, Pennsylvania 15219
> June 14, 1978
>
> Dear Mark,
>   You are invited to attend my
> birthday barbecue on Friday, June 28,
> at 5:00 P.M. The party will be
> held at my house.
>   I sure hope you can be there.
>   Sincerely,
>   Barb
>
> R.S.V.P.

R.S.V.P. is an abbreviation for a French phrase that means "please respond." The person sending the invitation needs to know how many people are attending, so that enough food and supplies can be provided. Sometimes there will be a telephone number after R.S.V.P.; in that case, all you have to do is call. Usually, however, you should send a note of acceptance or regret to inform the person whether or not you are coming. Always answer an invitation as soon as possible.

The following examples will guide you in writing either a note of acceptance or a note of regret.

A Note of Acceptance

June 16, 1978

Dear Barb,

What a great time to have a party – as soon as school is out. You can count on my being there. It sounds like a great way to start the summer.

Your friend,
Mark

A Note of Regret

June 16, 1978

Dear Barb,

I sure wish I could attend your birthday party. It sounds like great fun. Unfortunately, our family will be leaving for vacation that week, so I won't be able to come.

I'll call you when I return. Have a happy birthday and a great party.

Sincerely,
Mark

Writing Notes of Invitation, Acceptance, and Regret

Write an invitation to a party. Include R.S.V.P. in your invitation. Exchange your invitation with someone in the class. Then write a note of acceptance, and a note of regret in reply to the other student's invitation.

Folding a Friendly Letter

Folding a friendly letter depends on the stationery you use. Many types of stationery are prefolded, and packaged or boxed with envelopes to match. Whatever the size, fold the paper neatly so that the reader can open the letter easily. If the stationery is too wide for the envelope you are using, fold the letter in half from the bottom and then into thirds from each side.

Addressing the Envelope

When addressing the small square envelope that is usually included with invitations and note cards, you may put your return address on the flap on the back of the envelope, with the receiver's name and address centered on the front.

Ms. Julie Stewart
849 Selmer Road
Philadelphia PA
19116

Mr. Tim Goodman
205 Walton Place
Chicago IL 60611

When you use state abbreviations in capital letters in addressing an envelope, you do not need to use a comma to separate the city from the state. However, you must include the zip code.

Exercise   Addressing Envelopes

Draw the fronts and backs of two 5″ × 5″ envelopes on plain sheets of paper. Address the fronts of each envelope to two of your friends or relatives. Write the correct return address on the back flaps of each envelope.

Part 3   Writing Business Letters

Many times you will need to write a letter requesting information, ordering products, or complaining about a product. Such letters are called business letters. A business letter is written for a specific purpose and requires a different kind of writing and a different form from a friendly letter.

A good business letter should be brief and to the point. The form of a business letter requires certain information that is a form of courtesy. The remainder of the information you supply should be specifically related to the information you require.

Business Letter Forms

The two types of business letter forms are **modified block form** and **block form.** Look carefully at the examples on pages 149 and 150.

The modified block form is always used when a letter is handwritten. It may also be used for a typewritten letter. In this form the paragraphs are indented, and the closing and signature are in line with the heading, just as in a friendly letter.

Modified Block Form

1205 Brunswick
Baltimore, Maryland 21233
October 4, 1978

Television Information Office
746 Fifth Avenue
New York, New York 10019

Ladies and Gentlemen:

Yours truly,

Maria Perez

Maria Perez

Block Form

1205 Brunswick Street
Baltimore, Maryland 21233
October 4, 1978

Inside Address

Television Information Office
746 Fifth Avenue
New York, New York 10019

Dear Sir or Madam: **Salutation**

                              Body
_____
_____
_____
_____
_____
_____

_____
_____
_____
_____

Sincerely,   **Closing**

Maria Perez   **Signature**

Maria Perez

The block form for a business letter is used only when the letter is typewritten. Notice that all parts of the letter begin at the left margin. The paragraphs are not indented. Instead, there is a double space between paragraphs.

Parts of the Business Letter

The parts of a business letter are different from those of a friendly letter because a business letter is written formally. Follow these suggestions for writing the parts of a business letter:

1. **Heading.** The heading of a business letter is the same as the heading for a friendly letter. Write your street address on the first line. Write your city, state, and zip code on the second line. Write the date on the third line. Remember to use punctuation and capitalization rules, and do not abbreviate.

2. **Inside Address.** In a business letter, the name and address of the firm or organization to which you are writing appear in the letter itself. This address follows the same punctuation and capitalization rules as the heading. The inside address comes below the heading and begins at the left margin. This inside address should always be exactly the same as the address on the envelope.

3. **Salutation.** The salutation of a business letter is more formal than that of a friendly letter. If the letter is being written to a specific person, use *Dear* and then the person's name:

    Dear Ms. Garland or
    Dear Mr. Grigsby

    Usually, when writing a business letter, you don't know the name of the person to whom you are writing. In this case, you use a general greeting such as *Dear Sir or Madam* or *Ladies and Gentlemen*. All salutations begin two lines after the inside address and end with a colon (:).

4. **Body.** The body of a business letter is usually short. It should be courteous and state very clearly the subject you are writing about. When ordering products, be especially careful to include the name of the item, the quantity, the catalog number, and the price. If you are enclosing anything with your letter, such as a coupon, a subscription form, an order form, or an entry blank, mention it in the letter.

5. **Closing.** The closing appears on the first line below the body. The most common closings for a business letter are these:

Sincerely,   Very truly yours,
Yours truly,   Respectfully yours,

Notice that only the *first* word of the closing is capitalized and that the closing is followed by a comma.

6. **Signature.** Type or print your name four spaces below the closing, then write your signature in the space between. This way the reader will have no trouble reading your name so that he or she can reply to you.

It is best to make a copy of your business letters so that you will have a record of what you wrote and when you wrote them. You can do this easily by using carbon paper. Mail the original and keep the carbon copy for yourself.

Study the following example of a business letter to see how all of the parts work together to form a well organized, clearly stated letter.

1104 Balsam Avenue
Boulder, Colorado 80302
April 27, 1978

Postmatic Company
Dept. BHG-877
Lafayette Hill, Pennsylvania 19444

Dear Sir or Madam:

In the March issue of <u>Better Homes</u> and <u>Gardens</u>, I read your advertisement for the personalized hand embosser and your catalog. I would like to purchase both items. Please send the following items as soon as possible:

1 hand embosser	$10.95
1 catalog	.25
postage and handling	1.25
	$12.45

I am enclosing a money order for the amount of $12.45. Also, please inscribe the embosser with the following name and address:

Douglas Williams
1104 Balsam Avenue
Boulder, Colorado 80302

Sincerely,
Douglas Williams

Exercises   Writing Business Letters

A. Choose one of the following items and write the letter described. Make up any names and facts needed for a complete letter, but sign your own name.

1. You would like to order a ship model of the *U. S. S. Constitution* for the price of $14.95 plus $1.50 postage and handling, and a free catalog. The company is Prestom's, 601 Westport Avenue, Norwalk, Connecticut 06851

2. You would like a T-shirt with a picture of your dog reproduced on the front. Give the size and color of the T-shirt you want and enclose a picture of your dog. The price is $4.95 plus $.75 handling. The company is T-Shirts, Inc., 1130 Nicollet Avenue, Minneapolis, Minnesota 55403. You want your picture returned.

3. You are interested in going on a canoe trip offered by Camp Greenburg, Box 478, Ypsilanti, Michigan 47197. You would like to know the dates, costs, and equipment needed for the trip.

4. While on vacation you left your glasses in their case at the Villa Lodge, Box 527, Lake Zurich, Illinois 60047. You would like to know if they have been found and how they will be returned.

B. Bring to class an advertisement of an item you would like to buy or send for. Write a business letter to order this item.

Part 4   Preparing Your Letter for the Mail

How your letter is folded and how the envelope is addressed is an important part of writing letters. The letter should be folded so that it is easy for the reader to open and read it. The

envelope must be addressed accurately, or your letter may
never reach its destination.

Folding Your Letter

A business letter should be folded and inserted into the
envelope so that it can be removed and read without having to
be turned around and over. Use a 9½″ × 4″ white business
envelope that matches the width of the stationery. Fold the
letter like this:

How To Fold a Business Letter

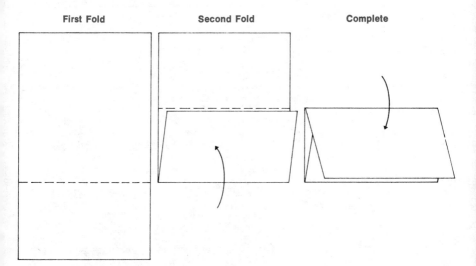

First Fold   Second Fold   Complete

Addressing the Envelope

Addressing the envelope accurately will get your letter to the
right place. A simple mistake such as using the wrong abbreviation for a state or forgetting a zip code could cause your
letter to end up in the Dead Letter Office in Washington,
D. C. If you don't know the approved abbreviation for a state,
or the zip code, call your local post office.

Take the following steps when addressing your envelope:

1. Make sure the envelope is right-side up.
2. Put your return address on the envelope.
3. Double-check all numbers to make sure they are in proper order.
4. Include the correct zip code.

In each example that follows, notice the placement of the return address on the envelope.

Business Envelopes

Ms. Laura Daniels
2202 Sunnyside Avenue
Salt Lake City, Utah   84108

                              Walters Drake Interiors
                              P.O. Box 12684
                              Dallas, Texas   75225

When writing to a particular department within a large company, specify the department on the envelope for faster service.

Mr. Joseph Culter
3016 Maryland Avenue
Columbus, Ohio 43209

Montgomery Ward & Company
Sporting Goods Department
Randhurst Shopping Center
Mt. Prospect, Illinois 60056

Exercise Addressing Envelopes

Put each of the addresses below in proper three- or four-line form as it should appear on an envelope. Capitalize, abbreviate, and punctuate correctly.

1. the athlete's foot 825 chicago avenue evanston illinois 60201
2. g b enterprises 6635 north clark street chicago il 60626
3. the harper company 1252 fairwood avenue columbus ohio 43216
4. bach and laurence ltd 15 park avenue new york ny 10022
5. campfitters inc p o box 6745 providence rhode island 02940

Chapter 10

Using the Library

Every year in school you have been surrounded by books. They line the shelves of most of your classrooms and fill the walls of every library you have ever used. Much of what you have already learned has come from books. However, many students do not know how to find all the information that a book has to offer. In fact, students often have trouble in locating a book in the library.

This chapter explains the classification and arrangement of books on library shelves. It also explains the use of the card catalog. Finally, it describes the many kinds of reference materials that are available in the library. The information in this chapter will help you make efficient use of the library.

Part 1   The Classification and Arrangement of Books

Because there are so many books in a library, you may be confused when you first start looking for a particular book. However, by learning the classification and arrangement of books, you will be able to locate any book quickly.

The Classification of Books

All the books in any library can be divided into two groups: *fiction* and *nonfiction*. Each group is classified in a different way for your convenience in finding individual books within a group.

Fiction

Fiction books are stories that the author has imagined or invented. Some fiction books may be partially true, as the author may have based the story on his or her own experiences or on actual events and then invented other elements to make a good story. Fiction books are all classified in the same way. Remember this one important rule:

Fiction books are arranged alphabetically according to the author's last name.

If an author has written more than one book, the books by that author are placed together on the shelf and then arranged alphabetically according to title.

If two authors have the same last name, they are alphabetized by their first names.

Exercise   Arranging Fiction Books

On a separate sheet of paper, number these fiction titles and authors in the order in which they should appear on the

160

shelves. Use the rules just given to check your work. (If a title begins with *a, an,* or *the,* it should be alphabetized by the second word in the title.)

1. Richter, Conrad. *Light in the Forest*
2. Lee, Mildred. *Fog*
3. Neville, Emily C. *Berries Goodman*
4. Cleaver, Vera and Bill. *Where the Lilies Bloom*
5. Walsh, Jill Paton. *Fireweed*
6. Zindel, Paul. *The Pigman*
7. Lipsyte, Robert. *The Contender*
8. Neville, Emily C. *It's Like This, Cat*
9. Hinton, S. E. *Rumble Fish*
10. London, Jack. *The Call of the Wild*

Nonfiction

Nonfiction books are factual resources about every subject you can imagine. Most libraries classify nonfiction books according to the **Dewey Decimal System.** The system is named for its originator, the American librarian Melvil Dewey. This system classifies all books by an assigned number in one of ten major categories. The ten categories are these:

The Dewey Decimal System

000–099	**General Works**	(encyclopedias, almanacs, handbooks, etc.)
100–199	**Philosophy**	(conduct, ethics, psychology, etc.)
200–299	**Religion**	(the Bible, mythology, theology)
300–399	**Social Science**	(economics, law, education, commerce, government, folklore)
400–499	**Language**	(languages, grammar, dictionaries)
500–599	**Science**	(mathematics, chemistry, physics, biology, astronomy, etc.)

600–699	**Useful Arts**	(farming, cooking, sewing, radio, nursing, engineering, television, business, gardening, etc.)
700–799	**Fine Arts**	(music, painting, drawing, acting, photography, games, sports, amusements)
800–899	**Literature**	(poetry, plays, essays)
900–999	**History**	(biography, travel, geography)

As you can see, the Dewey Decimal System places all books on the same subject together. By taking an even closer look, you can see how detailed a particular category actually is. The following is a breakdown of the Fine Arts category (700–799).

700	**Fine Arts**
710	Civic & landscaping art
720	Architecture
730	Sculpture
740	Drawing
750	Painting
760	Graphic arts
770	Photography
780	Music
790	Recreation

790	Recreation
791	Public entertainment
792	Theater
793	Indoor games & amusements
794	Indoor games of skill
795	Games of chance
796	Athletic outdoor sports
797	Aquatic & air sports
798	Equestrian sports & animal racing
799	Fishing, hunting, boating

Exercises   The Dewey Decimal System

A. Using the Dewey Decimal System classification (shown above), assign the correct classification number for each of the following books:

1. *First Book of the Supreme Court*, Harold Coy
2. *World Book Encyclopedia*
3. *Tennis for Beginners*, B. and C. Murphy

4. *Great Religions of the World*, ed. Merle Severy
5. *Weather in Your Life*, Irving Adler
6. *How Personalities Grow*, Helen Shacter
7. *The Art of Africa*, Shirley Glubok
8. *America*, Alistair Cooke
9. *New Faces of China*, Willis Barnstone
10. *Modern English and Its Heritage*, Margaret Bryant

B. Draw a floor plan of your school library. Mark carefully each section that represents a classification of the Dewey Decimal System. Also, include the section where fiction books are shelved.

Call Numbers

At first, the Dewey Decimal System seems to have just too many numbers to learn. In fact, few people, with the exception of librarians, ever learn them all. You will find, however, that the more reports you work on, and the more interests and hobbies you develop, the more numbers you will learn and remember. Every nonfiction book has its Dewey Decimal number on its spine. This classification number then becomes part of what is known as the **call number.** Look closely at the call number of the following book, and the explanation of the call number.

Book: *The World of Champions*
Author: Anthony Pritchard

Call Number: **796.72**
      P961w

Dewey Decimal classification number **796.72** — first letter of book title

first letter of author's name **P961w** — author's assigned number

Since libraries usually have many books within each classification number, the lower part of the call number helps to keep the books organized by using the first letter of the author's last name with that classification.

Both the Dewey Decimal number and the call number identify books as precisely as possible in order to make it easier for you to find them. Within this system, there are three sections that deserve special mention: biography, short story collections, and reference books.

Biography. A biography is the true story of a person's life, written by another individual. An autobiography is the true story of a person's life written by himself or herself. Both are nonfiction books classified together and shelved in a special section of the library. The class numbers reserved for biography are 920 and 921.

920 This class number is reserved for collective biographies. These books contain the life story of more than one person. The call number of a collective biography is 920, plus the initial of the author's or editor's last name. For example:

> *Americans in Space* by Ross Olney
>
> Call number   920
>
>   O

921 This class number is used for individual biographies and autobiographies. These books are arranged differently on the shelves. They are arranged alphabetically by the last name of the *person written about*. For this reason, the call number is composed of 921 and the initial of the person the book is about. For example, this would be the call number for a biography about Abraham Lincoln:

> 921
>
> L

Short Story Collections. Most libraries keep the fiction books that contain several stories in a separate section. They are usually marked *SC*, which stands for "Story Collection." The initial of the author's or editor's last name is usually placed below the *SC* on the back of the book. The books are arranged alphabetically by the author's or editor's last name. For example:

> *I Couldn't Help Laughing* by Ogden Nash   SC
> N

Reference Books. Reference books of particular types or on specific subjects are also shelved together, with the letter R above the classification number:

> R
> 423.1
> D56

Exercises   Call Numbers

A. Each of the following books belongs in one of the special categories of *biography, collective biography,* or *short story collection.* Read the title carefully before deciding on the proper category. Then assign the correct call number code to each special category.

> *Mickey Mantle of the Yankees,* Gene Schoor
> *Heroines of the Early West,* Nancy W. Ross
> *Rembrandt: A Biography,* Elizabeth Ripley
> *Thirteen Ghostly Yarns,* Phyllis Fenner
> *Shirley Chisholm,* Susan Brownmiller
> *A Million Guitars and Other Stories,* Paul D. Boles
> *Ten Who Dared,* Desmond Wilcox
> *Neil Diamond,* Suzanne K. O'Regan
> *Perilous Ascent: Stories of Mountain Climbing,*
> Phyllis Fenner
> *They Gave Their Names to Science,* D. S. Halacy, Jr.

B. Arrange the following call numbers for nonfiction books in correct order, the way they would appear on a library shelf.

918.6	635	919.8	300	623.74
H38p	P22g	P31o	P93k	P39g

536.51	623.74	917.1	395.8	300
P22t	E25m	H38g	A45n	P83b

Part 2   Using the Card Catalog

The **card catalog** is a cabinet of small drawers in which a card for each book in the library is filed alphabetically. Each card has a **call number** in the upper left-hand corner of the card to make it easier for you to find the book on the shelves.

There are usually three cards for the same book in the card catalog: the *author card*, the *title card*, and the *subject card*. Each of these cards has the same information. However, each would be found in a different section of the card catalog. Look carefully at the following examples for the book *Instant Photography* by Lou Jacobs.

The Author Card

When you know the author of the book you want to read, use the card catalog to look up the name of the author. The author card will tell you the call number of the book. In addition, the titles of all the other books that the author has written and that are in that library will be listed on separate cards and filed alphabetically by the first word in each title. (*A, An,* and *The* do not count as first words). Here is an example of an author card for the book *Instant Photography:*

```
770.28    Jacobs, Lou
JAC
              Instant photography. Illus. with
              photos.
              N. Y., Lothrop, Lee & Shepard, © 1976

                 127p., illus., index

              1. Polaroid Land Camera
              2. Photography

                          O
```

Notice also that cards for books *about* the author are filed *behind* his or her author cards.

The Title Card

When you do not know the author of a book but know its correct title, look up the title of the book. (Remember that A, *An,* and *The* do not count as first words in a title.) Here is an example of a title card for the same photography book:

```
770.28    Instant photography
JAC
          Jacobs, Lou

              Instant photography. Illus. with photos.
              N. Y., Lothrop, Lee & Shepard, © 1976

                 127p., illus., index

              1. Polaroid Land camera
              2. Photography
                          O
```

The location of the title card in the card catalog is always determined by the first word in the title.

The Subject Card

Perhaps you just received a camera for your birthday, or you want to learn a new technique for taking photographs. The best way to find a book to help you would be to look under the subject heading, Photography, in the card catalog. One such card would look like this:

```
770.28      PHOTOGRAPHY
JAC

       Jacobs, Lou
              Instant photography. Illus. with photos
              N. Y., Lothrop, Lee & Shepard, © 1976

                 127p., illus., index

              1. Polaroid Land camera
              2. Photography

                        ○
```

When you look up a particular subject in the card catalog, you will find all of the books on that subject filed alphabetically by the authors' last names. This complete listing helps you to find the book that suits your purposes best. The card used in the above example also lists at the bottom one or more additional subject headings that you may want to investigate.

One important thing that you need to remember about the system used for card catalog cards is that only proper names and the first word of the title are capitalized. To find the title of a book, look at the entry immediately following the author's name. The title of the book in the example is *Instant Photography*.

Card Catalog Information

Notice that all three types of catalog cards (author, title, and subject) give the same information. This information includes the following:

1. The call number

2. The title, author, publisher, and date of publication

3. The number of pages, and a notation on whether the book has illustrations, maps, an index, or other features

Often the card catalog will also provide:

4. A brief description of the material in the book

5. A listing of other catalog cards for the book

Cross Reference Cards

Sometimes when you look up a subject, you will find a card that reads *See* or *See also*. The "See" card refers you to another subject heading in the catalog that will give you the information you want. Let's say that you want a book on jobs, and that you find a card that reads as follows:

```
Jobs
  see
Employment




                O
```

This "See" card means that the library catalogs all books on Jobs under the subject heading of Employment.

The "See also" card refers you to other subjects closely related to the one you are interested in. These subjects will help you find complete information on the topic. A "See also" card will look like this:

```
Animals
   see also
Desert animals
Domestic animals
Fresh-water animals
Marine animals
Pets

also names of individual animals, e.g., Dogs



               O
```

Guide Cards

Inside each drawer of the card catalog you will find some guide cards that extend higher than the other cards in the drawer. These cards may have letters of the alphabet, complete words, or general subject headings printed on them.

These cards are placed in the drawers to guide you to the correct place in the alphabet for the word you are looking for. For example, if you wanted a book about basketball, you would find a particular book by means of alphabetically arranged guide cards.

Exercises Using the Card Catalog

A. For each group below, number the entries in the order in which you would find them in the card catalog.

1. a. LAW
   b. The last frontier
   c. Last race
   d. The law of life
   e. The last out

2. a. The new math
   b. Newman, James R.
   c. NEWSPAPERS
   d. NEW YEAR
   e. New tall tales of Pecos Bill

B. What subject cards would give you information about the following topics? Discuss your answers in class.

1. Painting a van
2. How to make slides
3. How to sail a boat
4. Cures for diseases
5. How to enter a rodeo
6. Houdini's best magic tricks
7. Olympic medal winners
8. Wilderness camping
9. Television commercials
10. Grooming your dog

C. Use the card catalog to find the title, author, call number, and publication date of a book on one of the following subjects.

1. A book on metrics
2. A book about the Boston Marathon
3. A collection of stories by Arthur Conan Doyle
4. A book on World War I uniforms
5. A book about mountain climbing
6. A book on holidays
7. A book of short stories by Alfred Hitchcock

8. A book about country and western music
9. A book of science fiction stories
10. A book about Beverly Sills

D. Using the card catalog, list title, author, call number, and publication date of all books about two of the following people.

1. Robert Frost
2. Marie Curie
3. Frank Lloyd Wright
4. Queen Elizabeth II
5. Joan of Arc

6. Helen Keller
7. Eleanor Roosevelt
8. Martha Graham
9. Sarah Bernhardt
10. Amelia Earhart

Part 3　Using Reference Materials

Let us say that you are doing an assignment on solar energy for a science class or a social studies report on the Panama Canal. You might use only one or two encyclopedias and write your paper from these sources. However, you would probably be limiting yourself to a rather dull, ordinary report if you decided to use only two encyclopedia sources. There are many different kinds of reference materials that would provide you with more detailed, interesting, and up-to-date information on these as well as many other topics you may be looking for.

Every library has either a reference room or a reference section. It is here that you will find just about everything you want, from a *Time* magazine article on rock music to a map of camping areas in the state of Maine.

Reference works include the following:

dictionaries	biographical references
encyclopedias	pamphlets, booklets, and catalogs
almanacs and yearbooks	magazines
atlases	

Each of these reference books is used for a certain purpose, and each has its own particular organization. The uses and purposes of the basic types of reference works are described in this section.

Dictionaries

General Dictionaries. The dictionary is one of the best general references you can use. A dictionary tells you the spelling, pronunciation, and meaning of a word. It also gives you brief information about many subjects such as people, places, abbreviations, and foreign terms.

There are three major types of dictionaries:

Unabridged Dictionaries. These are the largest and most complete dictionaries. They contain well over 250,000 words in the language, with the complete history of each word and every definition and use available for each word. The best known unabridged dictionaries are the following:

> *Webster's Third New International Dictionary*
> *The Random House Dictionary of the English Language,*
> *Unabridged Edition*

You will find at least one, if not both, of these in your school or community library.

Abridged Dictionaries. These dictionaries are often called "desk" or "collegiate" dictionaries. They contain about 130,000 to 150,000 words. These dictionaries contain the information you would normally need about definitions, spelling, pronunciations, and matters of usage. In addition, they usually provide special sections that contain information such as biographical and geographical references.

Your school or local library probably carries several different abridged dictionaries. The best known are the following:

> *The American Heritage Dictionary of the English*
> *Language*
> *The Macmillan Dictionary*

The Random House Dictionary of the English Language,
   College Edition
Thorndike-Barnhart Dictionary
Webster's New Collegiate Dictionary
Webster's New World Dictionary of the American
   Language

Pocket Dictionaries. These dictionaries are limited in the number of words they contain. They should be used mainly to check the spelling of ordinary words or to give you a quick definition of an unfamiliar word you may come across in your reading.

Dictionaries on Specific Subjects. Many dictionaries deal with specific subjects, such as music, geography, art, and science. The following list includes the names of some of these dictionaries. There are far too many to list, so investigate the many different kinds that your library offers.

Compton's Illustrated Science Dictionary
Dictionary of Economics
Dictionary of American History (5 Volumes)
Grove's Dictionary of Music and Musicians (10 Volumes)
Harvard Dictionary of Music
An Illustrated Dictionary of Art and Archaeology
Mathematical Dictionary
Webster's Biographical Dictionary
Webster's Dictionary of Proper Names

Dictionaries About Language. Another group of dictionaries available to you deals with specific aspects of the English language, such as synonyms and antonyms, rhymes, slang, Americanisms, and etymology. Some of the most commonly used language dictionaries are the following:

Abbreviations Dictionary
Brewer's Dictionary of Phrase and Fable
Dictionary of Literary Terms
A Dictionary of Slang and Unconventional English
A Dictionary of Word and Phrase Origins (3 Volumes)

Mathew's Dictionary of Americanisms
The Oxford Dictionary of English Etymology
Wood's Unabridged Rhyming Dictionary

One additional type of language dictionary that is particularly useful to you as a young writer is the **thesaurus.** A thesaurus is a dictionary of words that have similar meanings. It is sometimes called a dictionary of synonyms. Using a thesaurus will help you in both your writing and in your speaking. It is important to remember, however, that although synonyms have similar meanings, synonyms are *not* identical. Each synonym has a slightly different meaning, and you need to study each meaning carefully to select exactly the right synonym for what you are trying to say.

A list of reliable thesauruses follows:

Roget's International Thesaurus
Roget's Thesaurus in Dictionary Form
Webster's Collegiate Thesaurus
Webster's Dictionary of Synonyms

Exercises   Using the Dictionary

A. Using your classroom dictionary or the desk dictionary that you have at home, list all of the sections of information that the dictionary contains. Be thorough.

B. Using only dictionaries as a reference, write answers to the following questions. Use different types of dictionaries, and after each of your answers write the title of the dictionary you used.

1. What is the origin of the word *cereal?*
2. These words may be spelled more than one way. Write the other spelling.

    ax   hiccup   chili   ketchup   busses

3. Where is Victoria Falls? How high and wide is it?
4. For what is Roald Amundsen famous?

5. Find the meanings of the words in italics and answer these questions.

Could a castle have a *keep*?

Is a *decibel* an orchestral instrument?

Can you fire a *pistil*?

Would an airplane be in an *aviary*?

6. When was James Madison President of the United States?

7. Name six words that rhyme with *ark*.

8. What is the military definition of the word *leapfrog*?

9. Define the word *verbose* and use it in a sentence.

10. What parts of speech are each of these words?

run   flash   round   set

C. Use a thesaurus or dictionary of synonyms to complete the following exercises.

1. Rewrite each sentence, using a more precise synonym for the words in italics.

It was an *old car*.

The *house* was on a *hill*.

2. List four synonyms for *disgrace* and define each one.

3. The nine words in the box are common names for colors. Look up each word in your thesaurus. Then match each of the colors with their synonyms in the two columns at the right.

red	emerald	cinnamon
blue	ivory	raven
black	amethyst	plum
white	pearl	sapphire
brown	tangerine	ochre
yellow	ebony	azure
purple	vermillion	topaz
orange	apricot	umber
green	saffron	claret

Encyclopedias

An encyclopedia contains general articles on nearly every known subject. This information is organized alphabetically into volumes. There are guide words at the top of each page to help you find information. Each set of encyclopedias also has an index, which you should check before looking for your information. The index is usually in the last volume of the encyclopedia or in a separate volume. Some encyclopedias also publish a yearbook that reviews current events and subjects for a particular year.

The following encyclopedias are used frequently by young people:

General Encyclopedias

Collier's Encyclopedia (24 volumes)
Compton's Encyclopedia (26 volumes)
Encyclopaedia Britannica (29 volumes)
Encyclopedia Americana (30 volumes)
World Book Encyclopedia (22 volumes)

The library also has many encyclopedias that deal with specific subjects. Here are some of them:

Encyclopedias on Specific Subjects

The Baseball Encyclopedia
Better Homes and Gardens Encyclopedia of Cooking
The Encyclopedia of American Facts and Dates
Encyclopedia of Animal Care
Encyclopedia of Careers and Vocational Guidance
The Encyclopedia of Folk, Country, & Western Music
Encyclopedia of World Art (15 volumes)
Family Life and Health Encyclopedia (22 volumes)
The Illustrated Encyclopedia of Aviation and Space
The Illustrated Encyclopedia of World Coins
LaRousse Encyclopedia of Mythology
McGraw-Hill Encyclopedia of World Biography (12 volumes)
The Mammals of America

The Negro Heritage Library (9 volumes)
The Ocean World of Jacques Cousteau (19 volumes)
The Pictorial Encyclopedia of Birds
Popular Mechanics Do-It-Yourself Encyclopedia (16
  volumes)
Rock Encyclopedia

By no means is this list complete. Check the encyclopedias in your library's reference section and take note of the many kinds of encyclopedias that are available to you.

Exercises   Using Encyclopedias

A. In finding answers to the following questions, what key word in each question would you look for in the encyclopedia?

1. What new volcano appeared in Mexico in 1943?
2. Who invented the game of basketball, and when?
3. Can a living person be elected into the Baseball Hall of Fame?
4. What country first tried to dig the Panama Canal?
5. In what year did the United States set up standard time zones?
6. When did West Point first begin to train soldiers?

B. Select a subject of interest to you, such as a person or an invention. Using three different encyclopedias, compare the information that is given. First, write down the name of each encyclopedia and the basic information given in it. Then compare the information by looking at the specific details each contains. Decide which was the best resource. Then write a composition on your topic in *your own words.*

Almanacs and Yearbooks

Almanacs and yearbooks are published annually. They are the most useful sources of information, facts, and statistics on current events and historical records of government, sports, entertainment, population, and many other subjects. The information in an almanac is not arranged in any one particular order, so you will have to use both the table of contents and the index to find what information you need. Here is a partial list of the most widely used almanacs and yearbooks:

Guinness Book of World Records
Information Please Almanac, Atlas, and Yearbook
World Almanac and Book of Facts
World Book Science Yearbook
World Book Yearbook of Events

Exercise   Almanacs and Yearbooks

Answer the following questions by using the current issue of the *World Almanac:*

1. Which bridge in the United States has the longest span?

2. Who are the two present Senators from Florida?

3. What were the lowest and highest temperatures ever recorded in your state?

4. Which two baseball teams played in the World Series in 1975, and who won?

5. How many women, including officers and enlisted personnel, are in the U.S. Marines?

6. What is the world's largest city, and what is its population?

7. In what year and for what movie did John Wayne win an Academy Award?

8. Which state in the United States produced the most wheat last year?

9. How much does it cost to send a letter to Greece by ordinary mail (not over 1 oz.)?

10. What is the address of the Environmental Protection Agency?

Atlases

An atlas is a reference book that contains many large, detailed maps of the world. It also contains other sources of geographical information, such as statistics about population, temperatures, oceans, and other specific areas. Some atlases publish different information, so it is a good idea to study the table of contents and any directions to the reader before you try to use it. The following is a list of some reliable atlases:

Atlas of World History
The Britannica Atlas
Collier's World Atlas and Gazetteer
Goode's World Atlas
Grosset World Atlas
The International Atlas from Rand McNally
National Geographic Atlas of the World
The Times Atlas of the World
Webster's Atlas with Zip Code Directory

Exercise   Using the Atlas

Using a world atlas, answer the following questions:

1. What countries make up Central America?
2. What is the weight of the earth?
3. What does the foreign term *zaki* mean?
4. How are volcanoes helpful to humankind?
5. What are the five largest islands in the world?
6. What is the population of Canberra, Australia?
7. In what states does Glacier National Park lie?
8. How many states have a city or town named Lexington?

Special Biographical Reference Books

Both the dictionary and an encyclopedia will give you information about people. However, the best references to use when you need detailed information about a specific person are biographical references. They are specific subject books that deal only with information about people. Some of the most commonly used biographical references are these:

Current Biography
Dictionary of American Biography
Dictionary of National Biography
Twentieth Century Authors
Who's Who
Who's Who in America
Who's Who in the East (and Eastern Canada)
Who's Who in the Midwest
Who's Who in the South and Southeast
Who's Who in the West
Who's Who in American Women

Exercise Using Special Biographical References

After the answer to each of the following questions, write the title of the reference you used.

1. Who is Doug Henning, and what did he do?
2. Is Carson McCullers a man or a woman? What is the best-known work of this author? Is the author living?
3. Identify the following Americans: Robert Williamson Lovett and Antoine Robidou.
4. Who is Alice Paul?
5. List three important works written by Carl Sandburg.
6. Where was Johnny Carson born?
7. What reference contains information on the following: Pearl Buck, Sinclair Lewis, Ray Bradbury, and Harper Lee? Tell when and where each was born.
8. What is Frank Borman's claim to fame, and what does he do now?
9. Who is Bella Abzug, and for what is she well known?
10. Who is Martha Graham, and for what is she well known?

The Vertical File

Many libraries have a file cabinet in which they keep an alphabetical file of pamphlets, booklets, catalogs, handbooks, and clippings about a variety of subjects. Always check the vertical file when you are writing a report or looking for information, especially information on careers.

Magazines

The *Readers' Guide* is a monthly index of magazine articles. It lists the articles alphabetically by subject and author. It is issued twice a month from September to June, and once a month in July and August. An entire year's issues are bound in one hardcover volume at the end of the year. There are two forms of the *Readers' Guide*. The unabridged edition indexes over 135 magazines and is found mainly in high school and public libraries. The abridged edition of the *Readers' Guide* indexes 45 magazines and is usually used in junior high school libraries.

The *Readers' Guide* is a valuable source of information. It is important to read the abbreviation guide in the preface to the *Readers' Guide* so that you will understand how to read each entry. The excerpt from the *Readers' Guide* shown on page 183 illustrates how articles are listed.

Exercises   Using the *Readers' Guide*

A. Write the meanings of the following symbols used in the *Readers' Guide:*

    il   +   ed   m   w   no   Je

    bibl pub Jl Mr abr D   rev

|HAIRCUTTING|
    Above all, the cut. M. Lynch. il Ladies Home J 94:108-13   — subject entry
    Ap '77
HAIRDRESSING
    24 spring hairdos. il Good H 184:108-17+ Mr '77
|HALEY, Alex|
    Haley's Rx: talk, write, reunite; interview, ed by W. Marmon.   — author entry
    il Time 109:72+ F 14 '77
    |My search for roots|: excerpt. il por Read Digest 110:148-52   — title of article
    Ap '77
    Roots; condensation; reprint of 1974 article. il Read Digest
    110:153-79 Ap '77

                           about

    After Haley's comet. |H. F. Waters.| il por Newsweek 89:97-8   — author of article
    F 14 '77
    Alex Haley: the man behind Roots. H. J. Massaquoi. il pors
    |Ebony|32:33-6+ Ap '77   — name of magazine
    Uncle Tom's Roots. M. Greenfield. il Newsweek |89|:100 F   — volume number
    14 '77*
HALL, Alice J.
    Dazzling legacy of an ancient quest. il Nat Geog 151:|202-311| — page reference
    Mr '77
HALL, Beverly
    Wild bunch. il Nat Wildlife 15:4-11 |Ap '77| — date of magazine
HALLEY'S comet
    Sailing to Halley's comet. il Time 109:54 Mr 14 '77
HALLMARK, Clayton L.
    Multimeters for electronics (cont) il Pop Electr 11:31-2+ F '77
HALOS (meteorology)
    Form and origin of the Parry arcs. R. G. Greenler and others,
    il Science 195:360-7 Ja 28 '77
HAM
    |See also
    Cookery-Meat| — "see also"
HAM radio.   cross reference
    |See Radio. Amateur|
HAMAMATSU, Japan   — "see"
    Japan's warriors of the wind: city's annual tribute to its   cross reference
    first-born sons. J. Eliot. |il|Nat Geog 151:550-61 Ap '77   — illustrated article
HAMBERLIN, Emiel
    Chicago teacher makes his classes come alive. B. Rhoden.
    il pors Ebony 32:43-6+ Mr '77*

B. Read carefully the following excerpt from the *Readers' Guide.* Then answer the questions following the entry.

> Hooping it up; women's basketball. B. Weber. Sr Schol 109:27 Ja 27 '77

1. What is the name of the article?
2. In what magazine is the article published?
3. In what issue of the magazine is the article printed?
4. Who wrote the article?
5. Is the article illustrated?
6. On what page of the magazine is the article?

C. Use the excerpt from the *Readers' Guide* on page 183 to answer the following questions:

1. What two magazines featured articles *about* Alex Haley?
2. What magazine and what issue of the magazine featured an article about haircuts?
3. On what page in *Time* magazine can you find an article about Halley's comet?
4. Give the complete magazine title of the following abbreviations:

> *Nat Geog*   Good H
> *Read Digest*   *Ladies Home J*

5. What magazine featured an article about a Chicago teacher?

D. Choose a current subject or person of importance. Using the *Readers' Guide,* make a list of four articles that would be a good reference for writing about your subject. Be sure to list all of the necessary information.

Chapter 11

Developing Your Speaking and Listening Skills

Speaking is the most common form of communication. You probably feel comfortable when you're talking with your friends because you do that on a daily basis. You can communicate with them because they know and understand you. Your voice and what you say are an important part of your identity.

But what happens when you have to talk to a group of people who are not all your best friends? That is when fear usually sets in. You know the symptoms: dry mouth, sweaty palms, shaky legs, and quivering voice. This nervousness happens to everyone at one time or another. The best way to overcome this condition is to learn the speaking skills that help to prepare you and put you at ease.

Part 1 Speaking Informally

There are many times both in and out of school when you will be asked to speak informally to a group of people. Informal talks usually take only a few minutes. Because they are short, you don't have much time to make a good impression with what you say. That is why the two most important skills in speaking informally are your preparation and your presentation.

Preparation

Even though informal talks are short, it may be necessary to do some background work so you are sure you have all the information you need. The kind of background work will depend, of course, on the subject of your talk and your audience. You may need to interview the person sponsoring a particular event, or you may need to go to the library to check a reference book for any facts you need. When doing any kind of background work, you should always take accurate notes. Having to rely on your memory only adds to your nervousness in a talk. Accurate notes give you confidence and help you to organize your talk.

It is a good idea to practice giving your talk, preferably in front of a mirror, so you can watch yourself and correct any movements you might not like. When you give your actual talk, you may be permitted to use a note card or two for a quick glance at your main points.

Here are the three points to remember:

1. Do some background work to find the information you need.
2. Take notes to organize your material.
3. Practice delivering your talk orally to gain confidence in what you are saying.

Presentation

When you finally give your talk, you want to be as relaxed and confident as possible. Naturally, you are going to be a bit nervous because you want to do a good job. The following steps will help you deliver a talk that your audience will enjoy.

1. **Preparation.** Be well prepared. Be sure of your information. Be ready with any extra materials you may need.

2. **Eye contact.** It may be hard at first to look directly at your audience, but be sure to keep your head up. You can start by looking over the heads of your audience. Then gradually look directly at them as you feel more confident. Good eye contact helps to keep the audience interested. You may, of course, refer briefly to your notes when you need to.

3. **Posture.** It is important to appear relaxed—even if you are not. If you act nervous, your audience will pay more attention to your nervous habits than to what you are saying. If you try to stand comfortably straight, with your legs slightly apart for good balance, your voice will project better, and your audience will think you are at ease.

4. **Voice.** If the audience cannot hear you, you have wasted your time and theirs. The important things to remember about your voice are these:
   Keep your head up so that you can be heard.
   Speak slowly enough to be understood.
   Vary the tone of your voice to keep your audience interested.

5. **Gestures.** Gestures are facial expressions and movements you make with your hands and body to help emphasize what you are saying. Gestures should be natural, such as pointing to an illustration or nodding your head to emphasize the truth of a statement. Gestures keep your audience alert, but too many gestures are distracting.

Both preparation and presentation are basic to speaking in front of people. *The way you present your information and yourself affects the interest of your audience and determines the success of your talk.*

Part 2 Types of Informal Speaking

Making Announcements

In school you hear announcements several times a day. Some of them you remember, but others never seem to catch your attention. Announcements are short and simple, but the information should be clear and include the following details:

Who is involved or sponsoring the event?
What is happening?
Where is it taking place?
When is it happening (time)?
Why should the listener be interested?

Many people don't listen until they hear something in particular that interests them. That's why it is important to get their attention first. Always repeat the most important facts, especially the *where* and *when.*

Announcements fall into two basic categories: those about future events and those about events that have already taken place. With events that have already happened, you can add many more details. Look at the following examples of each:

Announcement of a Future Event

Have you ever seen your name in print? Do you know who made basketball and cheerleading tryouts? Are you up-to-date on the latest gossip? Now you have the chance to find the answers to these questions and many more. Tomorrow, Wednesday, October 15, the first issue of the school paper, *The Eagle's Eye,* will be sold in the school cafeteria during all lunch periods. The cost is only 10¢. Don't forget—tomorrow, Wednesday, the school paper will be sold in the cafeteria. There's something in it for everyone, so don't forget your dime.

Announcement of a Past Event

Last Saturday, April 12, at Heritage Park, our baseball team won its first victory by slaughtering the Holmes Lions, 12 to 5. Bob Jansen struck out ten batters while infielders Campbell, Juarez, and Lee pulled off six double plays. The team really worked together for this great victory. Everyone come to the next game and support our team. Be there on Saturday, April 19, at 7 P.M. at Heritage Park and watch our Eagles stampede those McArthur Mustangs. That's Saturday, April 19, at 7 P.M. at Heritage Park. See you there.

Announcements can be fun. Be sure to include all of the necessary details and review the information on preparation and presentation.

Exercises   Making Announcements

A. Make an announcement to the class using two of the following events or two events that are going to take place in your school. If you wish, make up events, but be sure to include the specific information that is required.

a student council event	tryouts for a play
a club meeting	an assembly
a bake sale	talent show competition
an athletic event	a field trip

B. With a small group of three or four other people, plan a short newscast using both the announcement of a future event and a past event. You can center your newscast around one subject area, such as sports or politics, or you can present a typical newscast with several subject areas.

Giving Directions

Remember your first day in school, when you seemed totally lost? You probably received directions like these:

> Oh, the music room. Just go down the hall, through the double doors, and it's on your right.

You followed the directions and ended up at a janitor's closet, not a very good start for your first day. With this kind of experience, you can see the importance of using complete and accurate details. Look at the difference details can make:

> To get to the music room, continue going down this hall. As soon as you pass the entrance to the gym you will see a hall on your left. Go down that hall and through the double doors. The music room is the first door on your right, across from the water fountain.

With these details you have a much better chance of finding your way.

When you give directions, remember that you know where the location is but that the other person does not. Do not take any clue for granted. Use accurate details and be as clear as possible. To be sure that you have given good directions, either repeat the directions or have the person repeat them to you.

Exercises Giving Directions

A. Give directions on how to get from the school to your house. Assume that no one knows the town. Calculate your distances carefully and point out landmarks that might be helpful.

B. Each member of the class is to write out directions for another class member to follow. Try to make the directions as exact as possible. Your directions should be limited to activities inside the classroom. Do not try to trick anyone. Just give accurate directions about what to do. Try to include several different tasks, such as selecting books, sharpening pencils, or opening windows. Don't leave out important details, such as opening a closet door. When it's your turn, follow only the directions on the paper—not what you think the person meant.

Giving a Demonstration Talk

How do you ride a bike?

Just hold on to the handlebars, push the pedals with your feet, and go.

It sounds easy enough, but if you explain it that way to a child who has never done it, he or she will fall right over.

When you demonstrate how to do something, you have to be as exact as when you are giving directions. The following steps will help you to give an informative demonstration:

1. **Know your subject.** The best demonstration will be about something you know how to do well. Also, choose a subject in which you know your audience will be interested.

2. **Organize your material.** Your audience will understand your demonstration best if the information is presented in the proper order. If you present each step in the order it occurs, your demonstration will make sense.

3. **Check your equipment.** Most demonstrations involve some form of equipment. Some require many utensils or tools. To keep yourself organized, make a list of the equipment you will need for each step. However, try to choose a subject that is not too complicated.

4. **Be interesting.** Start with a positive statement that gets

your audience immediately involved. Your audience needs to know why they should be interested in your subject. Look at the difference in these two beginnings. Which is more interesting?

> I'm going to show you how to make a pizza.
> I've discovered an easy way to make a great-tasting pizza that I know you're going to like.

Once you have gained everyone's attention, keep it with a clear, interesting, step-by-step explanation. If you need to use difficult terms, write them on the board. Do not pass around objects that will distract your listeners.

Exercise   Giving a Demonstration Talk

Give a demonstration talk to your class. Follow the steps carefully. The following list might help you to think of a good activity:

swing a tennis racket	make a candle
fix a bicycle chain	carve wood
set your hair	do a scientific experiment
set up an aquarium	repot a plant
macramé a plant holder	play a flute

Making Introductions

When someone introduces you, you certainly do not want to be embarrassed. That is why you should give other people the same courtesy. Begin with something positive about the person you are introducing. Next, add some interesting details to support your first comment. This information usually shows what you have in common.

> This is my good friend and neighbor, Brad Morris. He and I have played on the same baseball team for four years. He's a great hitter.

With details like this, the people who have just met each other will feel more comfortable and will have something to talk about.

When you have to make a more formal introduction, such as the introduction of a guest speaker, you will need some background information. The information you decide to use should be related to why the person is a guest. Here is an example:

> I am pleased to introduce Sharon McHale, president of the freshman class at Grover High School. As some of you may remember, Sharon was vice-president of the student council here at Stevenson last year. She has obviously learned a great deal from that experience. Sharon is here to tell us about the powers and responsibilities of the student government in high school and how we can become involved. Thank you for coming, Sharon.

Exercises Making Introductions

A. Introduce a member of your class. Even though you may know each other, try to find some new, positive information that will catch the interest of the class.

B. Write an introduction for a member of your family or a relative. You may decide on a particular occasion or assume that the person is going to speak to your class.

Part 3 Speaking Formally

When you are asked to speak about a specific topic, to a specific group, for a specific purpose, you are presenting a formal talk. A formal talk is longer and requires more preparation than an informal talk. You might think that speaking formally is harder and more complicated than speaking informally, but if you follow the step-by-step procedures in this chapter, you will soon learn the routine.

There are eight basic steps for preparing a formal talk. Learning these steps will help you to be a better speaker whenever the occasion arises.

1. Know your audience
2. Select a topic
3. Define your purpose
4. Select your theme
5. Gather your material
6. Organize your material
7. Practice your presentation
8. Present your material

Step 1 Know Your Audience

Most of the formal talks that you give are to your classmates. Since this group of people is the same age as you, and has the same common interests, it will be easier for you to approach your subject. But suppose you have given a successful formal talk in your social studies class. It was so good that your teacher has asked you to give it again both to a fifth-grade class and to the PTA. To do this successfully, you will have to change the approach to your subject so that each group will understand and be interested in what you are saying. To determine how to approach your subject, you should consider the following facts about each group:

1. **The purpose of the group.** Is this group meeting to learn something new, or is the group expecting you to support its ideas? Is the group meeting merely to relax and have fun? If you know the purpose of the group, you can include in your talk the ideas and information that will help the group to achieve its purpose.

2. **The composition of the group.** How many people are there in the group? Are they alike or different in age, sex,

education, or occupation? The more differences a group has, the more you will have to consider what to include in your talk.

3. **The experience of the group.** How well will the group listen? Is the group used to hearing speakers? Are you one of a series of speakers? How can you relate your material to the experience of the group?

4. **The occasion for the group to meet.** Is the group meeting for a social occasion such as the Fourth of July or the presentation of awards? If so, you should try to relate your material to the occasion, in such a way that it will be both relevant and interesting.

Exercise   Knowing Your Audience

Name three different audiences to which you might have the opportunity to speak. For each audience, list the chief characteristics that you should consider in approaching your subject for each group.

Step 2 Select Your Topic

There will be occasions when you are assigned a specific topic for a speech. In that case, you can begin your research immediately. At other times you will be given a general subject area such as football. In that case you will need to limit your subject to one specific topic about the subject area, such as Famous NFL Quarterbacks. This decision can be made according to the make-up of the audience. There is also the possibility that you will have the chance to choose your own topic. More than likely you will select a topic that you know well, but don't be afraid to choose a new topic in which you are interested. Your new experience could add excitement to your talk.

Following are a few suggestions that will help you to select a topic:

The unusual appeals to everyone. Consider a new topic or one seldom discussed that would be of interest to the group.

A familiar topic is one about which your audience already has general information. Look for new details to interest your audience, because sometimes a familiar topic can be dull.

A factual topic is informative, and it contains details. To keep these details interesting, look for new sources that might supply you with unexpected highlights.

Contrasts are also interesting, such as a talk showing the differences between American and British television.

Exercises   Selecting a Topic

A. Select two topics that would be appropriate to speak about to each of the following groups.

1. your science class   3. a scout troop
2. the PTA   4. an athletic award banquet

B. For each of the following topics, suggest an interesting title. Before you decide, consider the unusual, the familiar, the factual, and the contrast approaches. Label the approach used for each of the titles you choose. Be sure to limit your topic before you think of a title.

| democracy | education | weather |
| cooking | stars | music |

Step 3 Define Your Purpose

Once you have chosen an appropriate topic for the group, you need to define exactly what you wish to achieve with your talk. Defining your purpose will help you to organize your material and to plan the response you want from your audience. Formal talks generally fall into one of the following categories. Decide which of these three purposes your talk involves.

To inform

Most formal talks that you are required to give in class are informative. Your purpose is to help your audience to understand or appreciate what you are telling them. Talks to inform might include the following:

a report on a book
an explanation of voting procedures
an explanation of how the heart works

To persuade

When the purpose of your talk is to persuade, you have chosen a topic that has two sides to it. Some people in the audience will feel the same way you do. If so, your main purpose will be to persuade the others to your point of view. Make sure that your information is accurate and that you have many strong points to support your opinion. To be successful, your talk should lead to some change in the listener's point of view, attitude, or course of action. The following are examples of topics for persuasive talks:

the election of a candidate
the dangers of drug addiction
city living *versus* suburban living

To entertain

Certainly you want your audience to enjoy any talk you give. Talks that are given at special occasions are frequently for the purpose of entertainment. A talk to entertain might be one of the following:

a humorous or unusual personal experience
a visit to an unusual place
living with a pet

Exercise Defining Your Purpose

Identify what you think the main purpose should be in each of the following topics:

Bicycle Lanes Should Be Built Along Major Streets and Highways

New Laws Against Vandalism

The Day a Fish Caught Me

Vote Kathy Caldwell for President

How an Engine Works

Step 4 Select a Theme

The theme is the main idea you want to get across to your audience. Selecting a theme also helps you, the speaker, to plan your talk. To make sure that the theme is clear in your mind, write out the theme in a full sentence. For example:

Students who are taking a foreign language do not have enough opportunities to use that language.

As a career, the Air Force offers many hidden opportunities.

John Steinbeck's novel *The Pearl* is an excellent example of how greed can destroy a person.

All of the information that you gather and present should support your theme in some way. You may even want to use your theme sentence as part of your speech to make sure that the theme is clear to your audience.

Exercise Selecting a Theme

Suggest a possible theme for each of the following subjects. Write out the theme in a full sentence.

voting   movie ratings   kite flying

Compare your themes with those of others in the class. Each of these subjects has numerous possibilities.

Step 5 Gather Your Material

Once you have decided on your theme, you can begin to gather material to support your main idea. Using a variety of information, such as illustrations, facts, quotations, and charts will make your talk more interesting. Most of your material will come from these three main sources:

Firsthand experience. Personal experience adds life to your talk. If you have had an interesting experience, it is possible that others in the audience may have had a similar one. A personal experience might also help you to think of other sources, either people or books, to investigate.

Experience of others. If you have not had a personal experience related to your subject, it is a good idea to interview someone who has. When you do interview someone, be sure to use a tape recorder or to take very good notes.

Research in the library. The library offers you the largest variety of information. Check carefully every possible resource, including the *Readers' Guide to Periodical Literature*, the vertical file, audio-visual aids, and the many varieties of reference books. Refer to Chapter 10, "Using the Library," for specific sources. Whatever resources you decide to use, be sure to take notes. The best procedure is to use 4″ × 6″ index cards to organize your information.

Exercise Gathering Material

Choose one of the following topics or one of your own. Find four different sources of information about the topics. If possible, use index cards to write down the name of the source, the page number, and the sample of information. The sources of information include interviews and personal experience.

macramé	American composers	kite building
astronomy	Olympic medal winners	pro quarterbacks

Step 6 Organize Your Material

Once you have gathered all of your information, you need to organize it so it will make sense. Begin by dividing your material into three parts: the *introduction*, the *body*, and the *conclusion*.

The Introduction

The purpose of the introduction is to gain the attention of the audience. There are four commonly used kinds of introductions:

1. **An anecdote.** This is a humorous beginning that helps to relax the audience. While it is a common beginning, it is not appropriate for every subject.

   I had no idea when I started doing research on the flea that I would need a truck to get home all of the information. Even my dog offered to help by lending me one of his fleas for an interview.

2. **An explanation of the title.** This introduction is particularly helpful if your title gives only a small clue to what the subject is.

   "The Day a Fish Caught Me" may sound like a joke or a science fiction story to you, but to me it was a real life or death experience. I had never before thought that a peaceful sport like fishing could be dangerous.

3. **A statement of your theme.** If you state your theme at the beginning of your talk, the audience will know immediately what your purpose is.

   This school needs an after-school activity bus so that more students can participate in extra-curricular activities. This will benefit both the students and the school, and will also improve the school spirit.

4. **An unusual fact.** If you can find some unusual information, especially about a common topic, it will help to get everyone's attention.

Did you know that there are more deaths caused by car accidents every year than there are by any disease? It certainly makes you wonder if it's safe to get a driver's license.

The Body

The body is the major part of your talk, and it must inform, entertain, or persuade your audience. After getting the attention of your audience with your introduction, you now give them the facts and details to support your theme. Here are some guidelines to help you.

1. **Determine your main points.** How much time you are given to speak will determine how many main points you will be able to use. The points you use must have details to support them. To organize your main points, arrange them in logical order in outline form.

   ### How Creatures Protect Themselves

   I. Their Speed
   II. Their Protective Coloring
   III. Their Protective Resemblance
   IV. Their Armor
   V. Their Weapons
   VI. Their Habits

2. **Develop your main points.** Each of your main points can be developed by using details from your notes, charts, graphs, illustrations, personal experience, or quotations from your sources. These details should be added to your outline under each main point. You might also include a notation when you want to show an illustration. You might underline the notation in red so you will be alerted ahead of time for its use.

How Creatures Protect Themselves

V. Some creatures carry weapons for protection.
    A. The porcupine has spines. (Show actual quill.)
    B. The swordfish has its sword.
    C. Lions, tigers, and leopards have claws.
    D. Some creatures use poison.
       1. The sea anemone shoots out poison darts.
       2. Bees and wasps inject poison with their sting.
       3. The black widow spider's bite is poisonous.
          (Show large poster of spider.)
    E. Some animals, such as the skunk, give out a bad odor.

The Conclusion

The conclusion is a summary of the main points of your talk. It should be brief and should not introduce any new information. It is a good place to repeat your theme for emphasis.

> Some creatures may not be our favorite friends. In fact, we humans seem to be the enemy of some. However, creatures must be able to protect themselves. They do this effectively, and in varying ways, by speed, coloring, resemblance to nature, armor, weapons, and habits.

By organizing your ideas in a logical order, you can help the listener follow them and understand your talk.

Exercise   Organizing Your Material

Arrange the following main points in the most logical order. After each main point, list the supporting details that would best explain that particular main point.

The Library

Main Points

Why the library is important
How you get books from a library
What a library is

Important because it is a place where books can be safely kept

Place where we can read

Important because it has maps, globes, and dictionaries

Important because we don't have to buy all the books we want to read

Next go to the appropriate section for the book, such as fiction, nonfiction, biography, or reference

To locate a library book, look up the book or subject or author in the card catalog

First you must get a library card

Place where we can borrow books

Then copy down the author, title, and number of the book

Go to the checkout desk to check out your book

Place where we can study and do research for reports

Step 7 **Practice Your Presentation**

After you have organized your material, you need to practice giving your talk out loud so that you will be familiar with the material and at ease in front of your audience. The following suggestions will help you in your oral practice sessions.

1. Read through the material several times until you are sure of the correct order in which the information should be presented.

2. Underline the material you particularly want to emphasize as a reminder to increase the expression in your voice at that point.

3. You may want to memorize as much of your talk as you can so you can speak directly to your audience. If your head is down because you have to read your notes, your audience will soon lose interest.

4. Practice your talk in front of a mirror to help you add facial expressions and gestures to your talk when they are needed. Do this several times until you feel that your expression and gestures are natural.

5. Finally, practice giving your talk to your family or a small group of friends so that you can see their reactions. They will be able to tell you if you need improvement in your voice, posture, eye contact, gestures, or information.

Exercise   Practicing Your Presentation

Once your material is well organized, follow the preceding steps and practice your talk. The best way to practice is to use the actual material you are going to present. Allow yourself plenty of time to practice before your presentation. Do not wait until the night before it is due.

Step 8 Deliver Your Talk

The guidelines for presenting a formal talk are basically the same as those for presenting an informal talk. The main idea is to appear as relaxed as possible so that your audience will listen to you carefully.

Review the following guidelines:

1. **Preparation.** Thorough preparation is important. Be sure of your information and have all of your materials ready.

2. **Rehearsal.** Rehearse your talk aloud many times. If possible, use a tape recorder to hear how you sound.

3. **Eye contact.** Refer to your notes when you need to, but be sure to keep your head up and look around at your audience to keep their attention.

4. **Posture.** Appear as relaxed as possible, but stand up straight to show your confidence. Limit your gestures to those you need for emphasis only.

5. **Voice.** Speak loudly enough and clearly enough for everyone to hear you. Use good expression to keep attention. Do not read your talk.

Exercise Delivering Your Talk

The best exercise for delivering your talk is to give one to the class. First practice in front of a mirror. If you have a tape recorder, use that also. Then present your talk to the class. Good luck!

Part 4 Evaluation

Having your talk evaluated is important to you. An evaluation helps you to learn how to improve your speaking, and by evaluating others, you also learn ways to improve your own presentation. There are several different elements to consider when you evaluate a speaker, such as information, purpose, preparation, organization, and presentation. Before you can evaluate others, however, there is one very important rule to learn:

Good listening is the key to good evaluating.

Since listening is so important, you can see that being a member of the audience requires as much responsibility as being the speaker. Following these guides to good listening will also help you to evaluate fairly:

Guides to Good Listening

1. **Be ready.** First, make sure that you are located in a position to hear the speaker well. Second, know your purpose for listening to the speaker. Is the speaker's purpose to inform, to persuade, or to entertain? The speaker's purpose for speaking will be your purpose for listening. Only a

good listener can make an intelligent evaluation of a speaker.

2. **Be attentive.** To be a good listener, you have to give strict attention to the speaker. To evaluate the speaker fairly, you can't miss any information, overall organization, or aspects of preparation that add meaning to the talk.

3. **Be open-minded.** Sometimes a speaker's subject may not be of special interest to you, or you may not have the same opinion as the speaker does. In either case, you still have the responsibility to listen carefully to everything the speaker has to say. Do not let your personal opinions affect your judgment of the speaker's abilities.

Once you have learned to follow the guides to being a good listener, you will be better able to evaluate the speaker fairly. When it is your turn to speak, you can expect to be evaluated fairly if the audience has followed these same guidelines.

Guides to Fair Evaluating

1. **Topic.** Was the topic interesting to the majority of the group? Do not judge the topic by your personal interests. Watch the response of the group before you decide whether the topic was appropriate.

2. **Purpose.** Was the speaker's purpose to inform, to persuade, or to entertain? Did the speaker achieve this purpose?

3. **Preparation.** Did the speaker have enough information about the subject? Was there too much unnecessary information? If the speaker was well prepared, all of the information will have had a purpose.

4. **Organization.** Did the speaker present the information in a logical order? If the information was well organized, you should not have had any trouble understanding it. Was the speaker ready with any equipment that was needed,

such as tools for a demonstration or an illustration to help explain? If the speaker forgot such materials, the information was not as well organized as it should have been.

5. **Presentation.** Several aspects should be considered in evaluating the presentation:

   a. **Eye contact.** Did the speaker look at the audience in order to keep their interest?

   b. **Posture.** Did the speaker appear relaxed, or did nervous habits distract the audience?

   c. **Voice.** Could you hear the speaker? Was there good expression in what was said?

   d. **Gestures.** Were gestures used when they were needed, especially facial expressions? Were the gestures too distracting to the audience?

   e. **Practice.** Was the speaker familiar with the material, or was more practice needed? Did the speaker read the material?

The most important point to remember in evaluating a speaker is to be *fair*. Speaking to a group is not a contest; it is a skill that you are learning to develop. Try to be as constructive as possible in your criticism. As an evaluator, you can help other people to become better speakers, and you can also help yourself to become both a better listener and a better speaker.

Exercise   Evaluating a Speaker

When your class is prepared to present individual formal talks, make out an evaluation form for each speaker. List the five categories for fair evaluation. Next to the categories make the following three columns: *Good, Fair, Needs Improvement*. When the speaker is finished, fill in a column for each category and return the form to the speaker. Remember, this is not a contest. You are trying to help each other become better speakers. When you receive the evaluation forms for your talk, you will know what to improve upon the next time you speak.

Grammar and Usage

The Mechanics of Writing

A detailed Table of Contents of Sections 1–12 appears in the front of this book.

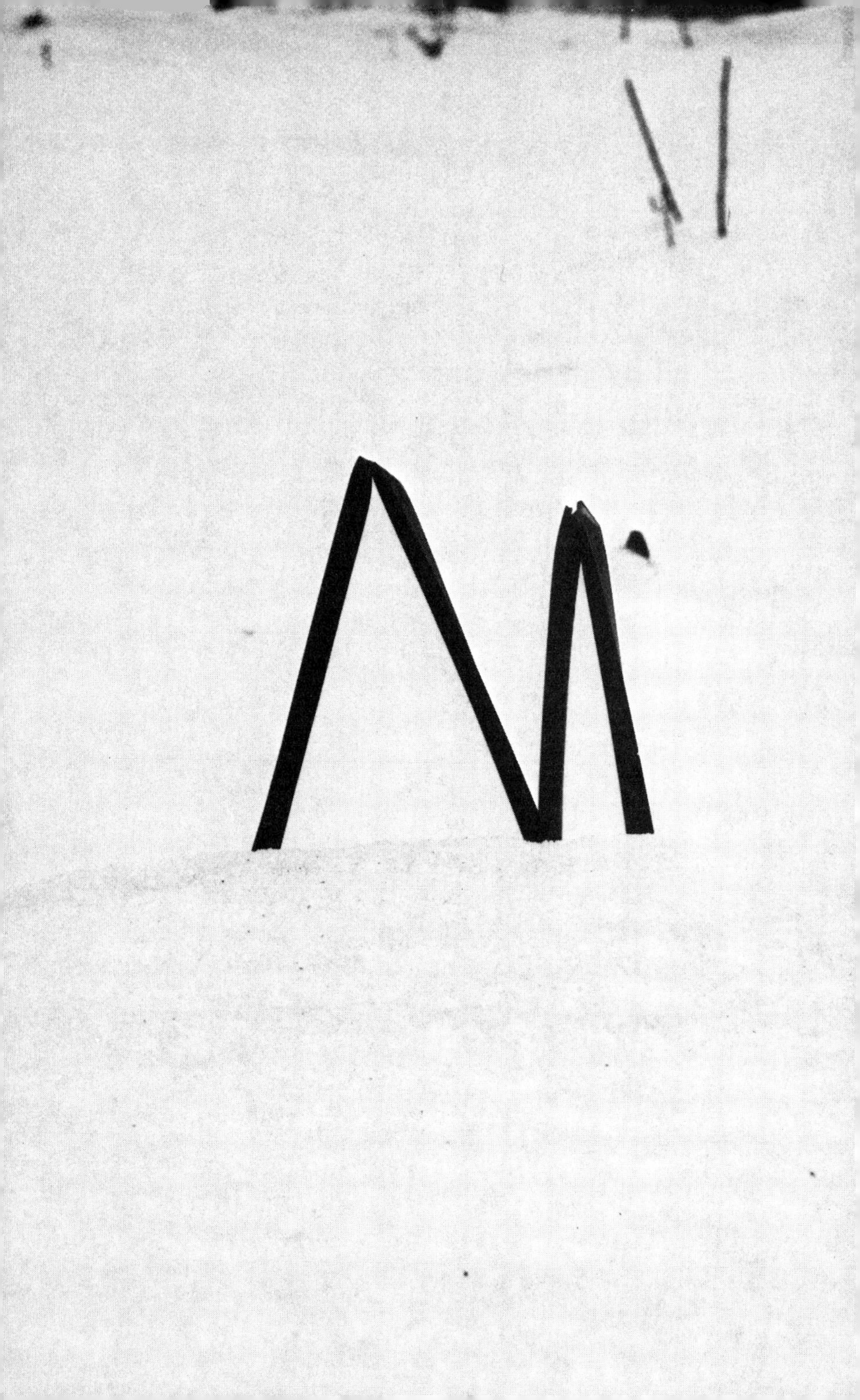

Section 1

The Sentence and Its Parts

What are sentences made of?

They are made of words, of course. But they are not made of words just jumbled together in any way at all. Sentences are made of a few different kinds of words placed in particular kinds of positions to mean specific things.

Sentences have structure. That is a way of saying that the arrangement of words in a sentence is itself important, just as is the choice of words. This chapter will help you understand the structure of sentences.

You will need to use English sentences day after day all the rest of your life. Learn to understand how they are constructed so that you can use them well.

Part 1 The Parts of a Sentence

A sentence expresses a complete thought; that is, it makes a complete statement, asks a question, tells someone to do something, or expresses strong feeling. It always has two grammatical parts. One part tells whom or what the sentence is about. This is the **subject.** The second part tells something about the subject. This is the **predicate.**

Subject (Who or what)	Predicate (What is said about the subject)
Beth	smiled.
The boys	had gone.
The two cars	nearly collided.
Each participant	received a certificate.

An easy way to understand the parts of a sentence is to think of the sentence as telling who did something or what happened. The subject tells *who* or *what*. The predicate tells *did* or *happened*. You can divide sentences, then, in this way:

Who or What	Did or Happened
Juanita	arrived.
The ice	melted.
The subway	was crowded with people.
A roar of anger	rose from the crowd.
The runner in the red shirt	won the race.

The subject of the sentence names someone or something about which a statement is to be made.

The predicate of the sentence tells what is done or what happens.

Exercises Find the subjects and predicates.

A. Copy these sentences. Draw a vertical line between the subject and the predicate.

Example: The whole crowd | cheered.

1. Karen wrote the weekly sports news.
2. Both dogs circled the water hole.
3. Thunder rumbled in the distance.
4. The boy across the street raises rabbits.
5. Terry saw the skydiving show on Channel 4.
6. A large crowd watched the basketball game.
7. My brother went home after the game.
8. Nancy collects foreign postage stamps.
9. Joe's Labrador retriever jumped the fence.
10. The yardstick snapped in two.

B. Copy these sentences. Draw a vertical line between the subject and the predicate.

1. An alligator slid into the water.
2. Elaine collects antique dolls.
3. The sand dunes baked in the sun.
4. Both of my sisters have graduated from high school.
5. Several students at Central School drew the posters.
6. My little brother knows the rules for the game.
7. Greg's brother builds historical model boats.
8. The girl in the yellow slicker missed the bus.
9. The man snored like a distant vacuum cleaner.
10. The two boys from our neighborhood went on a canoe trip.

Part 2   Simple Subjects and Predicates

In every sentence there are a few words that are more important than the rest. These are the key words that make the basic framework of the sentence. Study these examples:

1. A cold, driving **rain** │ **fell** throughout the night.

2.   **Rain** │ **fell.**

The subject of the first sentence is A *cold, driving rain.* The key word in this subject is *rain.* You can say *Rain fell throughout the night.* You cannot say *cold fell throughout the night.* Nor can you say *driving fell throughout the night.*

The predicate in the first sentence is *fell throughout the night.* The key word is *fell.* Without this word you would not have a sentence.

The key word in the subject of a sentence is called the simple subject. It is the subject of the verb.

The key word in the predicate is called the simple predicate. The simple predicate is the **verb.** Hereafter we will use the word *verb* rather than the phrase *simple predicate.*

The verb and its subject are the basic framework of every sentence. All the rest of the sentence is built around them. To find this framework, first find the verb. Then ask *Who?* or *What?* This will give you the subject of the verb.

Examples: Two girls in our class made puppets.
                Verb: made   *Who made puppets?* girls
                Subject of verb: girls

A deep snow covered the village.

Verb: covered   *What covered the village?* snow
Subject of verb: snow

Exercises Find the verbs and their simple subjects.

A. Number your paper 1–10. For each sentence write the verb and its subject.

Example: Lee worked hard yesterday.

Verb: worked
Subject: Lee

1. My cousins live in Indianapolis.
2. The swimmers waited for the starting whistle.
3. Nancy plays the flute in the band.
4. Almost all beekeepers wear protective masks.
5. Jack helped with the rink after school.
6. The two boys built a chicken coop.
7. Julie caught the fly easily.
8. The co-pilot radioed the tower.
9. Tall elms lined the avenue.
10. The three girls walked home together.

B. Number your paper 1–10. For each sentence write the verb and its subject.

1. A high fence enclosed the yard.
2. The operator adjusted his headphones.
3. The compass pointed north.
4. Iridescent bubbles floated over the sink.
5. Megan balanced on the high diving board.
6. The fans in the bleachers roared.
7. The helicopter landed on the hospital roof.
8. A heavy rain flattened our tomato plants temporarily.

9. Our group gave a report on solar energy.

10. An old black-and-white TV in the den takes all Dan's spare time.

Exercises   Add subjects and verbs.

A. Number your paper 1–10. Think of a subject and verb for each of the following sentences and write the completed sentences.

Example: Some (subject) (verb) guitars.

Some students own guitars.

1. A few (subject) (verb) porpoises.
2. (Subject) (verb) in the autumn.
3. His (subject) (verb) at midnight.
4. Pretty soon the (subject) (verb).
5. Her (subject) (verb) ping pong.
6. My (subject) (verb) on the telephone.
7. The big (subject) (verb) absentmindedly.
8. The (subject) on the runway (verb) to the control tower.
9. A (subject) of his (verb) the trip.
10. These (subject) (verb) the game on Friday.

B. Number your paper 1–10. Think of a subject and verb for each of the following sentences and write the completed sentences.

1. His (subject) (verb) a box of nails.
2. The (subject) of the needle (verb) him.
3. Not many (subject) (verb) French fries.
4. (Subject) never (verb).
5. (Subject) (verb) their newspapers.
6. Your (subject) (verb) a lot.

7. In our house (subject) (verb) the dishes.
8. The slow, old (subject) (verb) the bananas.
9. (Subject) (verb) noisily under the window.
10. The (subject) soon (verb) on the screen.

Diagraming Verbs and Their Subjects

A diagram helps you see how a sentence is put together. It shows which words go together. When you know which words go together, you can get the meaning easily.

A sentence diagram always begins on a horizontal line. The subject is placed at the left side of the line. The verb is placed at the right side of the line. A vertical line cuts the line in two and separates the subject from the verb.

Exercises Find the verbs and their subjects.

A. Show the verb and its simple subject in each of the following sentences. Use diagrams or any other method your teacher may suggest. Write only one word for the verb and one word for its subject.

1. A large, colorful umbrella shaded the chairs.
2. Curtis posted the results of the exam.
3. A squirrel in the attic started a nest.
4. The clock in the hallway needs repair.
5. The blower on the furnace stopped.
6. The photographs fell out of the folder.
7. Barbara's dresser fit next to the window.
8. The top drawer of the cabinet stuck.
9. Watermelon tastes good in hot weather.
10. Dr. Harvey's cat sported a tin bell.

B. Show the verb and its simple subject in each of the following sentences.

1. Pam collected the dues.
2. Unexpectedly, the engine stalled.
3. The pocket bulged with candy.
4. David builds kites in the garage.
5. The students in our class constructed a model space ship.
6. The end of vacation came too quickly.
7. We met Judy at the movie.
8. Maria's mother raises plants and flowers.
9. John visited the planetarium in Chicago last summer.
10. The Moores go to the photography show every year.

Part 3   Finding the Verb

To find the simple subject in a sentence, you first find the verb. Here are a few clues that will help you find the verb.

Some verbs tell about action:

> Tom *paddled* the canoe.
> Ann *caught* the ball.

Sometimes the action shown by the verb is an action you cannot see.

> Miki *had* a good idea.
> Jan *wants* a bicycle.
> Jim *remembered* the story.

Some verbs tell that something *is* or *exists*. We say that such verbs tell a *state of being*.

> The doctor *is* here.
> The test *seemed* easy.
> The road *looked* slippery.

A verb is a word that shows action or state of being.

Exercises   Find the verbs.

A.   Find the verbs in these sentences. They may be an action you cannot see or a state of being. Write only one word for the verb.

> Example: Rick thought hard.
>
> Verb: thought

1. Bill liked the program.
2. Skiers dream about snow.
3. I imagined the old fishing wharf.
4. The farmer noticed the vacant stall.
5. During the vacation we painted our garage.
6. Pam had time after supper.
7. The detectives considered the clues.
8. Debbie reacted quickly.
9. Their car is a compact.
10. The cards were here in the drawer.

B.   Find the verbs in these sentences. They may be an action you cannot see or a state of being. Write only one word for the verb.

1. I suppose so.
2. The desk top was uneven.
3. Raul and Maria are from Argentina.
4. The three boys were cousins.
5. All the campers have flashlights.
6. My dog never trusts the mail carrier.
7. The mail carrier, for that matter, never trusts my dog either.
8. The ice looked too thin.
9. Mark had an idea.
10. That record sounds scratchy.

Main Verbs and Helping Verbs

There are certain words that you always count on as verbs:

am	was	has	do
is	were	have	does
are	be	had	did

Sometimes these words are used alone. Sometimes they are used as **helping verbs** with other verbs:

> The neighbors *have* a new car.
> The girls *have finished* their work.
> Bill *has* the map.
> Sue *has painted* the porch.

A verb may consist of a **main verb** and one or more **helping verbs.**
Sometimes the main verb ends in *ing:*

> We *had been playing* the piano.
> The scouts *were gathering* driftwood.

To find the verb in a sentence:

1. Look for a word that tells action or state of being.
2. Look for words such as *is, am, are, was, were, be, been, have, has, had, do, does, did.* They may be helping verbs.
3. Look for all the words that make up the verb.

Exercises Main verbs and helping verbs.

A. Write down the helping verb and main verb for each sentence. Mark them HV (helping verb) and MV (main verb).

> Example: I am taking my camera.
>
> HV: am
> MV: taking

1. Ted is writing the script for the skit.
2. Nora has been in Florida.
3. Four students were serving refreshments.
4. Lou has returned your tape recorder.
5. My brother did arrive after the thunderstorm.
6. The weather is becoming cooler.
7. The next players are waiting for the court.
8. I have gone to the dentist's office once a week.
9. Patrick has eaten spaghetti twice today.
10. The key for the convertible is hanging by the back door.

B. Write down the helping verb and main verb for each sentence. Mark HV (helping verb) and MV (main verb).

1. The washing machine had stopped.
2. Ted was bracing himself against the shelf.
3. Two ducks were huddling near the pond.
4. The Mulligans have had a good time at Six Flags.
5. Kathy had been ready for over an hour.
6. The outcome had seemed uncertain.
7. Really, I do try.
8. At four o'clock the plumber was working on the drain.
9. The sky has looked stormy all afternoon.
10. Twice recently the car has needed a new front tire.

Separated Parts of a Verb

Sometimes the parts of a verb are separated from each other by words that are not part of the verb. In the following sentences the verbs are printed in red. The words in between are not part of the verb.

> That bus **has** often **been** late.
> The temperature **had** rapidly **dropped.**
> We **had** not **seen** the accident.

Exercises Find the verbs.

A. Write the verbs and their simple subjects in these sentences. Underline the subject once and the verb twice. Your teacher may ask you to use diagrams instead.

> Example: The cake had obviously fallen.
> <u>cake</u> <u>had</u> <u>fallen</u>

1. Ron was patiently sewing a patch on his jeans.
2. Her friend had intentionally left the window open.
3. That class is always going on a field trip.
4. Trudy was nearly laughing.
5. Sara will probably finish the posters by tomorrow.
6. Our family has never been to Mackinac Island.
7. Under the circumstances, Dad did permit the party.
8. The painter had carelessly tossed the brushes away.
9. With little effort, the salmon were leaping the rapids.
10. The class will surely go to the museum tomorrow.

B. Write the verbs and their subjects in these sentences. Underline the subject once and the verb twice. Your teacher may ask you to use diagrams instead.

1. She had recently photographed the Florida Everglades.
2. Chuck does not like chocolate ice cream.
3. The deer have often grazed on our lawn.
4. I will endorse this candidate.
5. We have never gone to the Milwaukee Zoo.
6. Jane's spirits were obviously rising.
7. Negotiations between the two countries have progressed well.
8. The waves were viciously splashing the deck.
9. The school will probably close because of the weather.
10. The elevators in our building are usually running.

c. On a sheet of paper numbered 1–10 write subjects and verbs for the sentences below. **s** stands for subject, **v** for verb, **hv** for helping verb, and **mv** for main verb.

1. The muddy ___**s**___ eagerly ___**v**___ his tail.
2. This red and white ___**s**___ usually ___**v**___ attention.
3. This ___**s**___ always ___**v**___ on time.
4. The ___**s**___ on the roof ___**hv**___ sometimes ___**mv**___ .
5. A long ___**s**___ of cars ___**hv**___ ___**mv**___ at the bridge.
6. ___**s**___ ___**hv**___ ___**mv**___ long enough.
7. The ___**s**___ ___**hv**___ frequently ___**mv**___ .
8. ___**s**___ quickly ___**v**___ the garage doors.
9. Those ___**s**___ from Deer Park Schools ___**hv**___ often ___**mv**___ the trophies.
10. ___**s**___ soon ___**v**___ the math book.

Part 4 Compound Subjects and Compound Verbs

Look at these two sentences. How do they differ?

1. Two boys went to the game.
2. Bob and Tony went to the game.

In the first sentence, the subject is *boys*. What is the subject of the second sentence? Both *Bob* and *Tony* are subjects. Such a construction is called a **compound subject.** The word *compound* means "having more than one part."

Verbs can be compound, too. How do these two sentences differ?

1. We worked.
2. We hammered and sawed.

In the first sentence the verb is *worked*. In the second, the verb is *hammered* and *sawed*. Such a construction is called a **compound verb**.

In the compound subject above, the word *and* joins *Bob* and *Tony*. In the compound verb, *and* joins *hammered* and *sawed*. Words that join words, and groups of words, in this way are called **conjunctions**. The word *and* is a conjunction.

Diagraming Compound Subjects and Verbs

To diagram the two or more parts of a compound subject, it is necessary to split the subject line. Put the conjunction on a connecting dotted line.

Example: Don and Mrs. Parish have left.

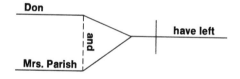

Compound verbs are similarly diagramed.

Example: Linda read, slept, and swam.

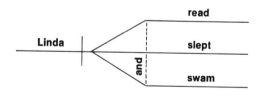

Exercises **Find the compound subjects and compound verbs.**

A. Show by diagrams, or as your teacher may direct, the subjects and verbs in the following sentences.

1. Phil and Jerry carried water for the garden.
2. Marie and her father skate and ski together.
3. Janet practiced the piano, studied, and read the newspaper.
4. Everyone swam, played ball, and then ate a big lunch.
5. The speaker's character and determination impressed the students.
6. Thunder and lightning preceded the rain.
7. The width and depth of the stage were unusual.
8. Ruth and Phil stood on the corner and waited two hours for the bus.
9. The wind and the tide were perfect.
10. Jack's boat rounded the buoy and finished first.

B. Show by diagrams, or as your teacher may direct, the subjects and verbs in the following sentences.

1. The workers pushed and shoved with their shoulders.
2. Trumpets and trombones accompanied the woodwinds.
3. Laura folded the picture and cut it.
4. His knees and ankles were slowly buckling under the weight.
5. Ann took some butter and then passed it.
6. The lamp and the candles threw shadows on the wall.
7. By that time Tracy and Luanne were home.
8. Jeff strode to the front, looked briefly at his notes, and began.
9. The Good-Humor man rang his bell and pedaled slowly.
10. Pete smiled and ducked behind the curtain.

Part 5   Subjects in Unusual Order

All the sentences we have so far considered in our study of subjects and predicates have been written with the subject first and then the verb. Are all sentences like that?

You won't have to look far in this book or any other to discover that the subject does not always come before the verb.

Giving Variety to Sentences

Placing the verb before the subject, occasionally, will make your writing more interesting. It will also give more emphasis to what you say.

Usual Order: An odd creature hobbled into the store.
Unusual Order: Into the store hobbled an odd creature.

Unusual order does not change the positions of subjects and verbs on diagrams.

Example: Down the street came the procession.

procession	came

Exercises   Find the subjects and verbs.

A. Show, as your teacher directs, the subjects and verbs in the following sentences.

1. Behind his sleepy face was a quick, intelligent mind.
2. From one end of the pipe scampered a frightened rabbit.
3. At the meeting were boys and girls from every class.
4. On the other side of the tracks stood the church.
5. High above our heads stretched the Bay Bridge.
6. From the committee at Boston came word of the prize.

7. Into Mr. Bevan's office strolled my scroungy dog.

8. From the sand along the shore came a curious glow.

9. In the corridor were models of boats and a special nautical exhibit.

10. Across the valley stretched fields of beautiful flowers.

B. Show, as your teacher directs, the subjects and verbs in the following sentences.

1. Over the housetops roared the wind.

2. Behind the kitchen was the entrance to the cellar.

3. Beyond the line of sleeping hills stood the crimson forest.

4. Suddenly out of the shrubs zoomed our dalmatian.

5. Over the used car lot flapped multi-colored pennants.

6. Under the table lurked the gerbil.

7. Far below our campsite lay the rapids.

8. Into the light of the campfire fluttered a rare moth.

9. Beyond the spaceship streamed the stars.

10. From the river rose three bickering flamingoes.

Part 6   Kinds of Sentences

You use language for several different purposes. Sometimes you want to tell something. Sometimes you want to ask something. Sometimes you want to tell someone to do something. Sometimes you want to show how strongly you feel about something. There is a different kind of sentence for each of these purposes.

1. A sentence that makes a statement is a **declarative sentence.**

> Her story was short.
> The sun is shining.
> Tom called the store about noon.

2. A sentence that asks a question is an **interrogative sentence.**

> Has anyone seen my dog?
> Are you going to the play?
> Do you know the final score of the game?

3. A sentence that tells or requests someone to do something is an **imperative sentence.** The subject is not usually stated but is understood to be "you."

> Finish the assignment for tomorrow.
> Be here at nine o'clock.
> Please raise the window.

4. A sentence that is used to express strong feeling is an **exclamatory sentence.**

> How Sherry yawned!
> Dad, that garage is on fire!
> Oh, what fun scuba diving was!

Punctuating Sentences

Every sentence begins with a capital letter. Every sentence ends with a punctuation mark. Notice the marks at the ends of the sentences above. Remember these rules:

1. Use a period after a declarative sentence.
2. Use a question mark after an interrogative sentence.
3. Use a period after an imperative sentence.
4. Use an exclamation mark after an exclamatory sentence.

Exercises   Learn the kinds of sentences.

A.   Number your paper 1–10. For each of the following sentences, write *Declarative, Interrogative, Imperative,* or *Exclamatory* to show what kind it is. Add the punctuation mark that should be used at the end of each sentence.

1. We found kindling for our fire in the woods
2. How do you do macramé
3. Cut a green branch and sharpen the end
4. Have you been here before, Sara
5. Hold my books for a minute, please
6. Yes, we took first place
7. Is your watch running
8. How the falls thundered
9. Kate, look out
10. Move to the rear of the bus, please

B. Follow the directions for Exercise A.

1. Please walk the dog after dinner
2. Has Joy ever jumped that far before
3. Dad always trims the lilac bush
4. Tell the joke about the slide rule again
5. Where did you put the Christmas tree lights
6. What big eyes you have
7. Keep your elbow stiff and watch the ball
8. When do the miners' shifts change
9. Willie, watch out
10. Have a good day

Part 7 Subjects and Verbs in Questions

Some interrogative sentences (questions) are written in normal order: The subject comes first, and the verb second.

Subject	Verb	
Who	bought	the lollipops?

But not all questions follow this order. Look at the following question, for example:

HV	Subject	MV
Do	you	know Ms. Fisher?

Here the verb is *do know*. The subject *you* falls between the helping verb *do* and the main verb *know*.

Diagraming Questions

When you diagram a question, show the subject and verb as if they were in normal order.

Example: Have you answered that letter yet?

you	Have answered

Exercises **Find the subjects and verbs in questions.**

A. Make two columns on your paper. Write *Subject* at the top of one column and *Verb* at the top of the other. Write the subject and verb for each of the following sentences.

1. Have you visited Lake Tahoe?
2. Have you heard the news?
3. Has Mrs. Simmons spoken to you about the paper?
4. Did you watch the television special last night?
5. Does Jim help in the print shop?
6. Has Pedro given his speech?
7. Is Andrea moving to Arizona?
8. Do the members of the committee know the date?
9. Does the team still need money?
10. Did the officer question the suspects?

B. Follow the directions for Exercise A.

1. Do Mike and Pam work at the pharmacy?
2. Have you completed your art project?

3. Have you looked in your bottom drawer?

4. Are winters in Tallahassee warmer than in Corpus Christi?

5. Do raspberries grow wild in the Midwest?

6. Did Nancy give you the message?

7. Have you gone to the dentist yet?

8. Are your parents going to the meeting?

9. Did you read this morning's paper?

10. Have you had dinner yet?

Part 8 Subjects and Verbs in Commands

Imperative sentences (commands) usually begin with the verb. For example, in the command *Open the window,* the verb is the first word, *Open.* What is the subject? There doesn't seem to be any, does there? The subject in the sentence is *you,* even though it is not expressed. We say that the subject *you* is *understood.*

One-Word Commands

Imperative sentences sometimes consist of only one word—the verb. *Think. Go. Stop.* These are single-word sentences. The subject is the same: (*you*) *Think.* (*you*) *Go.* (*you*) *Stop.*

Diagraming Imperative Sentences

When the subject of an imperative sentence is understood, show it on your diagram by writing (*you*).

Example: Hurry.

(you)	Hurry

Exercises   Find the subjects and verbs in commands.

A.   Indicate the subjects and verbs in the following imperative sentences. Use diagrams or any other method suggested by your teacher.

1. Bring your books to class with you.
2. Try a bottle opener.
3. Put some spruce boughs under your sleeping bag.
4. Tear along the dotted line.
5. Hold this for a moment.
6. Sit here.
7. Do try the doughnuts.
8. Measure the flour into this.
9. Take your time.
10. Return these books to the library.

B.   Follow the directions for Exercise A.

1. Look this over before the meeting.
2. Oh, take another.
3. Dismount from the parallel bars to your right.
4. Have the rest of the casserole for supper.
5. Ask Nicole her opinion.
6. Fold the paper here.
7. Do come before noon, please.
8. Put your hands behind your back.
9. Weed the vegetable garden this afternoon.
10. Have fun.

Part 9   Sentences That Begin with *There*

Study this sentence. What is the simple subject?

There were some pencils in my locker.

The word *there* is not the subject. When *there* is used [to] begin a sentence, it usually serves just to get the sentence moving. The subject is *pencils*.

Verb   **Subject**

There *were* some *pencils* in my locker.

Study the following sentences. Notice that the subject is not first in sentences with *there*. Point out the subjects.

1. **Are** there any **apples**?
2. There **are** some **apples** in the bag.
3. There **are** two **birds** at the feeding station.
4. **Were** there many **families** at the picnic?
5. There **were** two **people** in the car.

Diagraming Sentences with *There*

There is usually just an "extra" word. It is placed on a separate line above the subject in a sentence diagram.

Example: There were several people on the platform.

There

people | **were**

Exercises **Find the subjects and verbs in *there* sentences.**

A. Write on paper the subjects and verbs in these sentences.

1. There are some new notices on the bulletin board.
2. Are there any Canadian dimes here?
3. There were several questions after Helen's presentation.

4. There were two pet skunks in one cabin.
5. Are there any papers in the cellar, Mother?
6. There was a line at the theater.
7. Are there any diseased trees in the parkway?
8. There were two scouts on the pier.
9. Were there any brownies in the cookie jar?
10. There are new chairs in the science room.

B. Write on paper the subjects and verbs in these sentences.

1. There was dirt on the floor.
2. Are there pickles in the sandwich?
3. Were there telescopes in the tower?
4. Is there anyone home?
5. There have been hornets in the garage again.
6. There is really no reason for concern.
7. Were there any problems at the meeting?
8. There was an old bicycle in the abandoned garage.
9. There is a charge for children over five.
10. There were several eggs in the basket.

C. Write sentences using the following beginnings. Add the correct punctuation.

1. Were there . . .
2. There has been . . .
3. There has never been . . .
4. Has there ever been . . .
5. Will there be . . .
6. There is . . .
7. There would often be . . .
8. There will be . . .
9. Have there been . . .
10. Would there ever be . . .

Part 10 Avoiding Sentence Fragments

A group of words that is not a sentence is called a **sentence fragment.** A fragment is only a part of something. Avoid sentence fragments in your writing.

A sentence fragment leaves out something important. Sometimes it leaves out the subject. Sometimes it leaves out the verb. As you read a fragment, you may wonder either *What is this about?* or *What happened?*

Examples: Fragment: Bought some art supplies (*Who bought them?*)
Sentence: Bob bought some art supplies.

Fragment: In the sky last night (*What happened?*)
Sentence: In the sky last night there was a strange light.

Exercises **Recognize sentences.**

A. Number your paper 1–10. Write *Sentence* or *Fragment* for each of the following sentences.

1. The dog is playing under the porch
2. Just before the end of the game
3. In our back yard
4. Down at the pharmacy in the middle of the block
5. Before the end of the day
6. We can rent a canoe
7. Came up and spoke to us
8. Suddenly a fire siren screamed
9. Rain, wind, and hailstones
10. The uprooted trees landed on the garage roof

B. Correct the following fragments by adding the words needed to make a sentence.

1. for almost two hours
2. have snowball fights and build snowmen
3. walked cautiously through the dark corridors
4. because I really like to sing
5. a moped next to the street light
6. designed the yearbook cover
7. near the football field
8. takes care of his dog
9. caused us to be late
10. across the hall from the cafeteria.

Part 11 Avoiding Run-on Sentences

Two or more sentences written incorrectly as one are called a **run-on sentence.** Here are some examples:

> Incorrect (*run-on*): Pam came, we went cycling.
> Correct: Pam came. We went cycling.

> Incorrect (*run-on*): Aren't you through let me help.
> Correct: Aren't you through? Let me help.

The trouble with run-on sentences is that your readers don't know which words go together. Without a period and a capital letter to guide them, they read right along. They believe they are following one thought. Suddenly the words stop making sense, and your readers have to back up to find the start of a new idea.

Exercises **Correct the run-on sentences.**

A. Correct the following run-on sentences.

1. There were many balloons strung from the ceiling, they were torn down afterwards.
2. The noise stopped, they finished the rest of the work.
3. We all opened our presents, then we ate dinner.
4. Kay is the sports editor, she is my sister.
5. Everyone was busy, we all had assignments to complete.
6. It rained for days, the soccer field was soaked.
7. We stayed at Elinor Village, we were only two blocks from the ocean.
8. We skated for one hour, we came in to get warm.
9. I have read several biographies, I find them very interesting.
10. Monica and I aren't going skiing, the snow is too slushy.

B. Follow the directions for Exercise A.

1. Rachel and I ate at McDonald's, we went to the movies afterwards.
2. The skyline of Chicago is beautiful, the city has many unusual buildings.
3. It snowed throughout the night, most schools were closed the next day.
4. We had basketball practice until noon, we have a game tomorrow.
5. Our class had a bake sale, it was very successful.
6. Ken and Lynn are co-editors, they manage our school newspapers.
7. The doctor x-rayed my arm, she then put it in a cast.
8. Our plane arrived early, we took a bus into the city.
9. Anne is on the volleyball team, she is the captain.
10. Our class went on a field trip, we toured the newspaper plant.

Additional Exercises

The Sentence and Its Parts

A. Find the subjects and predicates.

Copy these sentences. Draw a vertical line between the subject and the predicate.

1. All the water leaked out.
2. Chris wound the thread around the bobbin.
3. His fishing box belongs in the shed.
4. The pies smell delicious.
5. Meredith followed the parade over the bridge.
6. The large brown dog breathed down my neck.
7. The gardner grafted the new branch onto an old tree.
8. Peter eased his bicycle over the ditch.
9. The sleet was falling at a 40° angle.
10. Everyone from our school attended the play-off.

B. Find the verbs and their simple subjects.

Number your paper 1–10. For each sentence write the verb and then its subject.

1. The door swung soundlessly on its hinges.
2. Ann's older sister babysat for the neighbors.
3. The bluejays zigzagged past the clothesline.
4. That little blue Volkswagen squeezed into our parking place.
5. An undercoating protects new automobiles from salt erosion.
6. The measurements of the room surprised my mother.

7. In April, the edges of the swamp reverberated with peeper frogs.

8. The computer revealed the mistake.

9. Warm weather makes me happy.

10. In the square, beautiful gardens surrounded the fountain.

C. Find the verbs.

The verbs may be an action you cannot see or a state of being. Write only one word for the verb.

1. The Campbells had guests for Thanksgiving.
2. The sky appeared calm.
3. The porch steps are dangerous.
4. Terry had a hard time.
5. Their suspicion is mutual.
6. Fran had a job at the pool for two years.
7. Mrs. Watson feels much better.
8. The farmers hoped for rain.
9. I am from Missouri.
10. The issues in the debate became interesting.

D. Find the main verbs and helping verbs.

Write down the helping verb and main verb for each sentence. Label them HV (helping verb) and MV (main verb).

1. The hikers have looked everywhere for the rope.
2. The actors in the school play were practicing in a Spanish accent.
3. Laura had done all the work before breakfast.
4. The pair had played badminton in the tournament.
5. Roberto did believe the story.
6. The typist had done everything by three o'clock.

7. Karen has had enough sleep.
8. Tomorrow both families are going on the tour.
9. The buyers have agreed on the price of the boat.
10. Dawn was waiting for the bus.

E. Find the separated parts of a verb.

Write the verbs and their simple subjects from these sentences. Underline the subject once and the verb twice.

1. Bill has always liked photography.
2. I have not cut the grass for weeks.
3. The award has in past years gone to an eighth-grader.
4. Nancy was nevertheless flying to California.
5. The boys at the refreshment stand have nearly finished.
6. Cindy was therefore chosen to our representative.
7. The crew will probably repair the road next week.
8. The swallows had in spite of the netting nested in the barn.
9. The game was consequently postponed until Friday.
10. The locks were mechanically raising the water level.

F. Find the compound subjects and compound verbs.

Show by diagrams, or as your teacher may direct, the subjects and verbs in the following sentences.

1. His shirt and tie matched.
2. Confetti and rice covered the church steps.
3. The Pep Club and the Student Council organized and presented the assembly.
4. Popcorn, apples, crackers, and cheese were in big bowls on the table.
5. The plane circled once and landed.

6. After the movie, we stopped and ate dinner.
7. The cauliflower and cabbage rolled out of the bin.
8. Stripes and spots decorated the poster.
9. Jim and Sandra took turns and skied.
10. Salt, pepper, and mustard are condiments.

G. Identify the kinds of sentences.

Number your paper 1–10. For each of the following sentences, write *Declarative, Interrogative, Imperative,* or *Exclamatory* to show what kind it is. Add the correct punctuation mark at the end of each sentence.

1. What a big lawn you have
2. Follow these instructions
3. Who wants my racket
4. Terry thought and thought
5. Where is the province of Ontario
6. Go to the corner, turn right, and go to the third house
7. Chocolate chip cookies always disappear fast
8. How empty the room seems
9. Please keep the change
10. How the mare snorted and whinnied

H. Find the subjects and verbs in questions.

Make two columns on your paper. Write *Subject* at the top of one column and *Verb* at the top of the other. Write the subject and verb for each of the following sentences.

1. Are you going to the gymnastics meet?
2. Have you finished the assignment already?
3. Are Steve and Kim going to the carnival?
4. Did the referee see it?
5. Have you asked Mary-Lou to the party?

6. Did you see that movie?
7. Have you ordered the decorations?
8. Is our team running in the district track meet?
9. Did you audition for the school play?
10. Are you coming in?

I. Find the subjects and verbs in commands.

Indicate the subjects and verbs in the following impera-tive sentences.

1. Play that record over again, please.
2. Always take the necessary precautions.
3. Take four cards.
4. Close the garage door, please.
5. Please give me the sports page.
6. Now disconnect the hose.
7. Preheat the oven to 350°.
8. Give Sandy another glass of milk.
9. Water the lawn and the garden.
10. Act fast.

J. Find the subjects and verbs in *there* sentences.

Write on paper the subjects and verbs in these sentences.

1. There were several people in line for tickets.
2. Is there any more room between the trees?
3. Has there ever been a January without snow?
4. There is an extra racket in the closet.
5. There have been increases in our taxes for three years.
6. Towards evening there is a drop in temperature.
7. Was there more paperwork than usual?
8. Have there been problems with this drill before?
9. There has been enough rain for the evergreens.
10. There was too much humidity.

K. Write complete sentences.

Add words to the following fragments to make them complete sentences. Write the sentences on a sheet of paper.

1. from the other room
2. hardly rained
3. near the school
4. weeded the garden
5. called the library
6. across the street
7. were reflected in the glass
8. Bill and Peggy
9. at the bottom
10. ate a late dinner

L. Avoid run-on sentences.

Pick out the run-on sentences in the following group and rewrite them. If a sentence does not need to be rewritten, write *Correct*.

1. We could hear the ball bouncing on the gym floor, it sounded like a basketball.

2. We had an assembly today, the high school jazz ensemble performed.

3. Where is the racket, I thought it was in this closet.

4. The lecturer spoke softly, we could hardly hear him.

5. I called John he didn't know rehearsal had been canceled.

6. A nighthawk has built its nest on the roof of the school this spring.

7. Do you have Nancy's phone number I didn't write it down.

8. Several birds had nests near the school we took pictures of some.

9. Autumn is a beautiful season everything is so colorful.

10. The train ride was long, I never thought we'd get to Atlanta.

Section 2

Using Verbs

So far you have learned the following things about verbs:

1. The verb is a key word in a sentence. Every sentence must have a verb.

2. A verb in a declarative sentence tells something about the subject.

3. Some verbs tell about action. Others tell about a state of being.

Now you will review what a verb is. You will also learn more about what it can do. You will also learn how verbs work with other words to express your ideas.

Part 1　The Work of Verbs

The verb is one of the main parts of every sentence. It is one of the eight parts of speech.

The verb may tell what the subject of the sentence does. This kind of verb shows action, but the action may not be one you can see.

> Gary *laughed*.　We *enjoyed* the show.

The verb may tell that something exists. It may tell about a state of being.

> Cheryl *is* here.　Jack *seems* happy.

Verbs such as *is, seem, become,* and *appear* are state-of-being verbs.

A verb indicates action or state of being.

Here are four sentences, with the verbs missing.

Without Verbs	With Verbs
The school band hard	The school band played hard
Lee over the hoe	Lee tripped over the hoe.
Mr. Miller silently	Mr. Miller laughed silently.
He his minibike	He raced his minibike.

Without verbs, there can be no sentences and not much sense.

When you are hunting for verbs, look for words that express action (*ran, walked, fished*) or state of being (*is, are, was, were, am*).

> Examples　Judy *found* the dollar in her pocket.
> We *are* good friends.

Exercises   Find the verbs.

A. Find the verb in each sentence.

1. Al Hutchinson's dog followed us to the movies.
2. He stayed outside.
3. The fire nearly destroyed the fieldhouse.
4. Our class decorated the hall for the South Sea Islands bazaar.
5. The orchestra broke into country western music.
6. Emily is a really good artist.
7. There were five kids in the pool.
8. Lisa's dog jumped into the pool with us.
9. Last Sunday, the newspaper printed a special section about rock musicians.
10. During intermission, Erin told us about her canoe trip.

B. The following groups of words have subjects but no verbs. Make each group a sentence by adding a verb. Write your sentences and underline the verbs. Add the correct punctuation at the end of a sentence.

1. The bumper sticker off
2. Miriam in a play at school
3. We all Saturday afternoon
4. Their jeans on the line
5. The boys the back steps
6. Randy very well
7. The library at noon today.
8. A car radio in the background
9. Several of my friends to the rink every Saturday.
10. The jet into the air
11. The thoroughbreds from the starting gate.
12. A loud cheer from the bleachers.

C. Rearrange each of the following groups of words into a sentence, adding a verb.

1. team, the, into, gym, the
2. over, hamburgers, fire, the, slowly, the
3. horse, the, the, through, fence
4. shelf, the, on, kitchen, the, in, package, the
5. library, the, records, we, the, in

Part 2 Verbs and Direct Objects

In many sentences the thought is complete when there are just a verb and its subject.

Subject	Verb
Snow	fell.
Everyone	laughed.
John	stared.

In other sentences the thought is not completed until other words have been added.

Roger cut _____
Linda closed _____

You wonder *what* Roger cut and *what* Linda closed. Suppose we completed the sentences as follows:

Roger cut the *rope.*
Linda closed the *door.*

In the first sentence, the word *rope* receives the action of the verb *cut.* It is the **direct object** of the verb.

In the second sentence, *door* receives the action of *closed.* It is the **direct object** of the verb.

The direct object tells what receives the action.

Recognizing Direct Objects

To find the direct object in a sentence, first find the verb. Then ask *what?* after the .verb. For example: Drew *what?* Caught *what?*

Subject	Verb	What? (direct object)
engineers	drew	plans
outfielder	caught	ball
doctor	performed	operation
carpenter	repaired	cabinet

Exercises   Add direct objects.

A. Number your paper 1–10. Write direct objects that will complete each of the following sentences.

1. The girls ordered the _____ .
2. The farmer drove his _____ into the field.
3. The police car carried a _____ .
4. Helicopters make short _____ .
5. Do you watch many television _____ ?
6. Marilee draws _____ of landscapes.
7. Christie plays _____ after school.
8. Please pass the _____ .
9. The paramedics drove the _____ to the accident.
10. Larry fell and fractured his _____ .

B. On a sheet of paper, write sentences using the following verbs. Put a direct object in each sentence. Underline the direct object that you have added.

1. bought	6. invented
2. will build	7. sees
3. has found	8. is washing
4. photographed	9. has made
5. is sending	10. buys

Find the direct objects.

A. Copy the following sentences. Underline the verb twice and draw a circle around the direct object.

Example: The veterinarian <u>scratched</u> her (head).

1. Mud splattered the windshield.
2. The players rushed the goalie.
3. Suddenly a breeze puffed the sail.
4. The jug contains pure water.
5. Dandelions covered the lawn.
6. He always starches his collars.
7. Allison designed the covers.
8. Pete mopped the floor.
9. Mrs. Marshall lost her watch.
10. Judge Harvey drives a Cutlass.

B. Number your paper 1–10. Find and write the direct objects in these sentences.

1. Pat and Sandra painted the wall together.
2. Protect the wildlife.
3. Why did Tina crumple all that newspaper?
4. The store pipes music into every department.
5. Please cut the pie now.
6. Bob raised his eyebrows.
7. Give an example.
8. Have you finished your project yet?
9. Mr. White was constantly wiping his brow.
10. Did you finish your report?

Part 3 Transitive and Intransitive Verbs

When a verb has a direct object, the verb is called a **transitive verb.** When a verb does not have a direct object, it is called an **intransitive verb.** Here are some examples that will show you the difference:

1. All birds sing. (*Sing* is intransitive; it is used without an object.)
2. Some birds sing beautiful songs. (*Sing* is transitive; the direct object is *song.*)
3. Kevin washed. (*Washed* is intransitive; it is used without an object.)
4. Kevin washed the car. (*Washed* is transitive; *car* is the direct object.)

If there is a word in the sentence that answers the question *whom?* or *what?* after the verb, it is a direct object, and the verb is transitive.

Notice that *sing* and *washed* in the sentences given above are used both as transitive and as intransitive verbs, depending on whether there is a direct object or not.

Some verbs are always used as transitive verbs. They must always have a direct object. An example is *bring.*

Other verbs are always used as intransitive verbs. They can never have a direct object. An example is *arrive.*

Most verbs can be used with or without direct objects. They can be transitive in one sentence and intransitive in another.

Here are some more examples of transitive and intransitive verbs.

Transitive	Intransitive
Maurita practices her diving.	Maurita practices.
Maurita practices her diving in the mornings.	Maurita practices in the mornings.

Find transitive and intransitive verbs.

A. Make two columns marked *Transitive* and *Intransitive*. Find the verb in each of the following sentences. If the verb has an object, write the verb under *Transitive* and put its object in parentheses after it. If the verb has no object, write it under *Intransitive*.

Example: John read the map.

Transitive   *Intransitive*
read (map)

1. Sally painted a chair.
2. The zookeeper lifted the barking seal.
3. Mark collects stamps.
4. René has just moved to Richmond.
5. The stamps are lying on the table.
6. A good architect designed this house.
7. Jennifer and I ordered a pizza.
8. His brow wrinkled.
9. Melanie wrinkled her nose.
10. Craig admired his grandmother.

B. Follow the directions for Exercise A.

1. The ball sailed through the window.
2. Kay took the keys.
3. Mr. Thomas laid the keys on the TV.
4. Rake the front lawn.
5. We are eating pancakes for breakfast.
6. A wind rippled the water.
7. I was unpacking my suitcase.
8. Do you like cheesecake?
9. Barbara stayed at home.
10. Darcy swam across the pool.

C. Each of the following verbs can be used either as a transitive verb or as an intransitive verb. For each verb write two sentences. Label the first of the two sentences (a) and the second (b). Make the verb transitive in the first of the two sentences and intransitive in the second. Write *Transitive* after the first sentence and *Intransitive* after the second.

> Example: 1. (a) Jack dried his hands. Transitive.
> (b) The paint dried. Intransitive.

1. grow	3. turn	5. write	7. fly	9. crumble
2. paint	4. drive	6. eat	8. ring	10. open

Part 4   Linking Verbs

Verbs that show a state of being are often called **linking verbs.** Look at these examples:

1. This story *is* exciting.

2. The cake *looks* good.

3. The room *seemed* empty.

Linking verbs connect the subject with a word in the predicate. In the examples given, they connect *story* with *exciting*, *cake* with *good*, and *room* with *empty*.

The words *is, am, are, was, were, be, become* are often used as linking verbs. The words *seem, look, appear, smell, taste, sound* are sometimes linking verbs.

The words that follow linking verbs and tell something about the subject are either adjectives or nouns. Here are some examples of nouns used after linking verbs:

1. Anne *is* a good swimmer.

2. Larry *was* my classmate.

3. The Crowners *are* my neighbors.

Do not confuse a linking verb with a transitive verb. In the examples just given, you can see that the words *swimmer*, *classmate*, and *neighbors* simply tell something about the subject of each sentence. They are not direct objects. Therefore, the verbs in these sentences are all linking verbs.

Exercises   Find the linking verbs.

A. At the top of three columns write: *Subject, Linking Verb,* and *Word Linked to Subject.* Find the three parts in each sentence. Write them in the proper columns.

Example: The fresh bread in the oven smells delicious.

Subject	Linking Verb	Word Linked to Subject
bread	smells	delicious

1. Carlos is an ambitious worker.
2. Mari became president.
3. Thursday was Diane's birthday.
4. The temperature is unbearable!
5. Do you ever feel lonesome?
6. The new store was open for business.
7. Do be careful!
8. Sam was by far our best pitcher.
9. The air feels warmer.
10. Before the game the team was restless.

B. Put the *subjects, linking verbs,* and *words linked to the subject* in three columns as you did in Exercise A.

1. Kristen is the manager.
2. Tracy feels fine today.
3. Sue and Linda seemed anxious at first.

4. Lauren and Josh became conscious of the metric system while in Germany.
5. Were you late for the races?
6. Soon Bill became sleepy.
7. Tony looks a little pale this morning.
8. The cost of the space module seemed astronomical.
9. Mrs. Meredith became the new principal.
10. Water is essential to life on earth.

c. Some of the verbs in the following sentences are linking verbs and the others are transitive verbs. Copy each of the sentences on a sheet of paper. Draw a circle around the linking verbs. Draw a straight line under the transitive verbs.

1. Kelly knows the secret.
2. Are you ready?
3. Pete has the measles.
4. The new puppies seem content.
5. The sky became threatening during the last inning.
6. The freshly baked cookies smell delicious.
7. The crowd seemed unconcerned.
8. These walnuts taste good.
9. Jan tasted the pecans.
10. The lake appeared calm.

Part 5 Parts of the Verb

A verb often consists of more than one word. A two-word verb consists of the main verb **mv** and one helping verb **hv**. Helping verbs are words like *is, do, has.* Some new helping verbs are shown in red type below:

will go	**may** go	**could** go
shall go	**would** go	**might** go
can go	**should** go	**must** go

Three-word verbs consist of a main verb and two helping verbs. *Have* is often the middle verb:

will have gone   would have played
could have gone   can have heard
may have gone   might have fallen
should have gone   must have taken

Separated Parts of the Verb

The words that make up a verb are not always a compact group, like *could have done* and *might have seen*. Sometimes the helping verbs and the main verbs are separated by other words that are not verbs:

can hardly **wait**   **could** not **have come**
did n't **understand**   **should** not really **have stayed**
will surely **write**   **may** already **have arrived**

The parts of the verb are in red. Notice that *not* and the ending *n't* in contractions are not verbs.

Exercises   Finding helping verbs and the main verb.

A. Label two columns *Helping Verbs* and *Main Verb*. Find all the parts of the verb in each sentence. Write them in the proper columns.

Example: He should have been home an hour ago.

Helping Verbs   Main Verb
should have   been

1. Will you take the bus?
2. I may not go to the movies tonight.
3. Jeff could have told you that.
4. Didn't you hear the bang?
5. Do you have the backpack with you?

6. You could have fooled me.
7. Who can have told him?
8. Shall I bring the brace and bit?
9. The team could never have played in all that mud.
10. The movie will have already started.

B. Follow the directions for Exercise A.

1. We will never forget his expression.
2. The parade must be on Central Street.
3. Vicki would like more blankets.
4. Our neighbors are always planning something.
5. The secretary must stay until five.
6. The driver may have put the package there.
7. I could not possibly have thrown my Disneyland T-shirt out.
8. The message may have fallen through the crack.
9. We have been planning the party for weeks.
10. We cannot go without him.

C. The following sentences have main verbs but no helping verbs. The spaces show you where helping verbs are needed to make complete verbs. On a sheet of paper numbered 1–10, write the helping verbs needed.

1. Mary _____ nearly finished her story.
2. Why _____ n't Sally help with the yard work?
3. _____ n't you eaten yogurt before?
4. _____ n't the Student Council member report first?
5. A koala bear _____ never been happy in captivity.
6. _____ David already gone?
7. The P.E. classes _____ most likely run the relay races today.
8. It _____ be later than that.
9. Phil _____ _____ heard the news by now.
10. They _____ already gone.

Part 6   Tenses of Verbs

Verbs change their forms to show the time that they tell about. These changes in form to show the time are called **tenses.**

The **present tense** shows present time: *I am. I see.*
The **past tense** shows past time: *I was. I saw.*
The **future tense** shows future time: *I shall be. You will see.*

Tense changes are made in three ways:

1. By change in spelling: *sing, sang, sung*
2. By change in ending: *walk, walked*
3. By changes in helping verbs: *has walked, will walk*

Here are five important tenses:

Present Tense	She walks	We choose
Future Tense	She will walk	We shall choose
Past Tense	She walked	We chose
Present Perfect Tense	She has walked	We have chosen
Past Perfect Tense	She had walked	We had chosen

You can see that three tenses are used to show different kinds of past time: *past, present perfect,* and *past perfect.* You will learn two things about them:

1. The past tense forms of a verb are used alone. They are never used with helping verbs.

> we cleaned   you ran
> they brought   she slid

2. The present perfect and past perfect tenses are formed by using helping verbs: *has, have,* and *had.*

> he has cleaned   you had run
> they have brought   she had slid

Exercises **Learn to recognize and use tenses.**

A. Name the tense of the verb in each sentence.

1. The catcher wore the helmet.
2. They said hello.
3. He has taken his bicycle.
4. Throw the ball.
5. Gayle is happy.
6. She has a new jacket.
7. She paid for it herself.
8. Shall we go too?
9. You will find it on the table.
10. We have eaten lunch.
11. We almost froze yesterday.
12. My father had spoken to the club.
13. Bob earned some money.
14. He will buy a record.
15. Has Rick already gone?

B. Number your paper 1–10. Write down the verb tense for each of the sentences.

1. Cathy (present of *like*) pecan pie.
2. The men (past of *move*) the piano.
3. We (present perfect of *choose*) new band uniforms.
4. Tim (past perfect of *do*) twenty pushups.
5. The PTA (future of *buy*) our school three new typewriters.
6. I (past of *win*) the prize.
7. Her mother (future of *pick*) the package up tonight.
8. The bird (past of *fly*) away.
9. The ship (past of *touch*) the iceberg.
10. The plants (past perfect of *grow*) much taller.

Part 7 The Principal Parts of Verbs

Look up the words *see* and *begin* in your dictionary. You will probably find something like this:

see; saw; seen; seeing

begin; began, begun; beginning

What are these forms? The first is the **present tense** (see, begin). Then comes the **past tense** (saw, began). Next is the **past participle** (seen, begun). And finally we have the **present participle** (seeing, beginning).

The first three of these forms are called the **principal parts** of the verb.

Present	Past	Past Participle
see	saw	seen
begin	began	begun

If you know the principal parts of a verb, you can make any tense by using the forms alone or with helping verbs.

The principal parts of a verb are the present tense, the past tense, and the past participle.

A Note About Your Dictionary: Some dictionaries include the names of the principal parts when they list the verbs. Such dictionaries might list *see* in a manner something like this: *See*, past tense *saw*; past part. *seen*; pres. part. *seeing*. The abbreviations p. for past and p.p. for past participle are also used.

Learning Principal Parts

There are several thousand verbs in the English language. Most of them cause no problems of usage at all. They are **regular verbs.** That is, the past tense is formed by adding *-ed* or *-d* to the present. The past participle is the same as the past tense forms and is always used with a helping verb.

Present	Past	Past Participle
talk	talk**ed**	(have) talk**ed**
print	print**ed**	(have) print**ed**
crawl	crawl**ed**	(have) crawl**ed**

There are a few commonly used verbs, however, whose past forms do not follow this pattern. They are **irregular verbs.**

The list on page 54 gives the principal parts of many irregular verbs. The past participle is always used with a helping verb.

In using irregular verbs, remember two important things:

1. The past tense is always used by itself, *without* a helping verb.

> I *gave* him a book.

2. The past participle is always used *with* a helping verb.

> I *have given* him a book.

It may help to learn the list, saying *have* in front of each past participle. Then you will not confuse words in the last two columns and say, "he seen it," "he done it," "she had stole it," or "she had broke it."

The same helping verb may be used with two or more past participles.

> I *have known* and *liked* Pat for a long time.

The helping verbs you will use most frequently are *has, have, had, is, are, was,* and *were.*

Irregular Verbs

Present	Past	Past Participle
begin	began	(have) begun
break	broke	(have) broken
bring	brought	(have) brought
choose	chose	(have) chosen
come	came	(have) come
do	did	(have) done
drink	drank	(have) drunk
eat	ate	(have) eaten
fall	fell	(have) fallen
freeze	froze	(have) frozen
give	gave	(have) given
go	went	(have) gone
grow	grew	(have) grown
have	had	(have) had
know	knew	(have) known
ride	rode	(have) ridden
ring	rang	(have) rung
rise	rose	(have) risen
run	ran	(have) run
say	said	(have) said
see	saw	(have) seen
sing	sang	(have) sung
sit	sat	(have) sat
speak	spoke	(have) spoken
steal	stole	(have) stolen
swim	swam	(have) swum
take	took	(have) taken
teach	taught	(have) taught·
throw	threw	(have) thrown
wear	wore	(have) worn
write	wrote	(have) written

Practice Pages on Irregular Verbs

Irregular verbs can cause problems in writing as well as in speaking. Pages 56–66, with red borders, provide practice in the correct use of irregular verbs.

How well do you use these verbs? The exercise below will tell you.

If the exercise shows that you need more practice with certain verbs, your teacher may ask you to turn to those verbs on the following pages. For each verb there are many sentences that will help you to "say it right," "hear it right," and "write it right."

Exercise   Using Irregular Verbs

Number your paper 1–20. For each sentence, write the correct word from the two given in parentheses.

1. The jury (bring, brought) in the verdict.
2. Nathan had (broke, broken) his leg while water skiing.
3. Ruth had (came, come) to the meeting with us.
4. Rosita has (chose, chosen) a biography for her report.
5. After we had (did, done) all the work, we went tobogganing.
6. Have you and Michael (drank, drunk) all the lemonade?
7. When I came home, everyone else had (ate, eaten) dinner.
8. The shallow lake had already (froze, frozen).
9. Mrs. Lorenzo has (gave, given) us our assignment.
10. All of us have (gone, went) to the science fair.
11. Have you ever (grew, grown) strawberries or raspberries?
12. How long have you (knew, known) the MacArthurs?
13. Sara and Rick have (ran, run) in the relay race.
14. At camp, the dinner bell (rang, rung) every night.
15. Do you know who (rang, rung) the doorbell?
16. I have never (rode, ridden) in a helicopter.
17. Linda Ronstadt had (sang, sung) at the Summer Festival.
18. Diana Ross (sang, sung) there, too.
19. I have (saw, seen) *Star Wars* three times.
20. Ms. Bell has (spoke, spoken) to me about a job at her shop.

Say It Right   Hear It Right

A. Say these sentences over until the correct use of *bring* and *brought* sounds natural to you.

1. What have you brought?
2. Did you bring your bicycle?
3. I brought mine.
4. Keith brought his lunch.
5. Laura will bring the Cokes.
6. We brought you a gift.
7. I wish I'd brought my jacket.
8. Did you bring the tickets?

B. Say these sentences over until the correct use of *broke* and *broken* sounds natural to you.

1. I broke the dish.
2. The dish is broken.
3. The window had been broken.
4. She broke the record.
5. The tool was broken.
6. They broke the news.
7. Jason had broken his arm.
8. Christie broke the lamp.

Write It Right

Write the correct word from the two words given.

1. Did you (bring, brought) your camera?
2. I (bring, brought) two rolls of film.
3. Have you (bring, brought) the reports to class?
4. Yes, I have (bring, brought) mine.
5. I have (bring, brought) you a surprise.
6. Haven't you (bring, brought) anything?
7. Peg (bring, brought) her new racket to class.
8. The paramedics had (bring, brought) him to the hospital.
9. Jill may have (broke, broken) her wrist.
10. Pat has (broke, broken) another window.
11. We have (broke, broken) five dishes.
12. Tammy's car had (broke, broken) down on the expressway.
13. The runner has (broke, broken) the previous record.
14. Ted's fishing pole was (broke, broken) in half.
15. That clock has been (broke, broken) for over a year.

Came
Come

Chose
Chosen

Say It Right   Hear It Right

A. Say these sentences over until the correct use of *came* and *come* sounds natural to you.

1. Jennifer came yesterday.
2. Has Jay come yet?
3. Amy and Tad came home.
4. He should have come.
5. Has the pizza come yet?
6. They came on Sunday.
7. We came on the early bus.
8. Eric has come for me.

B. Say these sentences over until the correct use of *chose* and *chosen* sounds natural to you.

1. The actors have been chosen.
2. Our band was chosen to play.
3. The class chose these books.
4. Everybody has been chosen.
5. Student Council chose Lou.
6. Was Liz chosen?
7. Have you been chosen?
8. Dick chose a yellow shirt.

Write It Right

Write the correct word from the two words given.

1. I saw the accident just as I (came, come) along.
2. The exhibit will (came, come) this way in July.
3. I wondered why the mail carrier (came, come) so early.
4. They had arrived long before we (came, come).
5. A loud cheer (came, come) from the fans.
6. My sister has (came, come) home from college this weekend.
7. She (came, come) last weekend, too.
8. We (chose, chosen) to go camping this summer.
9. I (chose, chosen) watermelon instead of pie for dessert.
10. Have you (chose, chosen) the color you want on your walls?
11. The team has (chose, chosen) Chris as captain.
12. We have (chose, chosen) new books for our library.
13. At camp we (chose, chosen) Pablo as our group leader.
14. Ruth has been (chose, chosen) as class president.
15. I (chose, chosen) to work on the mural.

57

Say It Right   Hear It Right

A. Say these sentences over until the correct use of *did* and *done* sounds natural to you.

1. Art did his homework.
2. Ellen has done hers.
3. Tim did his quickly.
4. Jo has done ten problems.

5. Darla did only three.
6. Mark has done only one.
7. I did the dishes.
8. Jim has done the laundry.

B. Say these sentences over until the correct use of *drank* and *drunk* sounds natural to you.

1. I have drunk the lemonade.
2. Ann has drunk three glasses.
3. Ray had drunk only one.
4. Carol drank iced tea.

5. Linda drank ginger ale.
6. Carla drank fruit juice.
7. Tim had drunk the Coke.
8. Kim and Lisa drank milk.

Write It Right

Write the correct word from the two words given.

1. The school band has never (did, done) so well before.
2. No one could have (did, done) those problems.
3. Have you (did, done) your homework?
4. The team (did, done) the best it could.
5. Have you (did, done) the math exercises yet?
6. Juan (did, done) a good job on that model airplane.
7. Jane (did, done) that scale model of a pyramid.
8. The seventh graders (did, done) well in the school contest.
9. I have (drank, drunk) eight glasses of water today.
10. Jamie and Steve (drank, drunk) the last Coke.
11. Have you ever (drank, drunk) coconut milk?
12. The baby has (drank, drunk) from a bottle since her birth.
13. We (drank, drunk) ginger ale at the picnic.
14. Josh has never (drank, drunk) iced tea.
15. The hikers (drank, drunk) water from the well on the farm.

Say It Right   Hear It Right

A. Say these sentences over until the correct use of *ate* and *eaten* sounds natural to you.

1. I ate breakfast.
2. Dana has eaten breakfast.
3. Sam ate later.
4. Beth ate slowly.
5. We ate hot dogs.
6. We had eaten dinner.
7. I ate very little.
8. Shelly had eaten a lot.

B. Say these sentences over until the correct use of *froze* and *frozen* sounds natural to you.

1. Mother froze the meat.
2. The yogurt was frozen.
3. The milk had frozen.
4. Rain froze into hail.
5. We nearly froze.
6. Bus windows were frozen.
7. My fingers froze.
8. The pond was frozen.

Write It Right

Write the correct word from the two words given.

1. We had (ate, eaten) before going to the game.
2. Sue (ate, eaten) slowly.
3. I (ate, eaten) very fast.
4. Scott has (ate, eaten) all the peanut butter.
5. Lucy had (ate, eaten) lunch at a friend's house.
6. She has (ate, eaten) there lots of times.
7. Dave had (ate, eaten) slowly.
8. We (ate, eaten) at my cousin's last night.
9. This is the first winter the river has (froze, frozen).
10. The water pipe has (froze, frozen).
11. We have (froze, frozen) the left-overs.
12. Waiting for the school bus, we nearly (froze, frozen).
13. Linda's toes were almost (froze, frozen).
14. The lake was (froze, frozen) halfway out from shore.
15. Dar's tears were almost (froze, frozen) on her cheeks.

59

Say It Right   Hear It Right

A. Say these sentences over until the correct use of *gave* and *given* sounds natural to you.

1. I gave my speech yesterday.
2. Jo gave her speech today.
3. Jim had given his speech last week.
4. My aunt gave me a watch.

5. She has given a party.
6. I gave the baby a toy.
7. I was given the day off.
8. Sue gave Bob a rare stamp.

B. Say these sentences over until the correct use of *went* and *gone* sounds natural to you.

1. Allison went skiing.
2. John had gone last winter.
3. I went to the museum.
4. We went swimming yesterday.

5. Have you gone to Disneyland?
6. I went there last summer.
7. Dee went this spring.
8. Mom went to play golf.

Write It Right

Write the correct word from the two words given.

1. Their team seemed to have (gave, given) up.
2. You should have (gave, given) better directions.
3. Sally (gave, given) me a jigsaw puzzle.
4. We (give, gave) our teacher a present.
5. Our coach has always (gave, given) us praise when we win.
6. Sometimes he has (gave, given) us a lecture.
7. Mrs. Hanke (gave, given) us a spelling test.
8. Jeremy and Beth (went, gone) to the meeting.
9. Jonathan and Liz have (went, gone) fishing.
10. I have (went, gone) fishing only once.
11. Rob has (went, gone) fishing every day this summer.
12. Mary has always (went, gone) to the show on Saturday.
13. The children (went, gone) down the street to get ice cream.
14. My sister has always (went, gone) to summer camp.
15. Ann has (went, gone) away for the summer.

Grew
Grown
Knew
Known

Say It Right   Hear It Right

A. Say these sentences over until the correct use of *grew* and *grown* sounds natural to you.

1. We grew a garden this year.
2. We grew our own lettuce.
3. Have you ever grown beets?
4. The tree has grown tall.
5. The grass grew quickly.
6. I had grown tired of weeding.
7. The house has grown shabby.
8. We have all grown a lot.

B. Say these sentences over until the correct use of *knew* and *known* sounds natural to you.

1. I knew the owner.
2. I have known her for years.
3. Ed had known the results.
4. I had known Jim in camp.
5. Sally knew Sue from band.
6. Have you known Kim long?
7. Kay knew her well.
8. They knew it would rain.

Write It Right

Write the correct word from the two words given.

1. George has (grew, grown) two inches since last fall.
2. The Jeffersons (grew, grown) their own vegetables.
3. Ana (grew, grown) ten kinds of plants for her experiment.
4. Our class (grew, grown) flowers for the army hospital.
5. We have (grew, grown) radishes every summer.
6. Mother (grew, grown) catnip for our cat.
7. The sunflowers have (grew, grown) six feet tall.
8. They have (knew, known) each other since fifth grade.
9. I have never (knew, known) a busier person.
10. We hadn't (knew, known) the game was postponed.
11. Mike had never (knew, known) anyone from Japan before.
12. We (knew, known) the Jacksons.
13. Clara has (knew, known) how to swim since the age of three.
14. The hikers (knew, known) they were lost.
15. Before she started school, Kathy (knew, known) how to read.

61

Say It Right   Hear It Right

A. Say these sentences over until the correct use of *ran* and *run* sounds natural to you.

1. We ran along the shore.
2. Al had run very fast.
3. They ran out of ice cream.
4. Has our time run out?
5. Barb ran the school store.
6. The joggers ran for miles.
7. Steve has run three miles.
8. Has the relay been run yet?

B. Say these sentences over until the correct use of *rang* and *rung* sounds natural to you.

1. Has the bell rung yet?
2. I thought it rang.
3. Who rang the doorbell?
4. The mail carrier rang it.
5. The church bells rang.
6. The victory bell rang.
7. The fire alarm rang again.
8. It had rung earlier.

Write It Right

Write the correct word from the two words given.

1. The car has (ran, run) out of gas.
2. Katie and Jeff (ran, run) four miles today.
3. The race was (ran, run) at the high school.
4. Who (ran, run) in the relays?
5. Ruth had (ran, run) until she was exhausted.
6. When my little brother saw Dad coming, he (ran, run) to meet him.
7. Have you ever (ran, run) in a three-legged race?
8. The telephone (rang, rung) before.
9. The cathedral bells (rang, rung) at Christmas.
10. The camp dinner bell had (rang, rung) twice.
11. The doorbell (rang, rung) three times.
12. All the church bells had (rang, rung).
13. The fire alarm had (rang, rung), but it was a false alarm.
14. The student who (rang, rung) the fire alarm was expelled.
15. When the ceremony ended, all the bells (rang, rung).

Rode
Ridden
Sang
Sung

Say It Right   Hear It Right

A. Say these sentences over until the correct use of *rode* and *ridden* sounds natural to you.

1. Pat has ridden a horse.
2. I rode one last summer.
3. We rode our minibikes.
4. We have ridden them before.
5. We rode to the lake.
6. Have you ridden a camel?
7. Josh rode the ferris wheel.
8. I have ridden it often.

B. Say these sentences over until the correct use of *sang* and *sung* sounds natural to you.

1. We sang in chorus yesterday.
2. She had sung that before.
3. They sang with the band.
4. Who sang at the concert?
5. The choir had sung.
6. Lola sang two songs.
7. George has sung one song.
8. Have you ever sung here?

Write It Right

Write the correct word from the two words given.

1. Have you (rode, ridden) in a 747 jet?
2. My brother (rode, ridden) in a dirt bike race Saturday.
3. Our club (rode, ridden) in the bike-a-thon.
4. My uncle (rode, ridden) his bicycle to work.
5. Garry has (rode, ridden) in many horse shows.
6. That jockey has (rode, ridden) in many races.
7. Have you ever (rode, ridden) in a rodeo?
8. The quartet (sang, sung) in the mall last weekend.
9. Have you ever (sang, sung) in a chorus?
10. Paul (sang, sung) a solo.
11. Roger and Donna had (sang, sung) a duet.
12. Sara, Lois, Sam, and Chuck (sang, sung) a medley.
13. Ginny (sang, sung) beautifully in her recital.
14. Her cousin had (sang, sung) just before she did.
15. We (sang, sung) around the campfire every night.

Say It Right   Hear It Right

A. Say these sentences over until the correct use of *saw* and *seen* sounds natural to you.

1. I saw you yesterday.
2. We haven't seen him before.
3. Jay saw the All-Star game.
4. Chris saw it, too.

5. We have seen that movie.
6. Eve saw us at the pool.
7. Michelle has seen the play.
8. Have you seen our new car?

B. Say these sentences over until the correct use of *spoke* and *spoken* sounds natural to you.

1. Has Don spoken to you?
2. He spoke to Julie.
3. The principal spoke to us.
4. We had spoken to her.

5. Mother spoke to my teacher.
6. The baby spoke one word.
7. Lou has not spoken to me.
8. Who spoke at the meeting?

Write It Right

Write the correct word from the two words given.

1. We (saw, seen) the World Series.
2. I (saw, seen) Mr. and Mrs. Barton at the Auto Show.
3. My family (saw, seen) the Olympic Games.
4. Darcy has (saw, seen) the film before.
5. We (saw, seen) the King Tut exhibit in Chicago.
6. I have never (saw, seen) a Big League baseball game.
7. Have you (saw, seen) the movie *Star Wars?*
8. Ian (saw, seen) the President last week.
9. Tim (spoke, spoken) to the new students.
10. The first speaker (spoke, spoken) on solar energy.
11. The second speaker (spoke, spoken) on nuclear energy.
12. They had both (spoke, spoken) to us before.
13. I have (spoke, spoken) to three movie stars.
14. The coach (spoke, spoken) to us enthusiastically.
15. He has often (spoke, spoken) to us that way.

Say It Right   Hear It Right

A. Say these sentences over until the correct use of *swam* and *swum* sounds natural to you.

1. Wayne and I swam in the pool.
2. Sherry has swum there too.
3. We swam after school.
4. Mandy swam for an hour.
5. I have swum three laps.
6. The salmon swam upstream.
7. Roy swam in the river.
8. Dozens of fish had swum by.

B. Say these sentences over until the correct use of *threw* and *thrown* sounds natural to you.

1. Luzinski was thrown out.
2. Bench threw him out.
3. The mayor threw out the ball.
4. He threw his cap in the air.
5. Who threw that pass?
6. Have you thrown it away?
7. Yes, I have thrown it away.
8. The pitcher threw a curve ball.

Write It Right

Write the correct word from the two words given.

1. Our team (swam, swum) laps for an hour.
2. Dolphins (swam, swum) around our boat.
3. We have (swam, swum) in that race every year.
4. Sally (swam, swum) faster than I did.
5. Only one goldfish (swam, swum) in the bowl.
6. Sharks (swam, swum) in those waters.
7. Curt has (swam, swum) in races for years.
8. The trout (swam, swum) toward the bait.
9. Our newspaper had been (threw, thrown) into the bushes.
10. Kent (threw, thrown) the winning pass.
11. They had (threw, thrown) out bread for the birds.
12. Lynn (threw, thrown) the ball to Tanya.
13. The wrestler has (threw, thrown) his opponent.
14. The cargo was (threw, thrown) out of the train by the blast.
15. We (threw, thrown) rice at the bride and groom.

Say It Right   Hear It Right

A. Say these sentences over until the correct use of *wore* and *worn* sounds natural to you.

1. I wore out my Adidas.
2. Ryan had worn his jacket.
3. José wore glasses.
4. Gail had worn out the battery.
5. Libby wore her jeans.
6. We all wore sandals.
7. They had worn T-shirts.
8. I have worn out my pen.

B. Say these sentences over until the correct use of *wrote* and *written* sounds natural to you.

1. Who wrote that play?
2. Shakespeare wrote it.
3. Rebecca has written a letter.
4. Who wrote this song?
5. Sue has written a song.
6. We wrote the assignment.
7. I had written two letters.
8. Doug has written a poem.

Write It Right

Write the correct word from the two words given.

1. We all (wore, worn) costumes to the party.
2. I have never (wore, worn) roller skates before.
3. Holly and Juanita were (wore, worn) out from the hike.
4. My sandals (wore, worn) out.
5. I have already (wore, worn) out my jeans.
6. My sister (wore, worn) her new blazer.
7. We had (wore, worn) our heavy gloves to shovel snow.
8. To whom have you (wrote, written)?
9. Who (wrote, written) "The Raven"?
10. Edgar Allan Poe (wrote, written) it.
11. We had (wrote, written) our friends in Indiana.
12. Emily Dickinson has (wrote, written) many poems.
13. Have you ever (wrote, written) to the President?
14. How many letters have you (wrote, written) now?
15. Adam (wrote, written) a science fiction story.

Part 8 Choosing the Right Verbs

Sometimes people confuse certain verbs. For example, they don't know whether to say, "Let me help," or "Leave me help."

In this part you will study several groups of verbs that are often confused. Learn to use these verbs correctly.

Let and Leave

1. *Let* means "permit." Example: *Let* me go.
2. *Leave* means "go away (from)." Example: They will *leave* the party early. *Leave* also means "cause to remain" or "allow to remain." Example: They are *leaving* a few books on the table.

The principal parts of these verbs are:

let, let, let   leave, left, left

Lie and Lay

1. *Lie* means "recline" or "rest." It has no object. Its principal parts are *lie, lay, lain*.
2. *Lay* means "put" or "place." It takes an object. Its principal parts are *lay, laid, laid*.

Look again at the principal parts of these verbs:

lie, lay, lain   lay, laid, laid

You use these verbs like this:

Lie

Present My dog lies on the porch when it's hot.
Past The cyclist lay under the tree for a rest.
Past participle How long has that shovel lain there?

Lay

Present Megan always lays her coat on that chair.
Past He laid his books on the table.
Past participle She has laid aside her work.

Sit and *Set*

1. *Sit* means "rest" or "be seated." *Sit* does not take an object.

Sat is the past tense of sit. It means "rested" or "was seated." Since *sat* is a form of *sit*, it does not take an object.

2. *Set* is a different word entirely. It means "put" or "place." *Set* takes an object.

The principal parts of these verbs are:

sit, sat, sat   set, set, set

You use these verbs like this:

Sit

Present Our cat sits in the sunlight.
Past Jay sat in the first row.
Past participle I have sat there many times.

Set

Present Set the bowl on the counter.
Past I set the packages there last night.
Past participle Carol has set the plants on the back porch.

Exercise   *Let* and *Leave*

Write the correct word from the two words given.

1. (Let, Leave) me take those packages.
2. Shouldn't we (let, leave) the others come?
3. Please (let, leave) these paintings dry.
4. We will (let, leave) a note for him.
5. Will you (let, leave) Mark and Trisha go with you?
6. Please (let, leave) me help you with that.
7. (Let, Leave) me hold one of the new puppies.
8. The Jansens will (let, leave) us stay at their house.
9. Did you (let, leave) your jacket in your locker?
10. Randi will (let, leave) the package in the hallway.

Exercise *Lie* **and** *Lay*

Write the correct word from the two words given.

1. We found a wallet (lying, laying) on the front walk.
2. Please (lie, lay) those photographs on the table.
3. I'm going to (lie, lay) on the beach for an hour or so.
4. Where did you (lie, lay) the scissors?
5. The kittens like to (lie, lay) under the rocking chair.
6. The nurse advised me to (lie, lay) down for a while.
7. Jill and Kris left their skateboards (lying, laying) in the driveway.
8. Unfortunately, much litter was left (lying, laying) all over the picnic area.
9. Several runners did (lie, lay) down after the long, strenuous race.
10. If you will (lie, lay) all of the drawings on this counter, we will choose the best one.

Exercise *Sit* **and** *Set*

Write the correct word from the two words given.

1. Do you want to (sit, set) in the balcony or on the main floor?
2. I would prefer to (sit, set) on the main floor.
3. Please (sit, set) the groceries on the table.
4. We (sat, set) in the front row for the outdoor concert.
5. Tim and Michelle will (sit, set) near the fifty-yard line.
6. Will you (sit, set) the luggage on the curb, please?
7. I thought I had (sit, set) my lunch on this table.
8. Sandy (sit, set) the mail on the buffet.
9. Won't you (sit, set) down and join us for dinner?
10. The drivers (sat, set) waiting for the race to begin.

Additional Exercises

Using Verbs

A. Find the verbs.

Find the verb in each sentence.

1. The deer appeared in the clearing.
2. Billie Jean King won the tournament.
3. Jack left about an hour ago.
4. The wind rustled in the palm trees.
5. There were not many stoplights.
6. Is Penny on the volleyball team?
7. Dorothy Hamill and the Ice Capades performed at the Amphitheater.
8. Just a bit of praise encouraged Jennifer a great deal.
9. The fog horn sounded all night.
10. Out on the driveway, a car suddenly appeared.

B. Find the direct objects.

Copy the following sentences. Underline the verb twice and draw a circle around the direct object.

1. Thaw the hamburger first.
2. Marcia and Janet were drinking lemonade.
3. Judi and I weeded the garden.
4. At the end of the month the treasurer banked the club's money.
5. Please close the locker.
6. Penny opened the trunk.
7. Marilee read several biographies.

8. Gabriel slowly washed and dried the dishes.
9. Some unknown person sounded the alarm.
10. The state police ticketed the speeder.

C. Add the direct objects.

Number a sheet of paper 1–10. Write direct objects that will complete each of the following sentences.

1. Karen touched the _____ easily.
2. Take _____ with you.
3. Craig broke his _____.
4. Lisa reached the _____ well before dark.
5. With his foot he toppled the _____.
6. Insecticides often endanger _____.
7. Mr. Maloney liked _____ better than Tennessee.
8. She put a _____ in her pocket.
9. Who owns this leather _____?
10. A spider spun its _____ over the opening.

D. Find the transitive and intransitive verbs.

Mark two columns *Transitive* and *Intransitive*. Find the verb in each of the following sentences. If the verb has an object, write it under *Transitive* and put its object in parentheses after it. If the verb has no object, write it under *Intransitive*.

1. The race horses rested for a while.
2. Rest your bicycle against the building.
3. The weeds spread over half the garden.
4. Turn the thermostat to 70 degrees.
5. The sun set at 6:20.
6. Carrie swept the front walk in a hurry.
7. Do you understand the arrangements?
8. He set the luggage in the trunk.

9. Outside the front door, students waited for the bus.
10. The librarian murmured a polite reply.

E. Find the linking verbs.

At the top of three columns write: *Subject, Linking Verb,* and *Word Linked to Subject.* Find the three parts in each sentence. Write them in the proper columns.

1. Those blue stripes look violet to me.
2. The sauerkraut smells strong.
3. During the sunset the pink clouds became brighter.
4. Jim seemed annoyed.
5. Look alive!
6. Stamp collecting is a most interesting hobby.
7. My older brother was a busboy last summer.
8. The goalie looked ready for anything.
9. The old tomcat remained absolutely motionless.
10. Does this can smell funny to you?

F. Find the helping verbs and the main verb.

Label two columns *Helping Verbs* and *Main Verb.* Find all the parts of the verb in each sentence. Write them in the proper columns.

1. May I take your coat?
2. They may have an extra outdoor thermometer.
3. Shall I put the fish in the freezer?
4. It might have happened anyway.
5. Bridget has been practicing her speech.
6. Our band is participating in the concert.
7. I would never have forgotten your birthday.
8. Jim would ordinarily have put the mitt in the hall closet.
9. Linda might possibly have taken Dad's camera with her.
10. The book must obviously have been out in the rain.

G. Identify tenses.

Name the tense in each sentence.

1. Brenda brought her backpack.
2. Rick stole a base.
3. The class will write to the newspaper.
4. Dennis has walked his dog.
5. They saw it last week.
6. Shall we freeze the leftovers?
7. The pitcher's arm gave out.
8. Have you already met?
9. Will you tape this?
10. Nancy had run a mile.

H. Use tenses.

Number your paper 1–10. Write down the tense of the verb for each sentence.

1. We (past of *see*) him.
2. The test (future of *begin*) now.
3. The teacher (past of *choose*) you.
4. Sally (present perfect of *be*) here before.
5. Kip (past perfect of *do*) the work.
6. The others (future of *ride*) with them.
7. He (present of *do*) it every time.
8. (Present of *walk*) faster.
9. Melinda (past of *hurtle*) around the corner.
10. Don (present perfect of *return*) your tennis racket.

Section 3

Using Nouns

Part 1   What Are Nouns?

Nouns are used to name persons, places, and things.

Persons friend, pilot, driver, Chris Evert
Places Charleston, beach, field, Disney World
Things shoe, football, cloud, bread

Things named by nouns may be things you can see:

bike   belt   guitar   spoon

Other things named by nouns may be things you cannot see:

pain   science   language   law

Still other things named by nouns are ideas:

friendship	courage	honesty	sadness
freedom	poverty	religion	Christianity

A noun is one of the eight parts of speech.

A noun is a word used to name a person, place or thing.

Exercises Find the nouns.

A. Number your paper 1–10. Write down the nouns in each of the following sentences.

1. Put your foot on the ladder.
2. A fuzzy orange caterpillar crept up the tree.
3. The rains made a pond by the side of the road.
4. An hour and ten minutes had passed.
5. The words were on the tip of his tongue.
6. Two waiters shoved the chairs and tables against the wall.
7. The wind blew the snow into enormous drifts.
8. The company pumps 80,000 barrels of oil a day.
9. There is a wide porch along the back of the house.
10. The meadow behind the barn was covered with wildflowers.

B. Number your paper 1–10. Write down the nouns in each of the following sentences.

1. The filling was banana.
2. Matthew joggled the machine for change.
3. The crowd had already left the auditorium.
4. On a clear day you can see the islands.
5. Temperatures in the Antarctic are almost never above zero.
6. Add the column up again.
7. That news calls for a celebration.
8. Tina waited for the bus for two hours in the pouring rain.

9. The truth of the matter is another story.
10. Two sparrows took baths in the puddle.

Part 2   Common Nouns and Proper Nouns

What do you notice about the italicized words in the following sentence?

> One *boy*, *José Rodriguez*, and one *girl*, *Jenny Thiem*, come from a nearby *city*, *Lansing*.

The italicized words are nouns. The words *boy*, *girl*, and *city* are called **common nouns.** A common noun is a general name. It does not name a special boy, girl, or city.

The words *José Rodriguez*, *Jenny Thiem*, and *Lansing*, on the other hand, name specific people and a specific city. They are called **proper nouns.** A proper noun always begins with a capital letter.

A common noun is the name of a whole class of persons, places, or things. It is a name that is common to the whole class.

A proper noun is the name of a particular person, place, or thing.

Common Nouns	Proper Nouns
singer	Beverly Sills
schedule	Golden Gate Bridge
encyclopedia	Africa
custom	Jordan Marsh Company
night	Finland

As the above list shows, a noun may consist of more than one word.

Exercises   Find the proper nouns.

A. Number your paper 1–10. Write down the proper nouns in each sentence and capitalize them correctly.

1. We live near the choctawatchee river in florida.
2. We stayed at the holiday inn on market street in san francisco.
3. The village called blue hills is near three small lakes.
4. Last summer we went camping in rocky mountain national park near bear lake.
5. We visited sequoia national park in california.
6. The jefferson public library was open on saturday.
7. We used to go to a library on michigan avenue in downtown chicago.
8. Our school is on the corner of north street and hickory avenue.
9. We sailed along long island.
10. That's ellis island and the statue of liberty over there.

B. Follow the directions for Exercise A.

1. The clerk was talking to dr. trent.
2. The schubert theater has closed.
3. My family went to toronto, montreal, and niagara falls last summer.
4. It was dr. peters who dug the first shovelful.
5. She was an employee of coca-cola bottling company.
6. My aunt vivian arrived yesterday on the train.
7. This is governor garfield's hometown newspaper.
8. I have never been to the everglades in florida.
9. Last night georgetown beat newport in basketball.
10. President carter often stays at camp david.

C. On a sheet of paper, head one column *Common Nouns* and another *Proper Nouns*. List the numbers 1–16 down the left-hand margin. Opposite each number, write the common noun which is given and then a proper noun which it suggests to you.

Example: *street   Market Street*

1. school   5. building   9. book   13. ocean
2. car   6. country   10. magazine   14. company
3. railroad 7. state   11. newspaper 15. lake
4. person   8. avenue   12. river   16. national park

Part 3 Nouns Used as Subjects

The subject of a sentence tells who or what is being talked about. Nouns are often used as subjects.

The goalie stopped the ball.
(The noun *goalie* is the subject of the verb *stopped*.)

Into the room came Ken and Martha.
(The nouns *Ken* and *Martha* are subjects of the verb *came*.)

In some sentences, the subject may not be right next to the verb. Other words may separate them.

The edge of the rink melted.
What melted? Not the whole rink, just the edge.
Edge is the subject of *melted*.

Exercises   Find the nouns as subjects.

A. Number your paper 1–10. Write the nouns used as subjects in each of the following sentences.

1. The heavy rains forced many cars off the road.
2. The kittens were playing with my macramé.
3. My mother drove slowly around the detour.
4. Our troop is sponsoring a party for the children in the hospital.

5. His pocket was full of nails and washers.
6. The handle of the screwdriver was yellow.
7. From the sky came the roar of a jet plane.
8. There was no time for homework.
9. The bottom of the bag was wet.
10. *Tapestries* by Carol King was a best-selling album.

B. Follow the directions for Exercise A.

1. The English like marmalade.
2. Our cafeteria serves the best lasagne.
3. Mrs. Maney sat near us at the concert.
4. His headlights were on.
5. Raindrops are falling on my head.
6. The steps could have been slippery.
7. The voices of the speakers did not carry over the mike.
8. In the shade of the pond swam a flock of Canadian geese.
9. The calendar on the wall was out of date.
10. The wild canary in the cage sang continuously.

Part 4 Nouns Used as Direct Objects

A noun used as a direct object receives the action of a transitive verb.

Examples: 1. The arrow hit the *target*.

2. Peggy threw the *basketball*.

The nouns *target* and *basketball* are direct objects. They answer the questions: *Hit what?* and *Threw what?*

Now study these examples.

1. You can buy magazines at the corner store.

   Question: Is there a direct object? Answer: Yes, *magazines.*

   Question: How do you know? Answer: It answers the question: *Can buy what?*

2. My sister built a bookcase in shop class.

   Question: Is there a direct object here? Answer: Yes, *bookcase.*

   Question: How do you know? Answer: It answers the question: *Built what?*

Diagraming Sentences Containing Direct Objects

When you diagram a sentence, place a direct object on the horizontal line following the verb. Separate it from the verb by an upright line that does not cut through the subject-verb line.

Example: Shari enjoys music.

Shari	enjoys	music

For compound direct objects, continue the horizontal line a little way beyond the verb and then split it. Make as many parallel direct-object lines as you need. Put the upright line before the split, to show that all the words that follow are direct objects.

Example: We met Jean, Jesse, and Eric.

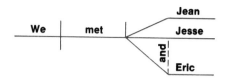

Exercises   Find the nouns used as direct objects.

A. Find the direct objects in the following sentences. Use diagrams or whatever method your teacher suggests.

1. Did you wash the car?
2. I've heard that song before.
3. The vaporizer cleared my head.
4. Adam took a big piece of pizza.
5. Barb suggested a possible solution.
6. The mechanic installed a new muffler.
7. Judy helped herself to more spaghetti.
8. The lighthouse keeper's daughter grimly climbed the stairs.
9. Bobbi dropped the book into the return slot.
10. Brenda could have found the way blindfolded.

B. Find the direct objects in the following sentences.

1. Release the clutch slowly.
2. Our coach clocked the race.
3. You should remove your glasses occasionally.
4. Mozart composed music as a child of five.
5. David took a swing at it.
6. You don't usually polish pewter candlesticks, do you?
7. The skyscraper shaded the whole street.
8. The worker removed the lid from the manhole.
9. Erica and her two cousins worked a jigsaw puzzle.
10. Three tugboats entered the harbor.

Part 5 Nouns Used as Indirect Objects

Thus far you have learned the three basic parts of the sentence: *subject-verb-object*. In the rest of this chapter, you will learn several other parts of the sentence. You will see that nouns can be used in all these sentence parts. The part you will examine first is the **indirect object** of the verb.

The indirect object tells to whom (or to what) or for whom (or for what) the action of the verb applies.

Examples:

Subject	Verb	Indirect Object	Direct Object
Sarah	gave	Renée	a kite.
Pam	told	Ray	the news.
Linda	showed	Sam	the pamphlet.

Usually, a sentence contains an indirect object only if there is also a direct object. The indirect object lies between the verb and the direct object. The words *to* and *for* never appear before the indirect object.

Diagraming Sentences Containing Indirect Objects

An indirect object is shown on a line below the main line of the sentence.

Example: Anne showed Tad her camera.

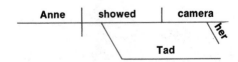

Notice that the indirect object is connected to the verb by a slanted line.

For compound indirect objects, continue the slanted line a little farther down. Then make as many parallel indirect-object lines as you need.

Example: Beth wrote Dave and Pat a letter.

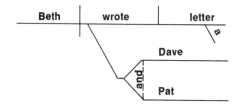

Exercises   Find the nouns used as indirect objects.

A. Indicate the indirect objects in the following sentences. Use diagrams or whatever method your teacher suggests.

1. Carl took the guests their coffee.
2. Mrs. Meyers gave the boys a few tennis pointers.
3. Bill got Eileen a dish of ice cream.
4. Tracy threw Mike a curve.
5. Marla taught her parakeet two new words.
6. Vicki sent Joe an invitation to the party.
7. We should have offered Pat a ride.
8. Ms. Bond gave our class the highest score.
9. Have you given the chair a second coat of paint?
10. Mr. Hall sent Ginny several postcards from Bolivia.

B. Find the nouns used as direct and indirect objects. Label two columns *Indirect Object* and *Direct Object*. Number your paper 1–10. Put down the indirect objects and direct objects in the following sentences. Not all sentences will have indirect objects.

Example: Give Jody a call after supper.

Indirect Object   Direct Object

Jody   call

1. Cindy gave the subject some thought.
2. Have you showed Jack your new watch?
3. Beth showed signs of progress.
4. Mrs. Jamison showed the Scouts some beautiful slides.
5. They sent Mr. McCorree flowers.
6. Mr. Hoffman sent Pete to the store.
7. Last week Rhoda showed her dog at the dog show.
8. Give Ellen a hint.
9. His little brother pestered Jim a while.
10. Mrs. Pettit baked Nancy some brownies for her birthday.

Part 6   Predicate Nouns

You remember that a linking verb links the subject to some word in the predicate. If that word is a noun, it is called a **predicate noun.** It usually means the same thing as the subject. It may explain the subject.

Examples: 1. This machine is a *drill.*
2. Jade is a very hard *stone.*
3. Sally became *chairperson* of the class today.
4. Sylvia has been my best *friend.*

The nouns *drill, stone, chairperson,* and *friend* are predicate nouns. In many sentences, the predicate nouns and the subject can be changed around without changing the meaning. The two parts are roughly equal.

Example: The boy is *Jack.* (Reverse the order and the sentence says: Jack is the boy.)

Diagraming Sentences Containing Predicate Nouns

The diagram for a sentence containing a predicate noun is different from that for a sentence containing a direct object.

Example: Mrs. Williams is the president.

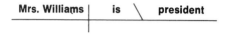

Notice that the predicate noun is on the horizontal line in the same position as the direct object. But the line that separates the predicate noun from the verb slants back toward the subject. This is to show its close relationship to the subject.

For sentences containing compound predicate nouns, use parallel lines.

Example: Tiger was a poor pet but a good watchdog.

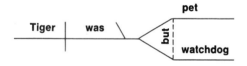

The slanting line comes before the main line is split.

Exercises Find the predicate nouns.

A. Find the predicate nouns in these sentences. Your teacher may ask you to diagram the sentences.

1. Dr. Patterson is a veterinarian.
2. My sister is a teller at this bank.
3. "Happy Days" is my favorite television program.
4. The library is the old building on the corner.

A. Write the plural of each of these nouns.

1. table	6. echo	11. tomato	16. cattle
2. dress	7. loaf	12. thief	17. stay
3. key	8. lady	13. deer	18. dormouse
4. daisy	9. coach	14. woman	19. way
5. desk	10. company	15. calf	20. Frenchman

B. Number your paper from 1–20. Write the correct form for the plural for each item. Some forms may already be correct.

1. patchs	6. thiefs	11. churches	16. skies
2. potatos	7. foxes	12. parties	17. donkies
3. buses	8. tattoos	13. crashs	18. citys
4. babys	9. joys	14. firemans	19. knifes
5. twos	10. wolves	15. moose	20. flies

Part 8 Possessive Nouns

When we speak of possession, we mean more than owner-ship. We may also mean that something belongs to a person or is part of him or her.

> *Jane's* sincerity   *Barbara's* ability   *Tom's* face

The italicized words above are nouns. They are called **possessive nouns** because they show possession of the noun that follows.

Forming Possessives of Singular Nouns

Do you see what it is about *Jane's* and *Barbara's* that is a sign of possession? It is the ending—the apostrophe and the *s*.

To form the possessive of a singular noun, add the apostrophe and *s*.

Singular Noun	Possessive Form
Sharon	Sharon's
Mrs. Hernandez	Mrs. Hernandez's
baby	baby's
waitress	waitress's
Charles	Charles's

Forming Possessives of Plural Nouns

There are two things to remember in writing the possessive of a plural noun:

1. If the plural noun ends in *s*, simply add an apostrophe after the *s*.

Plural Noun	Possessive Form
teams	teams'
ladies	ladies'
pilots	pilots'
drivers	drivers'
runners	runners'
contestants	contestants'

2. If the plural noun does not end in *s*, add an apostrophe and write an *s* after the apostrophe.

Plural Noun	Possessive Form
children	children's
men	men's
women	women's
alumni	alumni's

Diagraming Sentences Containing Possessive Nouns

In a diagram, possessive nouns are written on lines slanting down from the nouns with which they are used.

Example: This is Jeff's coat.

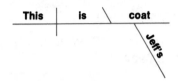

Exercises   **Show the possessive forms of nouns.**

A. On a piece of paper, write the possessive forms of these nouns.

1. day	6. photographer	11. secretary	16. horse
2. hour	7. Mr. Briggs	12. banker	17. farmer
3. James	8. Mrs. Holmes	13. Les	18. Peggy
4. Elyse	9. Charles Smith	14. Ms. Voss	19. printer
5. artist	10. customer	15. designer	20. architect

B. On a piece of paper, write the plural possessives of the following nouns.

1. teacher	6. minister	11. mother	16. animal
2. Smith	7. girl	12. journalist	17. captain
3. woman	8. principal	13. driver	18. catcher
4. ruler	9. father	14. leader	19. boy
5. group	10. Indian	15. Choctaw	20. governor

Additional Exercises

Using Nouns

A. Find the nouns.

Number your paper 1–10. Write down the nouns in each of the following sentences.

1. Turn the hamburgers, Shannon.
2. The state has passed laws against pollution.
3. The fans cheered the team vigorously throughout the game.
4. This recipe calls for a cup of walnuts or filberts.
5. A penguin waddled down the ramp.
6. Happiness is a warm blanket.
7. The afternoon brought more snow.
8. Energy has been the topic of many programs on television.
9. How high do jets fly?
10. That robin just flew away with a piece of bread.

B. Find the proper nouns.

Number your paper 1–10. Write down the proper nouns in each sentence. Capitalize them.

1. We visited the pentagon and the white house while in washington, d. c.
2. During our easter vacation, we went to the field museum in chicago.
3. Our high school is the largest in north carolina.
4. Two manufacturers of automobiles are general motors and chrysler.

5. The name of that science-fiction movie is *star wars*.

6. What large river flows through missouri?

7. Murray hill square is a new shopping center.

8. It is chris jansen who delivers *the huntstown daily news* before breakfast.

9. South of the border is mexico.

10. The new ford fiesta gets great gas mileage.

C. Nouns as subjects.

Number your paper 1–10. Write down the nouns used as subjects in each of the following sentences.

1. Clouds hid the top of the mountain from sight.

2. Plastic bags are lighter than paper ones.

3. Proper attention to details is a good idea.

4. A cool breeze aired the room.

5. The greenhouse was hot and humid.

6. Did Marilee and Frank come with you?

7. The third hole on the golf course is the longest.

8. The second chapter of the book is easier.

9. There were some pans and a glass on the picnic table.

10. The horn on Beth's bicycle sounded like a Model T.

D. Nouns as direct objects.

Number your paper 1–10. Write down the nouns used as direct objects in each of the following sentences.

1. The cat yawned and closed its eyes.

2. The police directed traffic around the accident.

3. A mockingbird built its nest in the tulip tree.

4. Dick simply couldn't believe his eyes.

5. The contractor calculated the cost of labor.

6. Grate the rind of one lemon.

7. Kimberly rode her bicycle from Milwaukee to Kenosha.

8. He had just transplanted the evergreens.

9. Gina owns the Sunshine Plant Shop.
10. Please bring your money for the tickets tomorrow.

E. Nouns used as indirect objects.

Indicate the indirect objects in the following sentences. Use diagrams or whatever method your teacher suggests.

1. Uncle Ted and Aunt Marie gave my brother a new football.
2. Joyce gave her sister a music box.
3. Carlos baked Donna a cake for her birthday.
4. Marsha might have offered the elephant some peanuts.
5. The mayor showed the visitors Riverside High School.
6. Phil cooked the family some supper.
7. The toothpaste gave the police their first clue about the suspect.
8. Barb offered Chris her umbrella.
9. Did you buy your cousin a birthday present?
10. The club members gave the room a thorough cleaning.

F. Find the predicate nouns.

Number your paper 1–10. List the predicate nouns in these sentences.

1. That van is really a camper.
2. Laura was the messenger.
3. The Sears Tower is the tallest building in the world.
4. Benji is a famous dog.
5. Susan became an architect.
6. The cherry blossom is the Chinese symbol for happiness.
7. Botswana is a country in Africa.
8. To his mother, Billy was a welcome sight.
9. Who is the owner of these sneakers?
10. Peaches and apricots are drupes.

G. Plural forms of nouns.

Number your paper from 1–30. Write the correct form of the plural of each word. Some forms may already be correct.

1. feet	11. crashs	21. coachs
2. valleys	12. lifes	22. securities
3. ashes	13. tusks	23. banjoes
4. keys	14. cuckoos	24. patchs
5. sheeps	15. toys	25. tomatoes
6. wolfs	16. buzzs	26. lilys
7. watchs	17. mans	27. pianoes
8. selfs	18. elkes	28. countrys
9. duos	19. bunches	29. citys
10. lobbys	20. ladies	30. leaves

H. Forming the possessives of nouns.

Write the following phrases, adding the possessive forms in the brackets.

Example: (singular possessive of Joan) towel
Joan's towel

1. the (plural possessive of *bird*) claws
2. (singular possessive of *Melinda*) calendar
3. Bobbie (singular possessive of *Jones*) house
4. the (plural possessive of *rainbow*) colors
5. the (plural possessive of *horse*) manes
6. the (singular possessive of *bass*) mouth
7. (singular possessive of *James*) clock
8. the (plural possessive of *woman*) club
9. the (singular possessive of *mouse*) whiskers
10. the (plural possessive of *baby*) habits
11. Mrs. (singular possessive of *Clarks*) hobbies
12. the (plural possessive of *child*) shoes

Section 4

Using Pronouns

Part 1 What Are Pronouns?

Study these sentences:

> When Roger saw Wendy, Roger spoke to Wendy.
> When Roger saw Wendy, he spoke to her.

The words *he* and *her* are pronouns because they stand for the nouns Roger and Wendy.

A pronoun is a word used in place of a noun.

A pronoun is a very useful word. It helps you write and talk smoothly and easily without losing track of your ideas and without repeating the same words too often. A pronoun is one of the eight parts of speech.

How Pronouns Differ from Nouns

Pronouns change form according to their use in the sentence. Study these pairs of sentences to see how the pronouns differ.

Nouns	Pronouns
1. *Jerry* pruned the tree.	1. *He* pruned the tree.
2. Mr. Barnes helped *Jerry*.	2. Mr. Barnes helped *him*.
3. Mr. Barnes is *Jerry's* father.	3. Mr. Barnes is *his* father.
4. The *books* came yesterday.	4. *They* came yesterday.
5. Mr. Franks brought the *girls*.	5. Mr. Franks brought them.

The Forms of Pronouns

Pronouns have three forms: *subject, object,* and *possessive.* Notice how the pronoun *she* changes as its use changes:

She came. (*She* is the subject.)
I saw *her*. (*Her* is the direct object.)
It is *hers*. (*Hers* is the possessive.)

The pronouns listed below are called **personal pronouns.** Here are the forms you should know.

	Subject	Possessive	Object
Singular:	I, you, she, he, it	my, mine, your, yours her, hers, his, its	me, you, her, him, it
Plural:	we, they	our, ours, your, yours, their, theirs	us, you, them

Substituting Pronouns for Nouns

Notice the pronoun chosen for each of the following sentences. The form of each pronoun depends upon the use of the pronoun in the sentence.

1. The girls are here. *They* arrived early. (subject)
2. The workers left later. Ann saw *them*. (direct object)
3. Sean was early. Terry showed *him* her new aquarium. (indirect object)
4. The Boyles have moved. Caryl has *their* address. (possessive)
5. Karen is my sister. *She* is older than I am. (subject)

Exercises　**Use pronouns correctly.**

A.　Rewrite the following sentences, changing all the proper nouns to pronouns.

> Example: Mrs. Vickers gave Debbie and Todd the game for Christmas. (You are Debbie. Use one word for Debbie and Todd.)
>
> She gave us the game for Christmas.

1. Joel is the owner. (You are Joel. Change the verb.)
2. Joyce and Craig are here. (You are Craig. Use two words.)
3. Pass Paula the pickle relish, please. (You are Paula).
4. Sherry and Shelley will lend John their tent. (You are Shelley.)
5. Sara and Sam were the main characters. (Use one word.)
6. Cindy and Marcia were the winners. (Use one word.)
7. The club presented Wayne with the book. (You are not Wayne.)
8. Kevin got *The Contender* and *Light in the Forest* from the library. (Use one word for the two books.)

9. Please direct Mrs. Slater and Claire to Ben's Texaco Station. (You are Claire. Use two words for the people.)

10. Jennie goes past La Grange City Hall and St. John's Church on the way home. (Use one word for the buildings.)

B. Rewrite the following sentences, changing all the proper nouns to pronouns.

1. Sandy and Emily are coming. (Use one word.)

2. Jon gave Bret his catcher's mitt. (You are Bret.)

3. Tracy and Marie walked home. (You are Marie. Use two words.)

4. Mr. Corona took Pat and Andrea to the hockey game. (You are Andrea. Use two words for the girls.)

5. Paul, Janice, and Bob are reporters for our school paper. (You are Bob.)

6. Matt handed Rhonda *Newsweek*. (You are Rhonda.)

7. Darnell gave Rita "Probe" for her birthday. (You are not Rita. "Probe" is a game.)

8. Dr. Gonzales gave Meredith two books on medicine. (You are Dr. Gonzales.)

9. Mr. Russell and Cheryl were the guests. (Use two words.)

10. Eric went home. (You are Eric).

Part 2   Predicate Pronouns

The subject forms of pronouns are used as subjects. They are also used as predicate pronouns. A **predicate pronoun** is a pronoun that follows a linking verb and is linked by the verb to the subject.

The correct use of predicate pronouns is not difficult. But you must be sure that you understand what these pronouns are and how they are used. Otherwise you may become confused.

Study these examples:

Subject			Predicate Pronoun
She and *I*	went.	The students were	*she* and *I*.
You and *he*	came.	The visitors were	*you* and *he*.

If you have trouble recognizing predicate pronouns, remember these points:

1. Predicate pronouns follow linking verbs such as *is, was, were* and *will be.*

2. The predicate pronoun usually means the same thing as the subject.

3. A sentence with a predicate pronoun will usually make sense if the subject and the predicate pronoun are reversed. Study the following example.

Subject	Verb	
He	was	the visitor.
The visitor	was	he.

Always use the subject form of a pronoun for subjects and predicate pronouns.

Exercises   Choose the right pronoun.

A. Number your paper 1–10. Choose the right pronoun in each of the following sentences.

1. Kathy and (I, me) work together.
2. Chrisy and (her, she) are coming.
3. The base runners were Mark and (I, me).

4. The boys are Al's brothers. Al and (they, them) live next door.

5. (We, Us) and the Bradleys play touch football.

6. It was Todd and (me, I) to the rescue.

7. It is (her, she).

8. There are Ginny and (I, me) on TV!

9. (Us, We) and about half the class were tennis players.

10. The baseball experts are (they, them) and their brothers.

B. Number your paper 1–10. Choose the right pronoun in each of the following sentences.

1. (Him, He) is the boy at the door.

2. The Big Hawk Pack and (us, we) became friends at camp.

3. The winners are Trudy and (me, I).

4. Scott and (her, she) are cousins.

5. Robin and (she, her) both roasted marshmallows.

6. (He, Him) and Michael are always together.

7. (Her, She) and (I, me) will see you tonight.

8. The boy on the right is (he, him).

9. Michele and (they, them) kept movie scrapbooks.

10. Peter and (us, we) were almost late to homeroom.

Part 3 Possessive Forms of Pronouns

The possessive forms of pronouns are these:

my, mine	our, ours
your, yours	
his, her, hers, its	their, theirs

Notice that possessive pronouns have no apostrophes.

Its **and** *It's*. Many people confuse the contraction *it's* (meaning *it is* or *it has*) with the possessive *its*. *It's* with an apostrophe always means *it is* or *it has*.

1. The dog lost its collar. (its = belonging to it)
2. It's been raining. (it's = it has)
3. The horse turned its head. (its = belonging to it)
4. Now it's clear again. (it's = it is)
5. The cat has left its kittens. (its = belonging to it)
6. The bird cleaned its feathers. (its = belonging to it)
7. Tell me when it's time. (it's = it is)

Exercises   **Use *its* and *it's* correctly.**

A. Copy the following sentences and insert apostrophes where they are needed.

1. Its raining again.
2. Give the dog its bath.
3. Its a little too hot.
4. The long run brought the crowd to its feet.
5. Its either yours or hers.
6. See if its melted yet.
7. The airline will page us when its cargo plane arrives.
8. Its about time for the news.
9. The bear could not find its cubs.
10. Its an old story.

B. Copy the following sentences and insert apostrophes where they are needed.

1. Its winter in Australia.
2. The chair was lying on its back.
3. That bat is theirs. Its much newer than ours.
4. The robin left its nest too soon.
5. According to the weather report, its supposed to rain tomorrow.

6. Its not an impossible dream.

7. The marathon is Sunday; its distance is 26 miles and 385 yards.

8. The new record shop opens Saturday, and all of its albums will be on sale.

9. Its that alarm clock again.

10. Bill thinks its his football, but its mine.

Part 4   Pronouns as Objects

Direct objects and indirect objects always take the object forms of pronouns.

Direct object: Ted saw *him* and *her*.

Indirect object: Lynn asked *me* a question.

Pronouns in Compound Objects

A compound object may consist of two pronouns joined by *and*, *or*, or *nor*. A compound object may also consist of a noun and a pronoun. The object form of pronouns is used in all compound objects.

Direct object: They saw *Terry* and *me*.
He directed *him* and *her*.

Indirect object: Please give *Alice* and *me* your address.
She gave *us* and *them* the records.

Exercises   Use the right pronoun as object.

A. Choose the right pronouns from the parentheses in the following sentences.

1. Eric was teaching (he, him) and his sister backhand.
2. The snow in their faces slowed (they, them) and the other hikers down.
3. Sharlene and (she, her) gave the best speeches.
4. Mrs. Janson bought (them, they) and their friends ice cream.
5. Have you seen John and (he, him) this morning?
6. General Mills sent (he, him) and (I, me) a frisbee.
7. Mrs. Folette asked (they, them) and Kent to dinner.
8. Mother gave (they, them) and (us, we) a lift to school.
9. The old man told Jack and (me, I) about the Louistown flood.
10. Give (he, him) and his friend tickets for the tournament.

B. Choose the right pronouns from the parentheses in the following sentences.

1. The parade delayed (we, us) and my grandmother.
2. You should have seen (he, him) and (me, I) on Saturday.
3. The architect drew (they, them) and the onlookers a brief sketch.
4. Will you give (she, her) and (I, me) some help?
5. The lawyer brought the jury and (her, she) positive proof.
6. Will you give Mary and (me, I) some fudge?
7. Tell Linda and (she, her) to wait.
8. Kirk helped (he, him) and (she, her) with the arrangements.
9. Curtis gave Barry and (I, me) his promise.
10. My mother will call Jim and (they, them) early in the morning.

Part 5   *We Girls* or *Us Girls;*
We Boys or *Us Boys*

When do you say *we boys* and *we girls?* When do you say *us boys* and *us girls?* You will make the correct choice if you try the pronoun alone in the sentence.

> Example: (We, Us) boys walked ten miles.
>
> > (*We* walked. Therefore, *We boys walked ten miles* is correct.)

Exercises   Use the correct pronoun.

A. Choose the correct pronouns in the following sentences.

1. (We, Us) girls are all on the team.
2. Did you see (we, us) boys in the pool?
3. Take (we, us) boys with you.
4. The winners were (we, us) girls.
5. At first (we, us) receivers were missing the passes.
6. Give (we, us) members a break!
7. Do (we, us) students have a spelling test today?
8. (We, Us) girls were chosen as representatives.
9. (We, Us) boys were selected as the finalists.
10. Ms. Gianetti picked (we, us) two for the parts.

B. Choose the correct pronouns in the following sentences.

1. (We, Us) girls are from Lincolnwood.
2. He is watching (we, us) boys on the bridge.
3. (We, Us) two are in the play-offs Saturday.
4. (We, Us) three did all the cleaning up.
5. Give (we, us) boys some help.
6. You never told (we, us) class representatives.
7. (We, Us) girls have all seen the movie.

8. Please take (we, us) boys on the boat, too.
9. (We, Us) girls have waited half an hour.
10. (We, Us) girls are the best.

Part 6 Pronouns and Antecedents

The **antecedent** of a pronoun is the noun or pronoun which it replaces or to which it refers.

> 1. *Larry* came today and brought *his* tools.
>   (*Larry* is the antecedent of *his*.)
>
> 2. *Debbie* and *Tom* came in. *They* were laughing.
>   (*Debbie* and *Tom* are the antecedents of *they*.)

The antecedent usually appears before the pronoun. Sometimes, as in the second example, the antecedent is in the sentence before it.

Exercises   Find the antecedents.

A. Number your paper 1–10. Make two columns and label one *Pronouns* and the other *Antecedents.* Place the pronouns in one column and their antecedents in the other.

> Example: Aunt Carol and Uncle Jim like Terry. They told her many stories about the old mining town.

> | Pronouns | Antecedents |
> |----------|-------------|
> | they | Aunt Carol |
> | | Uncle Jim |
> | her | Terry |

1. Owen had the pigeon with him. He carried it carefully.
2. Joan has had her bike repaired.

3. Tim and Rick didn't bring their raincoats.

4. Marsha and Jack are here now. She is cutting the lawn, and he is washing the car.

5. Even before Mary got there, Jay and Frank had started their breakfast.

6. Jim and Liz brought their dog. They had it on a leash.

7. Wayne sanded and painted the birdhouse. He had made it in shop class.

8. Peter put his camera on Nancy's coat. When she came in, she knocked it off.

9. Mrs. Foster bought all those bananas for a quarter. They were certainly worth it.

10. The Ohio River is used for freight. It moves more of it than the Panama Canal.

B. Follow the directions for Exercise A.

1. Carla grabbed her end of the rope.

2. The boys saw Nancy. They asked her how she liked the movie.

3. My father held the needle at arm's length. Then he poked the thread at it.

4. Here is the canoe Bill's grandparents lent him. He brought it on his car.

5. Steel mills can create a serious problem. They pollute the air.

6. The thief erased his fingerprints.

7. Mr. Mulligan planted more soybeans last year. They brought him a good price.

8. That tree lost all its berries overnight.

9. Rex showed Al his hockey stick. It was a gift from his aunt.

10. Andrea let Kevin try her skateboard. He found it hard to use.

Singular and Plural Pronouns

Use a singular pronoun for a singular antecedent. Use a plural pronoun for a plural antecedent.

1. Snow (singular) covered the hills. It (singular) was a foot deep.
2. Members (plural) of the class gave their (plural) ideas.

Exercises   Using the correct singular and plural pronouns.

A. Number your paper 1–15. Choose the right pronoun to fill each numbered space below.

1. Judy and ___1___ cousin are spending ___2___ holidays in New Orleans. ___3___ have both visited ___4___ before.
2. Erica takes ___5___ guitar lesson on Tuesday. ___6___ is the only day ___7___ is free after school.
3. Steve took the paddles and ___8___ father carried ___9___ tackle. Kathy carried ___10___ own fishing gear.
4. Janette brought a tiny white pine home with ___11___ from summer camp. ___12___ planted ___13___ in the backyard.
5. Julie bought ___14___ own kit and built ___15___ own showboat.

B. Number your paper 1–15. Choose the right pronoun to fill each numbered space below.

1. Janet had ___1___ pocket calculator along. ___2___ used ___3___ to calculate club dues.
2. Mr. O'Shea moved ___4___ lawn sprinkler. ___5___ was getting water on ___6___ car. ___7___ dragged ___8___ over near the bushes.
3. Mrs. Sherman put the beans in plastic bags. Then ___9___ tied ___10___ shut.

4. Kim and Heather put ___**11**___ return bottles on the counter. ___**12**___ got almost a dollar for ___**13**___. ___**14**___ used ___**15**___ money to buy a magazine.

Part 7 Indefinite Pronouns

There are some pronouns that do not refer to a particular person. They are therefore called **indefinite pronouns.** The following indefinite pronouns are singular:

another	each	everything	one
anybody	either	neither	somebody
anyone	everybody	nobody	someone
anything	everyone	no one	something

Because they are singular, we use the singular possessive pronouns *his, her,* or *its* to refer to them. Perhaps the words in italics in these sentences will help you to remember:

Everybody took *his* turn.
Someone left *her* raincoat.
Something had *its* burrow here.
No one had *his* shoes on.

Exercises **Use the correct possessive pronouns with indefinite pronouns.**

A. Number your paper 1–10. Choose the correct possessive pronoun from those in parentheses. Write the pronoun in the first column. In the second column write the antecedent.

Example: Someone left (their, his) sweater here.

Possessive Pronoun	Antecedent
his	Someone

1. Everybody does (his, its) own share of work.
2. Has everyone already gotten (his, their) drink?
3. No, no one here has lost (their, her) glasses.
4. Has anyone forgotten (their, his) raincoat?
5. No one has cleaned up (his, their) room yet.
6. At one time or another, everyone puts (their, his) foot in (their, his) mouth.
7. Has anyone brought (his, their) camera?
8. Everybody has (their, his) own idea of freedom.
9. Did somebody put (his, its) car in the driveway?
10. No one had (their, his) watch on.

B. Follow the directions for Exercise A.

1. Somebody upstairs just dropped (his, its) shoes.
2. Did anyone throw (his, their) sneakers into the wash by mistake?
3. Anybody can take (his, their) book home.
4. Something alive just poked (their, its) nose out of that hole.
5. Everybody has had (their, his) last chance.
6. Has each of the boys signed (its, his) name?
7. Doesn't somebody have (his, their) flashlight?
8. Somebody should have (its, his) head examined.
9. Each of the dancers took (their, her) turn.
10. No one brought (his, their) materials to class.

Additional Exercises

Using Pronouns

A. Use pronouns correctly for proper nouns.

Rewrite the following sentences, changing all the proper nouns to pronouns.

1. Give Joy Tim's coat.
2. Ryan gave *The Sunday Tribune* to his father.
3. Throw Fred the ball.
4. Will you lend Ron and Peg your basketball? (You are Peg.)
5. Mr. Leham took Dee's and Jill's picture. (Use one word for Dee and Jill.)
6. Maria gave the Selmers a macramé hanging. (Use one word for Selmers.)
7. Give Lana and Ginger the tape recorder. (You are Ginger.)
8. Flying Finish was Amy's and Brent's horse. (Use one word for Amy's and Brent's.)
9. Mrs. Rowe presented the *Time-Life Atlas* to the school. (Use one word for the *Time-Life Atlas*.)
10. Mr. and Mrs. Franklin took Kathy and Bill to the library. (Use one word for Kathy and Bill.)

B. Choose the right pronoun.

Number your paper 1–10. Choose the right pronoun in each of the following sentences.

1. Larry and (him, he) mowed the grass.

2. Ryan and (I, me) are naturally the best players.
3. (They, Them) and the two file clerks share an office.
4. (Us, We) and Ted are in the back row.
5. It might have been Frank and (I, me) after all.
6. (Him, He) and Paula raked the lawn.
7. The best cooks are (him, he) and (she, her).
8. (We, Us) and Mrs. Mooney won.
9. The first ones to leave the game were (they, them).
10. Dorinda and (I, me) finished the work.

C. Use *its* and *it's* correctly

Copy the following sentences and insert apostrophes where they are needed.

1. Its wing span is larger, too.
2. Leave the stapler in its box.
3. Its a good thing that the cat found its kitten.
4. Is this your mitt? George is sure its yours.
5. Its time to go.
6. This bat is ours. Its handle is taped.
7. Its 3:10 already.
8. Its about time to stop.
9. Our suburb buys its water from the city.
10. Its springtime in the Rockies.

D. Use the right pronoun as object.

Choose the right pronouns from those in parentheses in the following sentences.

1. The Kiwanians awarded the players and (we, us) the trophy.
2. Mrs. Phillips took (they, them) and (us, we) to the play.
3. My sisters and (they, them) organized the carnival.

4. The manager told Len and (he, him) the same thing.
5. The team chose (he, him) and (I, me) as co-captains.
6. Gail invited Joan, Jim, and (I, me) to the party.
7. The track outfits will fit both (they, them) and (we, us).
8. The time change confuses (me, I) and a lot of other people.
9. Mr. Litt dropped Kristie and (she, her) off at the art fair.
10. A strong wind blew Elaine and (I, me) off balance.

E. Use the correct pronoun.

Choose the correct pronouns in the following sentences.

1. (We, Us) students must stick together.
2. Mrs. McKlintock coached (we, us) girls.
3. (We, Us) girls will organize the art fair.
4. It would take (we, us) boys too long.
5. (We, Us) two did it.
6. (We, Us) three vice-presidents have signed a trade agreement.
7. They finally found (we, us) girls.
8. (We, Us) two tied for second place.
9. Please give (we, us) players some water!
10. (We, Us) girls beat the boys at tennis.

F. Find the antecedents.

Number your paper 1–10. Place the pronouns in one column and their antecedents in the other.

1. The chair has lost three of its rungs.
2. The girls have a new game. They were playing it last night.

3. Mother called Pete. She asked him to help her wash the windows.

4. The hikers were studying their maps and compass.

5. That book has its cover on upside down.

6. Tanya and Elyse bought some peacock feathers at a garage sale. They cut them short and made necklaces.

7. Grandfather wears a mask over his eyes every night.

8. Donna made Mrs. Pettinger a bookcase. She gave it to her on Tuesday.

9. Glen went through the steel mills. In two hours he saw everything in them.

10. Rosita rearranged the rec room. It looked great.

G. Use the correct possessive pronouns with indefinite pronouns.

Number your paper 1–10. Choose the correct possessive pronoun from those in parentheses. Write the pronoun in the first column. In the second column write the antecedent.

1. Nobody hits (his, their) stride in the first mile.

2. Somebody has (their, her) eyes shut.

3. Has anybody got (his, their) tools handy?

4. Nobody opens (their, his) present until dinner time.

5. No one has bought (his, their) tickets yet.

6. Has everybody made (their, his) bed?

7. Everybody gave (his, their) version of what happened.

8. Each of the girls was in (her, their) place.

9. Does everybody have (their, his) canteen full?

10. Everybody has (his, its) ups and downs.

Section 5

Using Adjectives

Part 1   What Are Adjectives?

When you write the noun *hills*, you probably have a picture of certain kinds of hills in your mind. Will your reader have the same picture? He or she may not. Do you mean *rolling* hills, *distant* hills, or *steep* hills? Do you mean *purple* hills, *bare* hills, or *rocky* hills? Each one of those words would be doing the work of an adjective.

Adjectives help to give your reader a clear picture of what you are talking about. They limit the meaning of another word and make the meaning more definite. When a word limits the meaning of another word, it is said to **modify** that word. It is called a **modifier.**

An adjective is a word that modifies a noun or a pronoun.

An adjective is one of the eight parts of speech. Noun, pronoun, verb, adjective—these are four of the eight parts of speech.

Adjectives can tell three different kinds of things about the words they modify:

1. *What kind: blue* sky, *hot* oven, *small* jar, *old* house, *beautiful* sunrise
2. *How many: four* bicycles, *several* cars, *many* people, *few* children, *more* letters
3. *Which one or ones: this* book, *that* jet, *these* shoes, *those* passengers

Diagraming Sentences Containing Adjectives

On a diagram, an adjective is shown on a line that slants down from the noun or pronoun it modifies.

Example: A lone tree shades the old cabin.

Exercises **Find the adjectives.**

A. Find the adjectives in the following sentences. Show in writing, as the teacher directs you, how they modify nouns. You need not bother with *a* and *the.*

1. This old car needs continual attention.
2. Sherry is an early bird.

3. Sheep and wriggly lambs crowded into the empty shed.
4. Round objects roll.
5. Rob whipped up a hot, ghastly, peppery sauce.
6. The fat, bespectacled clown led the parade.
7. The car had a flat tire.
8. The ancient windmill made a weird, screechy sound.
9. A young otter ruled the pond and terrorized the smaller inhabitants.
10. A playful young husky pranced ahead of the sled.

B. Copy the following sentences. Write a clear, exact adjective in place of each blank.

1. A _____ string dangled from the light fixture.
2. The _____ basket was full of _____ clothes.
3. The _____ clock has a _____ dial.
4. Have you ever seen such a _____ collection of bottles?
5. The _____ town had _____ buildings on the main street.
6. A _____ statue stood at the _____ intersection.
7. The sky was filled with _____ stars.
8. The _____ ship sailed rapidly through the _____ sea.
9. _____ gophers sat upright in the _____ pasture.
10. A _____ car was parked in front of the _____ house.

Part 2 Predicate Adjectives

Adjectives usually come before the words they modify:

The *tired* and *thirsty* Scouts crawled up the hill.

Sometimes they are put after the words they modify:

The Scouts, *tired* and *thirsty*, crawled up the hill.
(*Tired* and *thirsty* modify Scouts.)

In some sentences, an adjective is separated from the word it modifies by the verb:

The day is *clear*. (*Clear* modifies *day*.)
The election was *close*. (*Close* modifies *election*.)
Does the water look *deep*? (*Deep* modifies *water*.)

The words *clear, close,* and *deep* are in the predicate of the sentence. But each of the adjectives modifies the subject of its sentence. Each one is linked to the subject it modifies by a linking verb. For these reasons they are given a special name. They are called **predicate adjectives.**

A predicate adjective is an adjective in the predicate that modifies the subject.

Exercises **Find the linking verbs and predicate adjectives.**

A. Head three columns *Subject, Linking Verb,* and *Predicate Adjective*. Number your paper 1–10. For each sentence write the words under the appropriate columns.

Example: This water is salty.

Subject	Linking Verb	Predicate Adjective
water	is	salty

1. The plant looked dry.
2. The spinach tastes gritty.
3. The basement smelled damp.
4. My shoes felt sandy.
5. The possibilities are endless.
6. His story sounds fishy to me.
7. This cocoa tastes bitter.
8. The old rug looks clean.
9. Emily seemed sure.
10. That mosquito appears nonchalant.

Follow the directions for Exercise A.

1. That siren sounds close.
2. The rice looks sticky.
3. This board still feels rough.
4. My mother is busy on Thursday.
5. The deal seems questionable.
6. Is the hammer handy?
7. The applause seemed endless.
8. Sharon felt confident.
9. That canoe appears unsafe.
10. These flowers smell good.

Diagraming Sentences Containing Predicate Adjectives

You show predicate adjectives on diagrams just as you show predicate nouns. Place them on the horizontal line following the verb, and separate them from the verb by a line slanting back toward the subject.

Example: The stairs seem steep.

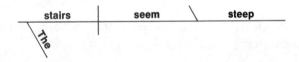

A slanting line shows the relationship between *steep* (predicate adjective) and *stairs* (subject).

Exercise   Find the predicate adjectives.

Copy the sentences and use an arrow to tie the predicate adjectives to the words they modify. Your teacher may wish you to diagram the sentences.

Example: John is musical.

1. That milk is sour.
2. This pencil is sharp.
3. That room seemed stuffy.
4. Does the raft look safe?
5. The teams appeared unequal.
6. Glenda's reply was frank.
7. Marshes always look scummy.
8. His knees felt wobbly.
9. The petals look rough.
10. Their nervousness was understandable.

Part 3 Pronouns Used as Adjectives

Possessive pronouns are often classed as adjectives. As you can see from the following, a possessive pronoun is a modifier because it makes the meaning of a noun more definite:

my book	*his* house	*its* foot	*their* school
your game	*her* ruler	*our* room	

The words *my, your, his, her, its, our,* and *their* are possessive pronouns used as adjectives.

Exercise   Find the pronouns used as adjectives.

Copy the following sentences and draw arrows from the possessive pronouns to the words they modify.

Example: Sue wrote her answer on the board.

1. My banjo is on the mantel.
2. I took my bicycle.
3. The horse has lost its rider.

4. Dick and Elyse brought their stamps.
5. My new book has a red leather cover.
6. The girls are repairing their bicycles.
7. These trousers need to have their cuffs fixed.
8. Their bicycles were chained to the parking meter.
9. The computer stored its information.
10. Jane left her bracelet on the chair.

Possessive Pronouns and Antecedents

Possessive pronouns have antecedents when they are used as adjectives. They must be singular if their antecedents are singular. They must be plural if their antecedents are plural. Look at the following examples:

The dog was chewing its bone.

The arrow is drawn to show that *dog* its the antecedent of *its*. *Dog* is singular; therefore, the singular possessive *its* must be used.

The students have completed their exams.

The arrow is drawn to show that *students* is the antecedent of *their*. *Students* is plural; therefore, the plural possessive *their* must be used.

Exercises **Find the antecedent for the possessive pronoun.**

A. Number your page 1–10. Label two columns *Antecedent* and *Possessive Pronoun*. Put the words in the correct column as shown in the following example.

Example: The parrot put its head on one side.

Antecedent	Possessive Pronoun
parrot	its

1. The book had lost its card.
2. Andy ate his breakfast in silence.
3. Mrs. Montoya threw up her hands.
4. Andrea went back to her embroidery.
5. Mr. Mantel was sweeping his sidewalk.
6. Marty tried his level best.
7. The partridge was trailing its wing.
8. Several pigeons were circling their coop.
9. Gerry didn't like his finished project.
10. The parade followed its usual route.

B. Follow the directions for Exercise A.

1. The students have started their homework.
2. The O'Sheas always opened their pool to the neighbors.
3. Karen caught her kite on the telegraph wire.
4. The ostrich obligingly put its head in the sand.
5. Brenda told us her side of the story.
6. The trees by the lane had lost their leaves.
7. Our car lost its muffler on that road.
8. The baby was always throwing her rattle out of her crib.
9. Tom watched his pet porpoise most of the afternoon.
10. Jessica had lent Jay her guitar.

Part 4 Adjectives in Comparisons

In a room there are three tall boys. Bob is five feet seven inches tall. Tom is five feet six inches tall. Meg is five feet four inches tall. How do we use the word *tall* to show the differences among them? We may say, "Meg is *tall*, Tom is *taller* than Meg, and Bob is the *tallest* of the three."

The Forms of Adjectives

Most adjectives change their forms by adding *-er* or *-est*. You saw how this works with the word *tall*. Notice that adjectives ending in *y* change *y* to *i* before adding *-er* or *-est*.

Adjective	Comparative Form	Superlative Form
old	older	oldest
small	smaller	smallest
shiny	shinier	shiniest
big	bigger	biggest

Notice also that these adjectives are short. Longer adjectives are usually compared by the use of *more* for the comparative and *most* for the superlative.

Adjective	Comparative Form	Superlative Form
beautiful	more beautiful	most beautiful
considerate	more considerate	most considerate

You will see why if you try saying "beautifulest" and "consideratest." These words would be difficult to say smoothly.

The Forms of *Good* and *Bad*

A few adjectives change their forms in other ways, with completely new words for the comparative and superlative forms. Here are two important ones to remember.

good	better	best
bad	worse	worst

Using the Correct Form

In speech or writing, use the comparative form to compare *two* things. Use the superlative form only when you are concerned with *three or more* things.

From these two, choose the one you like *better*.
Our *best* performance was the third one.

Exercises Use the correct form of the adjective.

A. Number your paper 1–10. For each of the following sentences, write the correct form of the adjective, following the directions in parentheses.

> Example: That clock is five minutes (comparative of *fast*) than my watch.

> **Answer:** faster

1. Jill was the (comparative of *young*) of the two.
2. These socks are the (superlative of *dry*).
3. Mr. and Mrs. Wilson's sports store was always (comparative of *busy*) on Saturday.
4. Of the two parks, I like this one (comparative of *good*).
5. This is the (superlative of *bad*) program I've ever seen.
6. My suitcase is (comparative of *heavy*) than yours.
7. It was (comparative of *warm*) in Texas than in Florida.
8. The expressway traffic is (comparative of *bad*) today.
9. Ian's room looks (comparative of *cluttered*) than mine.
10. That was the (superlative of *short*) night of the year.

B. Follow the directions for Exercise A.

1. We need a (comparative of *narrow*) board than this.
2. Lunch was (comparative of *good*) than breakfast.
3. The rinse water was (comparative of *soapy*) than usual.
4. That was the (superlative of *funny*) movie I have ever seen!
5. No school in town has (comparative of *beautiful*) grounds than ours.
6. Greg politely took the (comparative of *small*) piece.
7. That's the (superlative of *bright*) star in the whole sky.

8. This ice cream is (comparative of *hard*).

9. He was (comparative of *underweight*) than his brother.

10. The bus driver was (comparative of *careful*) than most I have seen.

Part 5   Demonstrative Adjectives

The words *this, that, these,* and *those* may be used as modifiers with nouns or pronouns to point out specific things. For example:

1. I liked *this* book, but I really didn't like *that* one.

2. *These* peas are fine, but *those* beans are tasteless.

When used as modifiers, these four words are called **demonstrative adjectives.** They tell *which one* or *which ones* about the nouns they modify. (When they are used by themselves, instead of as modifiers, these words are called **demonstrative pronouns:** I like *that. This* is better.)

Demonstrative Adjective	Demonstrative Pronoun
I liked *this* book.	I liked *this*.
We saw *that* play.	We saw *that*.

Using Demonstrative Adjectives

We use *this* and *that* with singular nouns. We use *these* and *those* with plural nouns.

this skateboard	these skateboards
that club	those clubs

The nouns *kind* and *sort* are singular. Therefore, we say *this kind* and *this sort*. We use *these* and *those* only with the plural: *these kinds* or *those sorts*.

> this kind of car   these kinds of chocolate bars
> that sort of shell   those sorts of programs

Exercises   Using demonstrative adjectives.

A. Find the demonstrative adjectives. Follow your teacher's directions for showing the words they modify.

1. That game of chess was close.
2. You should take some photographs of those puppies.
3. Are those books very interesting?
4. The peaches from that tree are the sweetest.
5. Those bands never come to Jacksonville.
6. This sort is more practical.
7. I like that kind very much.
8. We can use these kinds of things for props for our play.
9. All those dentists have just one receptionist.
10. You have come to the end of this exercise.

B. Fill in the blank with *this kind, that kind, that sort, these sorts,* or *those kinds.* Check that all words are singular, or that all three words are plural. Don't mix them.

> Example: _____ of spaghetti always tastes best.
> *This kind* of spaghetti always tastes best.

1. Mr. Glenn finds _____ of person tiring.
2. _____ of helmets are most expensive.
3. My father always prefers _____ of cars.
4. _____ of questions are too hard.
5. _____ of door is easy to close.
6. She took _____ of clothes to Alaska with her.
7. _____ of stormy day reminds me of last week.
8. _____ of doorknob comes from Hungary.
9. _____ of paint comes off easily.
10. _____ of ski requires a special wax.

Additional Exercises

Using Adjectives

A. Find the adjectives.

Number your paper 1–10. Put the adjectives in one column and the nouns they modify in the other column.

Example: A noisy owl disturbed the deep, silent forest.

Adjectives	Nouns
noisy	owl
deep, silent	forest

1. Dr. Klein is a good dentist.
2. The gold coin had strange words on it.
3. The old boat slid over the calm, smooth waters.
4. The tiny red wagon had been left out in the rain.
5. The bell had a tiny, tinny sound.
6. The immediate echo startled him.
7. There was a long line at the Dairy Queen.
8. I learned it from a reliable source.
9. That enormous jet cannot land at such a small airport.
10. High winds and a heavy surf damaged many vacant homes.

B. Find the linking verbs and predicate adjectives.

Head three columns *Subject, Linking Verb,* and *Predicate Adjective.* Number your paper 1–10. For each sentence write the words under the appropriate columns.

1. The ocean looked calm.

2. Those cookies taste stale.
3. Brooke and I were tired.
4. The big room appeared ready.
5. Our puppy is always excited.
6. The music sounded louder in the gymnasium.
7. Their future looks great.
8. A basic change appears certain.
9. Your cough sounds better this morning.
10. All reindeer are herbiverous.

C. Find the antecedent for the possessive pronoun.

Number your paper 1–10. Label two columns *Antecedent* and *Possessive Pronoun.* Put the words in the correct column.

1. Gretchen returned her books to the library.
2. The bluejay fed its young.
3. A cherub had its halo on crooked.
4. The automatic timer started its cycle.
5. Jeremy's sister is washing her car.
6. The returning tide brought its gifts.
7. Nan gave John her ice cream cone to hold.
8. The can has lost its label.
9. Randi and Marlene were showing the others their prizes.
10. The hailstorm certainly took its toll.

D. Comparative and superlative forms of adjectives.

Number your paper 1–10. Write the correct form of the adjective, following the directions in parentheses.

1. Kent is the (superlative of *short*) person on the team.
2. That trail was (comparative of *interesting*) than the other.

3. Sears Tower in Chicago is the world's (superlative of *tall*) building.

4. These questions are (comparative of *tricky*).

5. Mr. Berry had the (superlative of *pretty*) flowers in town.

6. Have you ever heard a (comparative of *good*) band than this?

7. That question seems a lot (comparative of *hard*).

8. These math problems are (comparative of *easy*) than the others.

9. This wall looks (comparative of *white*) than that one.

10. Her small car is (comparative of *economical*) than his.

E. Use demonstrative adjectives.

Find the demonstrative adjectives. Follow your teacher's directions for showing the words they modify.

1. This time of year is often hot.
2. Mrs. Cook always reads that kind of mystery.
3. Those gloves are too small.
4. That clock is way off.
5. Take those shoes with you.
6. Do you like working with those kinds of tools?
7. This sort of weather is fine with me.
8. This kind of rucksack doesn't hold much.
9. Those shoelaces are so long they trip me.
10. That batter is too runny.

Section 6

Using Adverbs

Part 1   What Are Adverbs?

Two parts of speech are used as modifiers. You have already studied adjectives, which modify nouns and pronouns. Now we come to the second kind of modifier: **adverbs.**

Adverbs Modify Verbs.

We walked.

How? We walked *slowly*.

Where? We walked *out.*

When? We walked *yesterday.*

Adverbs Modify Adjectives.

It was a *clear* day.

How clear? It was a *fairly* clear day.

I was *late.*

To what extent? I was *very* late.

The problem was *difficult.*

How difficult? The problem was *too* difficult.

Adverbs Modify Other Adverbs.

Joe talked *fast.*

How fast? Joe talked *extremely* fast.

Irene danced *happily.*

How happily? Irene danced *most* happily.

The ball rolled *away.*

To what extent? The ball rolled *far* away.

Adverbs are words that modify verbs, adjectives, and other adverbs.

Exercises   Find the adverbs

A. Copy each sentence. Draw an arrow from the adverb to the word or words it modifies.

Example: Ms. James had come early.

1. Our puppy barked eagerly.
2. He will leave tomorrow.
3. The rain fell heavily.
4. They ran swiftly.
5. The Warners had parked nearby.
6. Ben scored easily.
7. The water rose steadily.
8. Sandra plays tennis regularly.
9. Have you skied lately?
10. The skiers raced daringly down the slopes.

B. Copy each sentence. Draw an arrow from the adverb to the word it modifies.

Example: My shoes are too wet.

1. The closet is cleaner now.
2. His presentation was very long.
3. The gymnast gracefully performed her floor exercise.
4. Scott was extremely quiet.
5. A performance by that symphony orchestra can never be too long.
6. Luanne's speech was quite long.
7. The hat with that outfit looked simply ridiculous.
8. The movie was terribly funny.
9. Chris and Bruce are definitely running for office.
10. The base runner easily stole second.

The Position of Adverbs

When an adverb modifies an adjective or another adverb, it usually comes before the word it modifies: *very* hot, *quite* still, *not* often.

But when an adverb modifies a verb, its position is not usually fixed. I see *now*. *Now* I see. I *now* see.

Diagraming Sentences Containing Adverbs

Adverbs, like adjectives, are shown on diagrams on slanting lines attached to the words they modify. The following diagram shows an adverb modifying a verb:

Finally the lazy boy raised his hand.

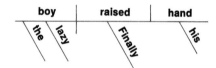

Notice that *Finally*, the first word in the sentence, keeps its capital *F* in the diagram.

The next diagram shows one adverb modifying an adjective and another modifying an adverb:

Some fairly young children play musical instruments quite well.

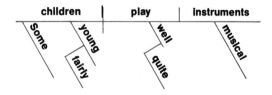

Notice how *fairly* is attached to *young*. Notice how *quite* is attached to *well*.

Exercises   Use adverbs.

A. Rewrite the following sentences, supplying adverbs that answer the questions. Indicate, as your teacher directs, what each adverb modifies.

> Example: Wash the dishes. *When?*
>
> Wash the dishes *now.*

1. Bring your books. *When?*
2. The monkey climbed. *How?*
3. The elevator started. *Where?*
4. The sunset was beautiful. *How beautiful?*
5. The damaged plane arrived. *When?*
6. The runners rounded the turn. *How?*
7. Jack slept soundly. *How soundly?*
8. The deer raised its head and looked. *Looked where?*
9. Did your cousin arrive? *When?*
10. The bird flew. *Where?*

B. Write sentences using the following adverbs. Use an adverb as the first word in half of your sentences.

1. closely	4. finally	7. quietly	10. fairly
2. speedily	5. forcefully	8. often	11. quite
3. now	6. nearly	9. away	12. soon

C. You saw on page 134 that certain adverbs appear in three positions: after the verb (I see *now*), at the beginning of a sentence (*Now* I see), and just before the verb (I *now* see). Can you change the position of other adverbs? Here are some to experiment with:

often	finally	away	over
in	there	sometimes	out
already	then	together	quietly

D. Do you say *We went together away* or *We went away together?* You say the second, and you do it naturally, without thinking about it.

Do you say *Then we went there out, There we out went then, Out we then went there,* or what? Again, there is a form that you use naturally.

Experiment with the adverbs in Exercise C to see how they fit with each other in two-adverb and three-adverb sentences.

Part 2 Adverbs in Comparisons

Most adverbs that end in *-ly* form the comparative with the word *more*. They form the superlative with the word *most*. For example:

Adverb	Comparative	Superlative
quickly	more quickly	most quickly
deeply	more deeply	most deeply
swiftly	more swiftly	most swiftly

Some adverbs add *-er* for the comparative and *-est* for the superlative. For example:

Adverb	Comparative	Superlative
soon	sooner	soonest
fast	faster	fastest

Some adverbs make their comparative and superlative forms by complete word changes. For example:

Adverb	Comparative	Superlative
well	better	best
much	more	most
little	less	least

Exercises Use the correct forms of adverbs.

A. For each of these sentences, write the correct form for the adverb, following the directions in parentheses.

Example: Avis tries (comparative of *hard*):

Answer: harder

1. He wrapped the next package (comparative of *carefully*).
2. Nobody can count money (comparative of *well*) than she.
3. I wished he would drive (comparative of *slowly*).
4. Our relay team could run the (superlative of *fast*) of all the schools.
5. I walked into the library (comparative of *quietly*) than before.
6. Follow this (comparative of *closely*).
7. We entered the library (comparative of *quietly*).
8. Ray cleared the high jump (superlative of *easily*).
9. My dog drinks (comparative of *noisily*) than any other dog I know.
10. Salina tried (comparative of *hard*) than all the others.

B. For each of these sentences, write the correct form for the adverb, following the directions in parentheses.

1. Our friends stayed (comparative of *long*) than usual.
2. A snail walks (comparative of *fast*) than Joe.
3. Ted usually wakes up (superlative of *early*).
4. Dr. Parr got home from Brazil (comparative of *soon*) than her postcards.
5. That package took the (superlative of *long*) to arrive.
6. No one draws (comparative of *well*) than Sue.
7. I reread the short story (comparative of *carefully*) the second time.
8. Speak (comparative of *distinctly*), please.

9. That driver approached the bridge (comparative of *cautiously*) than the others.

10. This door opened (comparative of *easily*) than the other.

Finding Adjectives and Adverbs

To use adjectives and adverbs correctly, you must learn to recognize them in sentences. When you see a word, ask yourself what it does in its sentence. Use this method:

1. Soon night came. *Problem:* Is *soon* an adjective or is it an adverb?

Question: Does *soon* tell what kind of night? Answer: No. Then it is not an adjective.

Question: Does *soon* answer a question about the verb? Answer: Yes—*came when? Soon.*

Answer to problem: Soon is an adverb, modifying *came.*

2. The situation is quite serious. *Problem:* Is *quite* an adjective or is it an adverb?

Question: What does *quite* do? Answer: It modifies *serious.* It tells *how serious.*

Question: What is *serious?* Answer: *Serious* is a predicate adjective modifying the noun *problem.*

Answer to problem: Then *quite* is an adverb modifying the adjective *serious.*

Using Adjectives and Adverbs Correctly

In the following sentences, notice the reasons for the choices between words.

1. He writes (good, well).
(The word *well* is an adverb modifying the verb *writes.*)

2. Roses smell (sweet, sweetly).
(*sweet* is a predicate adjective.)

3. We were (terrible, terribly) late.
(*terribly*, an adverb, modifies *late*, a predicate adjective.)

4. It tastes (good, well).
(*Good* is a predicate adjective.)

5. Rick is (bigger, more bigger) than Bob.
(The comparative of *big* is *bigger*. *Bigger* is a predicate adjective.)

Exercises   **Choose the right modifier.**

A. Write the correct word for each of the following sentences. Be ready to tell why it is correct.

> Example: White's Pond looks (clean, cleanly) enough for swimming.
>
> **Answer:** *Clean* is a predicate adjective modifying *White's Pond.*

1. The bread smells (fresh, freshly).
2. Are you (near, nearly) through?
3. This way is (more quickly, quicker).
4. That's a (real, really) tough question.
5. He lined up his airplane collection (neat, neatly).
6. May plays the piano (good, well), doesn't she?
7. The new girl watched the preparations (shy, shyly).
8. The puppy appeared (hungry, hungrily).
9. The graduates walked (quiet, quietly) through the corridors to the auditorium.
10. Ms. Kimball and Mr. Murphy felt (more strongly, stronger) about the council's decision.

B. Write the correct word in each of the following sentences and tell why it is correct.

1. The auctioneer gave the (most brief, briefest) nod.
2. That pie smells (wonderfully, wonderful)!
3. This building is (bigger, more bigger) than that one.

4. Your centerpiece looks (beautiful, beautifully).

5. Mrs. Becket answered (more gently, more gentle).

6. The squad looked (envious, enviously) at the first-place trophy.

7. My dog soon became (smarter, more smarter).

8. John felt (bad, badly) about the accident.

9. He didn't do so (good, well) this time.

10. The students moved (quiet, quietly) through the halls during the fire drill.

c. On a sheet of paper, write adjectives or adverbs that fit in the spaces in the following sentences.

1. A _____ _____ car came _____ down the road.

2. _____ stapler works _____ _____ .

3. _____ cake looks _____ and _____ .

4. _____ people _____ seem _____ .

5. Have you _____ ridden a _____ horse?

6. A _____ light shone across the _____ room.

7. The _____ bear stared _____ at the zoo visitors.

8. Miles of _____ beaches in Australia are _____ deserted.

9. The _____ noise was _____ annoying.

10. The little _____ Fiat moved _____ down the avenue.

Additional Exercises

Using Adverbs

A. Find the adverbs.

Copy each sentence. Draw an arrow from the adverb to the word it modifies. Watch for double adverbs.

Example: Their spaniel learned surprisingly slowly.

1. The man replied very warmly.
2. Her letter came amazingly quickly.
3. The helicopter landed quickly on the hospital roof.
4. Gretchen arrived too late.
5. He goes to Knoxville quite regularly.
6. The tomato plants will probably survive.
7. Surprisingly, the rain stopped.
8. They smiled at each other mischievously.
9. She hiccoughed rather loudly.
10. Emily moved to Talcott fairly recently.

B. Add adverbs.

Rewrite the following sentences supplying adverbs that answer the questions. Show the word or words each adverb modifies.

1. Katie and I walked _____. (*Where?*)
2. We went to the museum _____. (*When?*)
3. The neighbor's dog barks _____. (*How?*)
4. The horses are _____. (*Where?*)
5. Lynn and Tad arrived _____. (*When?*)

6. I will get it _____ (*When?*)
7. The snow melted _____. (*How?*)
8. Lee will bring you the package _____. (*When?*)
9. Leave your wet boots _____. (*Where?*)
10. Mr. Smalley replied _____. (*How?*)

C. Use the correct form of adverbs.

For each of these sentences, write the correct form for the adverb, following the directions in parentheses.

1. The parcel will come (comparative of *quickly*) by plane.
2. He went on (comparative of *quietly*) with what he was doing.
3. The boys ate (comparative of *little*) than he expected.
4. Beth got home the (superlative of *late*).
5. The tennis team practiced (comparative of *hard*) than ever before.
6. The guests stayed (comparative of *late*) than we had expected.
7. Penny and Mike reacted (comparative of *slowly*) than the others.
8. The day seemed to go (comparative of *fast*) than yesterday.
9. Of all the contestants, Michelle tried (superlative of *hard*).
10. It happens (superlative of *often*) in August.

D. Choose the right modifier.

Write the correct word for each of the following sentences.

1. The goat gave an (occasionally, occasional) bleat.
2. Just then Sandra looked up (brightly, bright).

3. Scotch tape is sometimes (usefuller, more useful) than glue.

4. He went (most recent, most recently) to Pakistan.

5. The backpackers grew (uneasy, uneasily) as they approached the summit.

6. Willie retraced his steps (more carefully, most carefully) the second time.

7. This calculator is (more better, better) than that one.

8. Kris came (more late, later).

9. (Occasional, Occasionally) Ms. Larson gave us an unannounced quiz.

10. My math grades have improved (considerable, considerably).

E. Add a suitable modifier.

Rewrite the following sentences, filling in the blanks with suitable modifiers.

1. The _____ motor ran _____ _____.
2. _____ _____ coat hangers clattered _____ to the floor.
3. The _____ airplane taxied _____ down the runway.
4. His _____ feet would not fit the _____ tennis shoes.
5. The _____ test was _____.
6. Skiing takes _____ _____ nerves.
7. Four _____ buses lined up by the _____ entrance.
8. The _____ cactus stood _____ in the sunlight.
9. Gail _____ flung her _____ jacket and books _____.
10. Their car looked _____ _____.

Section 7

Using Prepositions and Conjunctions

Part 1   What Are Prepositions?

The word *preposition* has two parts: *pre*, meaning "before," and *position*. A preposition is a word that stands before its object and shows the relationship between that object and another word in the sentence.

> Examples: to the store (*to* is the preposition; *store* is its object.)
>
> along the street (*along* is the preposition; *street* is the object.)

Standing before another word is only one function of a preposition. Its real job is to tie its object to some other word in the sentence. Usually this other word appears just before the preposition.

Examples: I walked *to the store.*   I strolled *along the street.*

In the first example, notice that *store* is connected with *walked* by the preposition *to.* In the second example, notice that *street* is connected with *strolled* by the preposition *along.*

A preposition is a word that relates its object to some other word in the sentence.

Of course we cannot tell what part of speech a word is until we see how the word is used in a sentence. But here are some words that we often use as prepositions:

about	at	but (except)	into	through
above	before	by	near	to
across	behind	down	of	toward
after	below	during	on	under
against	beneath	for	out	underneath
along	beside	from	outside	until
among	between	in	over	up
around	beyond	inside	past	with

Exercises   **Find the prepositions.**

A. Number your paper 1–10. Write the preposition in each of the following sentences.

Example: The robin balanced on the clothesline.

on

1. Lee stumbled up the steps.
2. Thursday comes before Friday.
3. Around three o'clock it got cooler.
4. In the box was a small tape recorder.
5. Chris always drives under the speed limit.

6. The apricots are on the table.
7. The pitchfork was leaning against the door.
8. Nobody is here but me.
9. The new church will be between these two houses.
10. Mr. Craig pulled his shopping cart down the street.

B. Complete the sentences that follow. How many prepositions can you find for each blank space? If you need a guide, refer to the list of prepositions given on page 148.

Example: Put the paper _____ the book. (in, on, under, beside, over, with)

1. Joe read the exercise _____ his sister.
2. The mice played _____ the woodbox.
3. I sat _____ Nancy and Bill.
4. Tony's Korean kite dived _____ the trees.
5. _____ the front door is the wreath.
6. The snow fell _____ the roof.
7. _____ the field we found a meadowlark's nest.
8. There was one white horse _____ many black ones.
9. That girl _____ the water swims well.
10. These five boys played _____ us.

Part 2 Using Nouns as Objects of Prepositions

Here are the words most often used as prepositions:

at	on	from	during
beneath	to	up	along
by	into	beside	
for	down	under	
in	of	about	

You have seen that nouns are used as subjects, direct objects, and indirect objects of verbs. Nouns are also used as objects of prepositions. Here are some examples:

> The boys stood behind the *flagpole.*
> Brian played with the *children.*
> The groceries are in the *car.*
> This play is by the younger *girls.*
> Ann talked to *Jerry.*
> What are we having for *dinner?*

Exercise Find nouns used as objects of prepositions.

Number your page from 1–10. Make two columns entitled *Preposition* and *Object.* For each sentence write the preposition and its object.

Example: There was the trail of a crab in the sand.

Preposition	Object
of	crab
in	sand

1. They walked along the edge of the lagoon.
2. Jay rushed into the room with the timetable.
3. Pat and Leslie walked along the beach with their dog.
4. Kevin looked closely at the big bluefish.
5. At a cry from its mother, the baby killdeer squats obediently on the ground.
6. Joan climbed up the ladder and onto the roof.
7. After school, we went to the pool.
8. Bob sat beside the fire and talked to his mother about the book.
9. A spider ran across the ceiling in a hurry.
10. All kinds of tropical fish were swimming in the tank.

Part 3 Using Pronouns as Objects of Prepositions

The object forms of pronouns are used for objects of prepositions.

Here are the object forms you need to know:

me   us   her   him   them   whom

Examples: 1. Bring the ball *to me*.
2. The dog sat *between us*.
3. There are four *of them*.

The word *whom* is the object form of the interrogative pronoun. *Who* is the subject form.

1. *Who* has the camera?
2. *To whom* did you speak?

Compound Objects

We seldom make a mistake in using a single pronoun directly after a preposition. But some people are confused when the object of a preposition is compound.

Simple Object	Compound Object
Take it to *her*.	Take it to *Mary* and *her*.
Come with *me*.	Come with *her* and *me*.
We worked for *him*.	We worked for *Homer* and *him*.

Here is a way to test compound objects:

Say the pronoun alone with its preposition. Then say it in the complete sentence.

Example: These tickets are for Pam and (he, him).

These tickets are for *him*.
These tickets are for Pam and *him*.

Using *Between* and *Among*

The prepositions *between* and *among* can sometimes be troublesome. We use *between* when we speak of two people or things. We use *among* when we speak of three or more.

1. Ginny sat between Nick and *me.*
2. There were several arguments between the referees and *us.*
1. Divide the profits among the French club, the Council, and *them.*
2. The final decision will be made among Allyson, Jon, and *me.*

Exercises   **Pronouns used as objects of prepositions.**

A. Choose the correct pronoun from the two given in parentheses. Write it with the preposition.

> Example: Look at Amanda and (he, him).
>
> **Answer:** at him

1. Give the tickets to Craig and (I, me).
2. This is for Glenn and (she, her).
3. Sit between Lisa and (he, him).
4. The folksong was sung by Marilu and (she, her).
5. Wendy arrived before Lin and (I, me).
6. Mrs. Cowles was looking for Sally and (she, her).
7. The scarf is from Elise and (we, us).
8. Dave and Kelly are coming with Terry and (I, me).
9. Jack always sits near Don and (he, him).
10. Mr. Walters was talking about Sue and (I, me).

B. Choose the correct pronoun from the two given in parentheses. Write it with the preposition.

1. Hal stood behind Tracy and (we, us).
2. We gave the score sheets to the coach and (he, him).

3. Finally the nurse looked at Bill and (I, me).
4. Beside Karen and (he, him) were their parents.
5. I almost fell over Amy and (she, her).
6. Mrs. Sims bought tickets for Judy and (I, me).
7. The presentation was given by Sara and (her, she).
8. Nobody was there except Mr. Parks and (I, me).
9. The ball fell between Steve and (he, him).
10. Roger was talking about Robin and (she, her).

C. Choose the correct pronoun from the two given in parentheses. Write it with the preposition.

1. from Ted and (I, me)
2. with Jack and (he, him)
3. for you and (we, us)
4. between Joy and (she, her)
5. beside them and (we, us)
6. toward Sally and (I, me)
7. between Carl and (he, him)
8. near Ellen and (I, me)
9. to Jim and (he, him)
10. at Sam and (I, me)
11. around Cathy and (she, her)
12. from Dan and (I, me)
13. beyond Peg and (she, her)
14. behind Penny and (he, him)
15. to him and (I, me)
16. past them and (we, us)
17. after Vicki and (she, her)
18. before Pete and (he, him)
19. beneath him and (I, me)
20. about them and (we, us)

Part 4 Using Prepositional Phrases

The group of words that includes a preposition and its object is a **prepositional phrase.** Words that modify the object are also part of the phrase.

Examples: Jim found my book *in his locker.*
The present was wrapped *in green paper.*

The prepositional phrases in these sentences are *in his locker* and *in green paper.*

If the preposition has two objects (a compound object), both are included in the prepositional phrase.

Example: My gift from Mother and Dad was a watch.

From Mother and Dad is a prepositional phrase with a compound object.

Exercises   Find the prepositional phrases.

A. On a separate sheet of paper write all the prepositional phrases in the following sentences.

Example: He ran to the door without shoes and socks.

to the door
without shoes and socks (a compound object)

1. A batting cage is behind home plate.
2. Terry slid into second base.
3. The picture fell off the wall during the night.
4. Behind the garage is a row of sunflowers.
5. The Cullens went from Seattle to San Diego by train.
6. Attach the shells to the frame with this glue.
7. Gail was waiting for the crackers and cheese.
8. There was dust under her bed.
9. The sailboat was drifting toward the breakwater and those sandbars.
10. Brad is waiting for you in the lobby.

B. On a separate sheet of paper write all the prepositional phrases in the following sentences.

1. Juanita fed the dollar to the change machine.
2. The program began after a brief announcement by the principal.
3. They built their bonfire by the light of the moon.
4. Go through that door and up the stairs, and leave the package there.
5. My brother was babysitting with Barb, Drew, and Jo.
6. Never look a gift horse in the mouth.
7. We visited Lincoln's home in Springfield.
8. Under the bridge the river flowed swiftly.
9. The group of skiers was taking the bus to Aspen.
10. The band marched briskly down the street.

Prepositional Phrases as Modifiers

Prepositional phrases do the same work in a sentence as adjectives and adverbs.

A phrase that modifies a noun or pronoun is an adjective phrase.

Examples: The bottom *of those jeans* was dirty.

He was washing the window *over the sink*.

The procession passed the statue *of Lincoln*.

A phrase that modifies a verb is an adverbial phrase.

Examples: They swam *under the bridge*.

The crowd ate *in shifts*.

The geyser erupted *at noon*.

Diagraming Sentences Containing Prepositional Phrases

Since a prepositional phrase does the work of an adjective or an adverb, you diagram it like an adjective or an adverb. Write the preposition on a line slanting down from the word modified. Then, on a horizontal line attached to the preposition line, write the object. Anything modifying the object slants down from it. Notice in the following diagram that the object of a preposition (*rim*) may be modified by another phrase (*of the volcano*).

Example: In the morning we walked to the rim of the volcano.

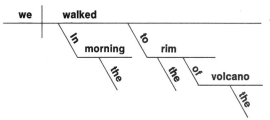

A prepositional phrase containing a compound object is diagramed in a similar way.

Example: Trucks with fruit and vegetables attracted the passers-by.

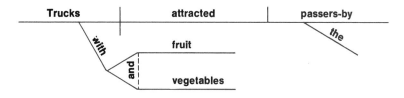

In this sentence, the phrase *with fruit and vegetables* is an adjective phrase modifying the noun *trucks*. The prepositional line therefore slants away from the word *trucks*. The line for the object of the preposition is split, because it is a compound object.

Exercises   Find adjective and adverb prepositional phrases.

A. Make three columns marked *Word Modified*, *Phrase*, and *Kind of Phrase*. For each prepositional phrase in the following sentences, fill in the information under the three columns.

Example: Under the planks, Gary could always find worms for bait.

Word Modified	Phrase	Kind of Phrase
could find	under the planks	adverb phrase
worms	for bait	adjective phrase

1. The doughnuts sizzled in the frying pan.
2. Someone called about noon.
3. At the corner they built a new sign.
4. The buttons on his sleeve caught in the door.
5. Four girls on the team waited in the office.
6. Put Jack's books behind the big chair.
7. In the afternoon, the class went to a bakery.
8. The closet beneath the stairs is for brooms.
9. Dad had already put the pizzas in the oven.
10. On his birthday he always has cake with chocolate icing.

B. Find the prepositional phrases in the following sentences. Tell whether each phrase is used as an adjective or adverb. Write the answers as your teacher indicates.

1. The Brown County art colony in Indiana is famous.
2. He didn't look under the couch.
3. Sheila stopped patiently on the landing.
4. After a while, the cars started at a snail's pace.
5. I saw a strange Siamese cat in the alley.
6. The hikers had blisters on their feet.

7. Gulls flocked around the fishing boats.

8. The Mannings went through the Blue Ridge Mountains on their trip.

9. In the greenhouse they grew three kinds of violets.

10. In the fifth inning, the first batter for the Tigers hit a home run.

Part 5 Preposition or Adverb?

A number of words that are used as prepositions are also used as adverbs.

Examples: 1. Tony walked *on*. (adverb)
Tony walked *on* the sidewalk. (preposition)
2. We went *down*. (adverb)
We went *down* the ladder. (preposition)

When you are in doubt as to whether a word is an adverb or a preposition, see how it is used. If it introduces a phrase, it is probably a preposition. If it is used alone, it is probably an adverb.

Exercises Prepositions and adverbs

A. In each pair of sentences that follows, there is one adverb and one preposition. Number your paper 1–10. After each number, write a and b. After each letter, write *preposition* or *adverb*, depending on which you find.

Example: (a) He heard a noise below.
(b) He heard a noise below the window.

(a) adverb
(b) preposition

1. (a) Come up the stairs. (b) Come up.

2. (a) The children stayed in the house all day. (b) The children stayed in.

3. (a) Terry walked along. (b) Terry walked along the shore.

4. (a) Behind came Joanne. (b) Behind us came Joanne.

5. (a) Above our heads shone the sun. (b) Above, the sun shone.

6. (a) The bear cub rolled over. (b) The cub rolled over his brother.

7. (a) We had not met before the game. (b) We had not met before.

8. (a) The blanket goes beneath. (b) The blanket goes beneath the saddle.

9. (a) We climbed out. (b) We climbed out the window.

10. (a) The ball fell through the net. (b) The ball fell through.

B. Follow the directions for Exercise A.

1. (a) The doctor is in. (b) Dr. Rayner is in her office.

2. (a) The dog ran beside the motorcycle. (b) The dog ran beside.

3. (a) Beyond lay the Smoky Mountains. (b) Beyond the town lay the Smoky Mountains.

4. (a) The picture fell off. (b) The picture fell off the wall.

5. (a) They went inside the model home. (b) They went inside.

6. (a) The train went through. (b) The train went through the village.

7. (a) They drove past. (b) They drove past the theater.

8. (a) The boys waited outside the gym. (b) The boys waited outside.

9. (a) We went inside. (b) We went inside the gymnasium.

10. (a) I've heard that song before. (b) I've heard that song before today.

Part 6   Beginning Sentences with Prepositional Phrases

Sometimes, for the sake of emphasis, or variety, we begin a sentence with a prepositional phrase. Study the following example.

> We saw a brilliant flash at that very moment.
> At that very moment, we saw a brilliant flash.

It is not necessarily better to start a sentence with a prepositional phrase. However, if the sentences in your composition have been starting pretty regularly with the subject, a different beginning will give variety. A variety of sentence openings makes more interesting reading.

Exercises   **Begin sentences with prepositional phrases.**

On a piece of paper, rewrite the following sentences so that each begins with a prepositional phrase. If the phrase is a long one, place a comma after it.

1. We left for the East on the following morning.
2. We drove along the lake for some time.
3. We saw nothing but sand dunes at one place.
4. We visited a glass factory in Indiana.
5. We came to the Ohio River after that.
6. We passed many coal mines in Pennsylvania.
7. We crossed the historic Delaware River at Trenton.
8. We arrived in New York on a very rainy day.
9. We spent several hours at the Bronx Zoo on Monday.
10. We took a wonderful boat ride around Manhattan on the last day of our visit.

Part 7 Putting Prepositional Phrases in the Right Place

You have seen that some prepositional phrases may be moved from one position to another in some sentences without changing the meaning. Sometimes, however, the position of a prepositional phrase makes a great deal of difference in the meaning of the sentence.

> Example: Patrick met the mail carrier in his robe.
>
> In his robe, Patrick met the mail carrier.
>
> Patrick, in his robe, met the mail carrier.

The first sentence is awkward because the phrase *in his robe* seems to modify *mail carrier*. The second and third sentences bring the phrase where it should be: closer to *Patrick*, the word it modifies. An adjective phrase should be placed either directly before or directly after the word it modifies.

Exercises Use prepositional phrases correctly.

A. The following sentences are awkward. By changing the position of one phrase in each sentence, you can make the meaning clear. Rewrite each sentence in this manner.

1. David mailed his request to the senator from Kansas in a great hurry.

2. Jean wrote several long letters to the director on her typewriter.

3. John stood on tiptoe and reached for the string beans with long arms.

4. The boys hurried after the ice cream truck on their bicycles.

5. With his big straw stomach Al laughed at the scarecrow.

6. There is some Fresca for the boys on the kitchen table.

7. We saw a big white horse beside a brook with a long flowing tail.

8. With his elephant gun the chickadee watched the hunter.

9. A rabbit ran across the street with long ears.

10. Grandpa picked up the baby with a pipe in his mouth.

B. Follow the directions for Exercise A.

1. Dan told everyone about his high dive at breakfast.

2. The woman looked at the book with the green umbrella.

3. That tall girl caught the ball with the striped T-shirt.

4. The game was played at the stadium between the Tigers and the Indians.

5. The clock stopped by the water fountain at 3:30.

6. Was he the only one who could do cartwheels on the gymnastics team?

7. The baby wanted its mother in the highchair.

8. Kathy has a letter from a friend in her desk.

9. Carol and I startled the mail carrier in our costumes.

10. That money is for the tollway on the dashboard.

Part 8   What Are Conjunctions?

What is missing in these sentences?

1. Jill's puppy ____?____ our cat like to play together.

2. John went, ____?____ Lee didn't go with him.

3. Either Bill ____?____ Sally has the tickets.

The missing words are **conjunctions.**

A conjunction is a word that connects words or groups of words.

A conjunction is one of the eight parts of speech.

Coordinating conjunctions join only words or groups of words that are of equal importance. Coordinating conjunctions are *and, but,* and *or.* Most words or groups of words joined by coordinating conjunctions are called **compound constructions.**

Conjunctions Join Words

These sentences show how coordinating conjunctions connect equal words:

1. Either **Mark** or **he** will fix it. (*or* connects *Mark* and *he,* making them a compound subject of the verb *fix.*)
2. Kent **shot** and **scored.** (*and* connects *shot* and *scored,* verbs that form the compound verb.)
3. We need **string** and **tape.** (*and* connects *string* and *tape,* making them a compound direct object of the verb *need.*)
4. Give **Susan** or **her** the mail. (*or* connects *Susan* and *her,* the compound indirect object of *give.*)
5. The suitcase was **light** but **awkward.** (*but* connects *light* and *awkward,* predicate adjectives.)
6. He spoke **briefly** but **well.** (*but* connects the adverbs *briefly* and *well.*)
7. Give it to **Andrea** or **her.** (*or* connects *Andrea* and *her,* the compound objects of the preposition *to.*)

Exercises Using compound constructions

A. Number your paper from 1–10. Write down the kind of compound construction you find in each sentence. Write the construction with its conjunction.

Example: Wear your dress or your jeans.

Compound direct object: dress or jeans

1. Barbara and Randy agreed.

2. The audience cheered and applauded.
3. The train whistle sounded faint and mournful.
4. We gave our coach and managers a trophy.
5. We play either South or Central next week.
6. The baby chicks were already up and about.
7. Diving lessons and tennis are Jill's main interests.
8. Part of the dress and jacket are cotton.
9. Sheer Music looked up and whinnied.
10. Bottles or cups will do.

B. Follow the directions for Exercise A.

1. The travelers waved and smiled.
2. Dad and Mother bought a rocking chair.
3. His story was unbelievable but true.
4. Lori carefully but quickly explained.
5. The lettering on the posters and banners is too small.
6. Slowly and thoughtfully he wound the clock.
7. Janette found the address and its location.
8. We waited throughout the afternoon and evening.
9. The biggest tractor on the lot was green and yellow.
10. She could have given you or Pat a chance.

C. Write sentences containing the constructions asked for.

Example: Compound direct object. Use two nouns.
Did you bring my *glove* and *bat?*

1. Compound direct object. Use a noun and a pronoun.
2. Compound indirect object. Use a noun and a pronoun.
3. Compound object of a preposition.
4. Compound subject. Use a noun and a pronoun.
5. Compound predicate noun.
6. Compound predicate adjective.
7. Compound verb.
8. Compound adjective.

Additional Exercises

Using Prepositions and Conjunctions

A. Find the prepositions.

Number your paper 1–10. List the prepositions in the following sentences.

1. That limerick was written by Shelly.
2. The oak tree is near the cemetery.
3. Ryan first looked through his tools.
4. Beside the river were several picnic tables.
5. Near the shore were two wet sailors.
6. During suppertime we received six phone calls.
7. The 747 flew over Saunders' farm.
8. Chris strolled past the bank.
9. There was a crate of watermelons in the truck.
10. Whom was he talking to?

B. Find the prepositional phrases.

On a separate sheet of paper, write all the prepositional phrases in the following sentences.

1. The helicopter rumbled across the sky.
2. We went to the restaurant near the theater.
3. She jumped on her bicycle and rode to the parade.
4. They were standing by the window eating tarts with blueberries on them.
5. She covered the rising bread with a cloth.
6. We were playing near the fieldhouse with Dan and David.

7. Two letters arrived for my grandfather.
8. The plane landed near San Jose.
9. The minibikes raced over the hill and toward the river.
10. For a minute the eagle stared at Sandy.

C. Find adjective and adverbial prepositional phrases.

Find the prepositional phrases in the following sentences. Tell whether each phrase is used as an adjective or adverb. Write the answers as your teacher directs.

1. The oven heats in a few minutes.
2. The music box in Murphy's store looks expensive.
3. An ant highway ran between the bucket and the pump.
4. The bear cubs went into their den.
5. Several boys in Peter's class work with Dr. Parker.
6. From the trunks of maple trees hung tin pails.
7. We built a greenhouse near the toolshed.
8. In all probability he will come around noon.
9. The umpire behind the plate is Mr. Edens.
10. The pilot of that plane is my sister.

D. Tell the difference between prepositions and adverbs.

In each pair of sentences, there is one adverb and one preposition. Number your paper 1–5. After each number write *a* and *b*. After each letter, write *preposition* or *adverb*, depending on which you find.

1. (a) Joy looked in. (b) Joy looked in the closet.
2. (a) Sylvia pedaled slowly by. (b) Sylvia pedaled slowly by the old mill.
3. (a) Laura and Tina looked around the shopping mall. (b) Laura and Tina looked around.
4. (a) We drove past the new office. (b) We drove past.
5. (a) We went across. (b) We went across the parkway.

E. Use prepositional phrases correctly.

The following sentences are awkward. By changing the position of one phrase in each sentence, you can make the meaning clear. Rewrite each sentence in this manner.

1. Does anyone know how to use a typewriter in this room?
2. Marsha told about her airplane trip in her speech class.
3. He put the pickles on the table for supper in the crock.
4. Can anyone fix this tape recorder in this class?
5. She leaned against the wall with a happy smile.
6. The convict revealed how he had escaped from prison in a letter.
7. There are some cookies for the children on the TV tray.
8. There is a letter from Grandma and Grandpa on the kitchen table.
9. The stereo was playing Peter Frampton's new album for the tenth time.
10. They let the water run through a misunderstanding.

F. Using compound constructions.

Number your paper from 1–10. Write down the kind of compound construction you find in each sentence. Write the construction with its conjunction.

1. Time and tide wait for no one.
2. Give me butter but no jam, please.
3. We visited Philadelphia and Hershey.
4. Should we go to the aquarium or to the museum?
5. Apparently money and security are important to him.
6. Sooner or later spring must come.
7. Marie ran up and down the stairs.
8. The countryside around Davisville was hilly and green.
9. I could tell you and Sherry the answer.
10. I will make you and Kris a deal.

Section 8

Compound Sentences

Part 1 What Are Compound Sentences?

Thus far in this book, you have been dealing with simple sentences.

A simple sentence is a sentence with only one subject and one predicate. Both the subject and the predicate may be compound.

You have learned that the word *compound* means "having two or more parts." You have worked with compound subjects, verbs, and objects. Note the following examples of compound constructions:

> *The co-captains* and *the coach* accepted the first place trophy.
> (Compound subject)
> We *sat* and *listened*.
> (Compound verb)
> Mr. Stalley took *cream* and *sugar*.
> (Compound object)

Now we come to a different kind of sentence, a sentence that has more than one subject and more than one predicate—the **compound sentence.**

A compound sentence consists of two or more simple sentences joined together.

The parts of a compound sentence may be joined by a coordinating conjunction or by a semicolon (;). Study the following examples:

> My uncle gave me a book, **and** I read it from cover to cover.
> We need scientists, **but** we need laboratory workers even more.
> You can take the course now, **or** you can wait until next year.
> Mother threw the coat away; it was worn out.

All of the main parts of the compound sentences above could be written as separate sentences without the conjunctions. For example:

> My uncle gave me a book. I read it from cover to cover.
> We need scientists. We need laboratory workers even more.
> Mother threw the coat away. It was worn out.

Why not, then, write only simple sentences? Why bother with compound sentences? You will see the answer as soon as you read this passage:

I earned four dollars last weekend. I decided to buy a Mother's Day present with it. My mother doesn't like candy. She does like flowers. My brother drove me into town. I went to the florist's shop. All the nice flowers cost too much. Finally I decided to buy a box of candy for the whole family.

A long series of short sentences is monotonous and dull. Joined into compound sentences, they sound much better:

I earned four dollars last weekend, and I decided to buy a Mother's Day present with it. My mother doesn't like candy, but she does like flowers. My brother drove me into town. I went to the florist's shop, but all the nice flowers cost too much. Finally I decided to buy a box of candy for the whole family.

Diagraming Compound Sentences

It is not difficult to diagram compound sentences if you can already diagram simple sentences. A compound sentence is really two, or more, simple sentences joined together. Therefore, you draw the diagram for the first half of the sentence, draw a dotted-line "step" for the conjunction, and then draw the diagram for the second half.

Example: John slept soundly, but the other boys didn't close their eyes.

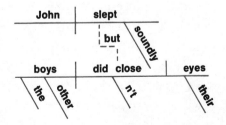

Exercises **Analyze compound sentences.**

A. Number your paper 1–10. Head three columns *Subject/ Verb, Conjunction,* and *Subject/Verb.* For each sentence, fill in the columns.

> Example: Greg went to the library, but I stayed home.

Subject/Verb	Conjunction	Subject/Verb
Greg/went	but	I/stayed

1. The bluejay called, and three other jays answered.
2. Five cars passed us, but we took our time.
3. Debby shut the curtain, and the crew changed the props.
4. Cheryl plays backgammon, but she prefers chess.
5. The commercial came on, and we headed for the kitchen.
6. The clouds are low, but it still isn't raining.
7. He's buying radish seeds, but I'm getting green beans.
8. Either I broke my watch, or it needs a new battery.
9. Tracy mowed the front lawn, and Jim weeded the flower bed.
10. Wendy washed the car, and Kim cleaned the garage.

B. Follow the directions for Exercise A.

1. The dog barked, but the cat just arched its back.
2. The program was on at eight, but we weren't home.
3. He painted the wall yellow, and his brother liked it.
4. Kate arranged the meeting, but Sue organized it.
5. Mom and I played chess, and Dad read the paper.
6. Bill painted the back porch, and he sanded the front steps.
7. The stars were out, but the southern sky was cloudy.
8. Scott flew to Miami, but we took the train.
9. The paintings were mostly acrylic, but there were several watercolors.
10. The nozzle came off, and Terry got all wet.

Part 2   Compound Predicate or Compound Sentence?

You will often need to know the difference between a compound sentence and a simple sentence with a compound predicate. Notice these sentences:

> 1. The girls *painted the posters* and *tacked them to the bulletin boards.*
> (This is a simple sentence. The conjunction *and* joins two parts of a compound predicate.)
>
> 2. *The girls painted the posters,* and *the boys tacked them to the bulletin boards.*
> (Here are two simple sentences, each with a subject and verb. They are joined by *and* into a compound sentence.)

Exercises   Compound predicate or compound sentence?

A. Number your paper 1–10. Decide whether the following sentences are compound sentences or simple sentences with compound predicates. Write *Compound Sentence* or *Compound Predicate.*

1. I enjoy movies but don't go often.
2. We started early for the game but got there late.
3. Julia and Jerry cleaned the garage and went home.
4. It is early, but we'd better get up anyhow.
5. They sat down and waited for the train.
6. We enjoyed the show, but it was too long.
7. Jan likes dramatics, and she enjoys singing, too.
8. The llama looked very proud and kept his long neck stiff.
9. Larry rang the doorbell twice, but no one came to the door.
10. In no time the elephant reached out for the hay and wheeled it into his mouth.

B. Follow the directions for Exercise A.

1. Our dog barks furiously at strangers, but he never bites.

2. Our bus was late, and we missed our flight.

3. We rowed out to the middle of the lake and fished until noon.

4. We called twice, but there was no answer.

5. The whistle blew suddenly, and everyone was quiet.

6. The tank was empty, and we were far from a gas station.

7. Laura closed the window and locked it.

8. Dave opened his wallet and took out his money.

9. Our wrestling team won the district meet, and they were second in the regionals.

10. Kristie and I went to the concert, but we missed the first group's performance.

Part 3 Commas in Compound Constructions

Since compound sentences are made up of two or more simple sentences, they may be long. To help the reader keep the thoughts in order, put a comma before the coordinating conjunction in a compound sentence.

> Example: Patti did a routine on the parallel bars, and Liz and Amy performed on the trampoline.

If the comma hadn't been used in the sentence just given, a reader might have been confused. The comma helps to clarify what *Patti* did, and then the reader can see that *Liz* and *Amy* did something else.

When Not To Punctuate

The only compound construction you have studied that requires a comma is the compound sentence. You do not need a comma to separate two direct objects, two predicates, or two of any of the other compound constructions you have studied.

Correct:

We walked into the office and talked with the manager.

Incorrect:

We walked into the office, and talked with the manager. (Do not use a comma between the parts of a compound predicate)

Correct:

The students from the seventh grade and those from the eighth formed a baseball team.

Incorrect:

The students from the seventh grade, and those from the eighth formed a baseball team. (Do not use a comma between the parts of a compound subject.)

Finally, the comma is not necessary in a very short compound sentence.

Example: We skated and we skied.
You can play ping pong or you can watch TV.

Exercises Punctuate compound constructions.

A. In the following sentences, commas have been omitted from all the compound constructions. Write the numbers from 1–10 on your paper. If a sentence is correct, write *Correct.* If it needs a comma, write the two words between which the comma belongs, and put in the comma.

Example: The class was preparing a program and the class sponsors were helping with it.

program, and

1. The walls were concrete and the windows were very narrow.

2. The old bathtub had legs on it and its feet were imitation lion's paws.

3. We could hear the rumbling of thunder and see flashes of lightning across the lake.

4. Ms. Hart and the members of the camera club will be putting on an exhibit of indoor photography.

5. The program was about the right length but we couldn't hear some of the speakers.

6. They took pictures of the activity groups and put them on display.

7. The Hiking Club has taken several training walks lately and it is planning a walkathon for next month.

8. The old pie chest had tin ends on it and Carrie was fascinated by the pie-top designs cut through the tin.

9. I like all sports but I really enjoy the World Series.

10. Dennis wears hip boots and fishes right in the stream.

B. Follow the directions for Exercise A.

1. They folded the raft and Mr. Russell stowed it in the trunk.

2. Steve was the villain in the play and he wore his sister's long brown cape.

3. A chain saw can be very dangerous and can cause accidents.

4. For a manual typewriter you need strong fingers or you will get tired.

5. An electric typewriter is very sensitive and types at the least touch.

6. We went to the drugstore for our photos but the film hadn't come back yet.

7. Americans will eventually use the metric system but we are having a hard time adjusting to it.

8. The smoke from his pipe settled in milky layers and obscured his armchair.

9. We repaired our bikes and we cycled to the lake.

10. Our tomcat chewed through the screen door and flies and mosquitoes got in.

Part 4 Combining Related Thoughts

We have said that the parts of a compound sentence are of the same importance—they are simple sentences. That means that they balance each other grammatically. They must also balance in thought. They must be related in thought.

Making Compound Sentences

Some pairs of sentences make good compound sentences, and some do not:

1. It looked like rain. We went anyhow. (Will these two simple sentences make a good compound sentence? Yes. Use *but*.)

2. I like horseback riding. Deep-sea fish are often big. (The ideas are not related; no compound sentence.)

3. Pete flew his kite. The rain got the car wet. (The ideas are not related; no compound sentence.)

4. Give me your boat. I'll give you my ski poles. (These two may be made into a compound sentence. Use *and*.)

Exercises   Make compound sentences.

A. Rewrite the following sentences as compound sentences. Pick the best coordinating conjunction for each.

1. Ann went horseback riding every weekend. She rode in the annual horse show every summer.

2. Dad has gone to PTA. Mom is going to the League of Women Voters.

3. The fan belt on the old Chevy was worn out. There was nothing wrong with the engine.

4. The car wash is open. The line is too long.

5. The rough-barked wood there is hickory. This pile is maple.

6. Builders use those concrete blocks for walls. My older brother uses them with boards for bookcases.

7. The swimming pool is too crowded. The water is too cold.

8. She put the announcements on the desk. The students picked them up.

9. Marilyn and Phillip were going to the carnival. The thunderstorm changed their plans.

10. Sharlene was talking to Joey. Joey wasn't paying any attention.

B. Find the six pairs of sentences that might be made into compound sentences. Indicate the coordinating conjunction that should be used.

1. Elizabeth has the mumps. She is not very sick.

2. The feature of the game was the raising of the flag. Our cheerleader sprained his ankle.

3. Cross-country skiing is a popular winter sport. Many Midwestern states provide excellent indoor skating rinks.

4. Have a good time in New York. See all you can.

5. You can make it this way. You can try another way.

6. The potatoes were raw. Some of the meat was burned.

7. Arizona is a beautiful state. New Mexico lies to the east of it.

8. Lori and Jovita walked to the basketball game. Lori's mother picked them up when it was over.

9. Most trees lose their leaves. Evergreens live up to their name.

10. Todd and Doug were the winners. It started to snow after the match.

C. The following paragraph could be improved by the use of some compound constructions. Using what you have learned about compound constructions, rewrite the paragraph. Remember to use a comma before a coordinating conjunction in a long sentence.

My friend Dick was going to the airport. I wanted to go, too. Mother objected. I hadn't mowed the lawn. I hadn't watered the garden. I could go to the airport. I had to work first. Dick was getting impatient. Then I had an idea. There was a watermelon in our garden. Dick loves watermelon. I talked my idea over with Mother. Then I talked it over with Dick. Soon Dick was watering the garden. I was mowing the lawn.

D. In the following sentences, the compound constructions are incomplete. Copy the sentences on your paper and complete them with one or more words so that they make sense. Do not change the punctuation.

1. After class Debbie talked to Andy and _____.

2. When we had finished lunch, Cory came over and _____.

3. We intended to do all our homework, but _____.

4. Scott and Carrie were adding up the cost, and _____.

5. The felt-tipped pens were not in the drawer, but _____.

6. He took off the tire and _____.

Additional Exercises

Compound Sentences

A. Analyze compound sentences.

Number your paper 1–10. Head three columns *Subject/ Verb, Conjunction,* and *Subject/Verb.* For each sentence, fill in the columns.

1. I collect Kennedy fifty-cent pieces, and Jim collects two-dollar bills.

2. The announcements were made, but the intercom didn't work.

3. She is singing, and her sister is playing the guitar.

4. We sometimes play miniature golf on Saturday, but last week my parents took us to the museum.

5. Last summer we went to the Grand Canyon, but this summer we will be backpacking in Maine.

6. John was property manager, and Jill was on the lighting crew.

7. We landed at O'Hare Airport at night, and we saw the beautiful Chicago skyline.

8. Melanie is coming, but Gil is staying home.

9. We went to the pool and we swam all afternoon.

10. The members of the cast were nervous at first, but they soon relaxed.

B. Compound predicate or compound sentence?

Number your paper 1–10. Decide whether the following sentences are compound sentences or simple sentences with compound predicates. Write *Compound Sentence* or *Compound Predicate.*

1. He discovered a worn-out washer in the tap and replaced it.

2. Sue arrived on time, but Dick was late.

3. The traffic was heavy, and we were late for the game.

4. Our plane arrived over the airport on time, but the fog kept it from landing.

5. The river had a swift current and was too dangerous for swimming.

6. Claire and I had a display at the science fair and received an honorable mention for it.

7. The moon rose, and the whippoorwill started its endless call.

8. The cable car ride up the mountain was fun, but I was frightened at first.

9. We had planned a party, but it was postponed.

10. Our homeroom won the intramural trophy for soccer, and we were victorious in floor hockey, too.

C. Punctuate compound constructions.

In the following sentences, commas have been omitted from all of the compound constructions. Write the numbers 1–10 on your paper. If a sentence is correct, write *Correct.* If it needs a comma, write the two words between which the comma belongs, and put in the comma.

1. The links in the chain were as big as saucers and they clanked against each other.

2. Our neighbors from Germany boil their Easter eggs and then dye them with red onion skins.

3. Trays of chicken-salad sandwiches and alfalfa sprouts were next to the dips.

4. We looked but the sawhorses were not in the shed.

5. Jack brought the school printing equipment and set it up on the stage.

6. An electric knife vibrates a lot but it works well on bread.

7. The grapefruit tree next door was in bloom and smelled tart and fresh.

8. The furnace clicked on but a moment later it stopped.

9. We all went to the baseball game and we later came home for a barbecue.

10. The photos of Mars didn't show much and Bob was disappointed.

D. Make compound sentences.

Make each of the following pairs of sentences into a good compound sentence. Use a suitable coordinating conjunction. Watch your punctuation.

1. Do you want a hot fudge sundae? Do you want a milk shake?

2. Many early attempts were made with a flying machine. The Wright Brothers are credited with the invention.

3. Jill, Linda, and I visited Universal Studios. We also went to Knotts Berry Farm.

4. Tierra del Fuego is at one end of the Pan-American Highway. Fairbanks, Alaska, is at the other end.

5. Green Lake, Wisconsin, is a great place for cross-country skiing. Door County is even better.

6. Our intramural softball game was postponed. We were able to play it on Friday.

7. We studied a unit on biographies and autobiographies. We were able to have some interesting guests visit our class.

8. In home economics class we baked cookies. At lunch we ate them.

9. The trip to Kings Island, Ohio, was fun. I really enjoyed the Great America amusement park in Illinois.

10. We filled out our schedule cards. We were able to choose two elective courses.

E. Use compound constructions.

The following paragraphs could be improved by the use of some compound constructions. Using what you have learned about compound constructions, rewrite each paragraph. Remember to use a comma before a coordinating conjunction in a long sentence.

1

It was rainy on the Fourth of July. Toward evening it cleared somewhat. We went to the roof garden of our apartment building. We watched the display. Little airplanes were flying around everywhere. There was even a helicopter. Two of the planes were sky-writing planes. The children were fascinated by them. They ran around with their sparklers, shouting at them.

2

The real show was along the lake front. You hardly knew where to look. There were big rockets bursting like emeralds. Some of them burst green. A fraction of a second later they turned pink. Some were a bright orange. They left a dripping, starfish-shaped cloud. Another kind was very bright. It was a burst of huge, multi-colored sparks. The rockets were mostly red, white, and blue. The very best rockets were brilliant bursts of fiery white stars.

Section 9

Making Subjects and Verbs Agree

Part 1 Singular and Plural Forms

When a noun stands for one thing, it is **singular.**

dog student city classroom

When a noun stands for more than one thing, it is **plural.**

dogs students cities classrooms

Verbs, too, have singular and plural forms.

Singular: The class *votes*. The team *practices*.

Plural: The classes *vote*. The teams *practice*.

Most verbs drop *s* to form the plural.

Exercises   Study singular and plural forms.

A. Write the words listed below on a sheet of paper. After each word, tell whether the word is singular or plural.

1. table	6. horses	11. game	16. jeep
2. foot	7. restaurant	12. sports	17. papers
3. building	8. town	13. mouse	18. school
4. I	9. television	14. operas	19. movie
5. they	10. holidays	15. fountain	20. duties

B. Write the numbers 1–10 in a column on a sheet of paper. Find the verb in each sentence. Write the verb and tell whether it is singular or plural.

1. Their friends come often.
2. He writes many letters.
3. A girl runs that press.
4. Your bike is here.
5. The radio warns the farmers.
6. Mrs. Morey is helpful.
7. The papers are ready.
8. Most kids like games.
9. It looks like rain.
10. Sports interest me.

Special Forms of Certain Verbs

A few verbs have special forms that you will need to keep in mind as you study this section:

Is, Was, Are, and Were. The verbs *is* and *was* are singular. The verbs *are* and *were* are plural.

Singular: Pat *is* here.   Pat *was* here.

Plural: They *are* here.   They *were* here.

Has and Have. The verb *has* is singular. The verb *have* is plural.

> Singular: She *has* a sailboat.
> Plural: They *have* a sailboat.

Does and Do. The verb *does* is singular. The verb *do* is plural.

> Singular: She *does* the driving.
> Plural: They *do* the driving.

Part 2   Agreement of Subject and Verb

When we say that a word is singular or plural, we are talking about whether there are one or more things, or one or more actions. This is called the **number** of the word. When we say that one word **agrees** with another, we mean that it is the same in number.

The verb must agree with its subject in number.

> The **boys** (plural) **were** (plural) fixing the toboggan.
> **She** (singular) **does** (singular) not have her coat.

Beware of Phrases

Often a phrase appears between the subject and the verb. The subject is never part of such a phrase. Look for the subject outside the phrase.

> **One** (of the glasses) **was** broken.
> The **horses** (in the barn) **were** restless.

The Pronoun *You*

Unlike other pronouns, *you* is the same for both singular and plural. But *you* is never used with a singular verb. It is always used with plural verbs.

> You have (*not* has) my best wishes.
> You were (*not* was) next on the list.

Exercises   Make the subject and verb agree.

A. Copy each sentence. Draw a circle around the phrase between the subject and the verb. Choose the right verb.

> Example: One of his feet (was, were) sticking out.
>
> One(of his feet)was sticking out.

1. Several houses in our block (is, are) for sale.
2. This group of skiers (give, gives) lessons to beginners.
3. The chances for a rerun (is, are) good.
4. This pair of gloves (look, looks) like yours.
5. The footprints in this cave (seem, seems) very large.
6. These sets of books (are, is) to be returned to the library.
7. One of my favorite programs (begins, begin) at eight o'clock.
8. The pond by the willow trees (were, was) deep.
9. The last bushel of apples (have, has) a name on it.
10. The paper on the walls (was, were) silvery.

B. Number your paper 1–10. Choose the correct form from the two forms given in parentheses.

1. Both of the boys (has, have) a soccer ball.
2. Two motors (is, are) running.
3. Two of the sheep (is, are) black.
4. The rungs in the ladder (was, were) loose.
5. Terri and Kate (works, work) at the dairy.

6. Each of the club members (was, were) going to bake something for the sale.

7. The bag of grapes (is, are) beside the nectarines.

8. This sort of sundae (is, are) best.

9. Both of her ears (were, was) red.

10. One of their starters (was, were) injured in last night's game.

Part 3 Verbs with Compound Subjects

A compound subject is two or more subjects used with the same verb.

A compound subject that contains the conjunction *and* is plural; therefore, the plural verb must be used with it.

Example: Marie and Lynn are here. (The compound subject is *Marie and Lynn*. The verb *are* is plural.)

Compound Subjects Joined by *Or* and *Nor*

When the parts of a compound subject are joined by *or* or *nor*, the verb agrees with the nearer subject.

Examples: Lisa or Ted *is* coming.
Neither Beth nor her sisters *are* here.
Three oranges or one grapefruit *makes* enough juice for the punch.

Exercises **Use the right verb with a compound subject.**

A. Number your paper 1–10. Write the correct form of the verb from the two given in parentheses.

1. Elyse and her mother (was, were) here.

2. The president or the vice-president usually (takes, take) charge.

3. Steve and I (is, are) both busy.

4. My mother or my older brothers always (meet, meets) Dad at the airport.

5. (Have, Has) either Carol or Brenda heard that record?

6. Either the Phillips or my parents (are, is) going on the hayride.

7. Neither the mushrooms nor that chicken (is, are) fresh enough.

8. The cottonwood trees and the elm (is, are) budding out.

9. The band and the chorus (is, are) performing at the assembly.

10. The older men and Jack (walk, walks) home along Plymouth Street.

B. Number your paper 1–10. Write the correct form of the verb from the two in parentheses.

1. Neither Alicia nor I (believes, believe) in ghosts.

2. My bedspread and rug (match, matches) the curtains.

3. (Do, Does) your mobile and that balloon always hang there?

4. Either my cousins or Kathy (phone, phones) every week from Boston.

5. (Do, Does) either Bob or Larry play soccer?

6. Neither Jane nor her sister (is, are) at home.

7. Sarah's pony and goat (don't, doesn't) like each other.

8. (Does, Do) either Colleen or her sisters come on Tuesday?

9. That hitching post and that horse (look, looks) inseparable.

10. The treasurer's figures and the secretary's report (agree, agrees).

Part 4 Agreement in Inverted Sentences

In most sentences, the subject comes before the verb. A person is likely to say, for example, "The glider soars over the hill." For emphasis, however, a writer or speaker may say, "Over the hill soars the glider." The second sentence is called an **inverted sentence.** In each sentence the subject is *glider* and the verb is *soars.*

In inverted sentences, as in ordinary ones, the subject and verb must agree.

> Examples: Up above flutter a thousand flags. (flags flutter)
> Through the museum stream tourists by the thousands. (tourists stream)
> In the yard is a pile of leaves. (pile is)

Exercises **Use the right verb in inverted sentences.**

A. Number your paper 1–10. Write the correct form of the verb for each sentence.

1. At the end of the two-by-fours (flap, flaps) a red shirt.
2. After the chapter on submarines (come, comes) one on oceanography.
3. On and on (go, goes) the story.
4. After all that baking (come, comes) the best part.
5. Out of the bird bath (jump, jumps) one goggle-eyed frog.
6. To each of you (go, goes) the speaker's thanks.
7. Down the road (thunder, thunders) the pony express.
8. Beside the bench (is, are) the tool box.
9. With each of the games (go, goes) an instruction booklet.
10. Underneath (rumble, rumbles) the subway.

B. Number your paper 1–10. Write the correct form of the verb for each sentence.

1. After the Marshfield band (comes, come) the 4-H float.
2. Round and round (go, goes) his thoughts.
3. Over the fire (hang, hangs) an old iron pot.
4. On either side of Trisha (sit, sits) her brothers.
5. Between the cushions (was, were) some change and a skeleton key.
6. Around 8 o'clock (come, comes) two buses.
7. Beside their house (flow, flows) the Wabash River.
8. Around her finger (curls, curl) a spoon ring.
9. High above the peaks (soar, soars) two eagles.
10. There on the windowsill (lie, lies) the stopwatch.

Part 5   Verbs with *There*

The word *there* often comes where you expect the subject to be. As you will remember from Section 1 (page 25), *there* is often used simply to get a sentence moving. When *there* begins a sentence, look for the subject farther on in the sentence.

> Examples: 1. There is a book on the table. (*book* is the subject.)
>
> 2. There are no questions. (*questions* is the subject.)

In the first example, notice that the correct verb is *is*, because the subject, *book*, is singular. In the second example, *are* must be used because the subject, *questions*, is plural.

When *there* is used at the beginning of a sentence, be careful to make the verb of the sentence agree in number with the real subject of the sentence.

Exercises **Use the correct verb with *there*.**

A. Choose the correct form of the verb. Write down the subject and verb for each sentence.

1. (Is, Are) there any oranges?
2. Sometimes there (is, are) taxis waiting here.
3. There (is, are) someone looking for you.
4. (Are, Is) there any toothpicks in the box?
5. (Was, Were) there no ushers?
6. There (is, are) a second-hand, three-speed bike for sale.
7. (Were, Was) there two windows in the stage set?
8. There (weren't, wasn't) many knobs on the stereo.
9. There (is, are) no reason for that.
10. Often there (is, are) people on the pier.

B. Choose the correct form of the verb. Write down the subject and verb for each sentence.

1. There (wasn't, weren't) another marina on the lake.
2. There (is, are) a chance of rain.
3. (Is, Are) there four rows of seats in the balcony?
4. (Is, Are) there any strawberry jam left?
5. There (were, was) extra hangers in the closet.
6. (Are, Is) there a second for the motion?
7. (Was, Were) there a cap on the 3-in-1 Oil?
8. (Weren't, Wasn't) there pyramids before the Egyptians?
9. There (is, are) just two pages left in my notebook.
10. There (was, were) several witnesses to the accident.

Additional Exercises

Making Subjects and Verbs Agree

A. Singular and plural forms.

Number your paper 1–20. Write down the subject and verb for each sentence. Tell whether they are singular or plural.

1. The computer works well.
2. Two cabbages are enough.
3. Most jeans have pockets.
4. Her photographs are beautiful.
5. She plays the piano with ease.
6. The windows face east.
7. The baby sleeps a lot.
8. Pete looks all right.
9. This T-shirt stretches too much.
10. The tulips are out.
11. The moose looks huge.
12. Lindsay does the planting.
13. The tomatoes taste delicious.
14. The anchor weighs a ton.
15. This plywood feels damp.
16. Sam has a coupon.
17. That dessert was absolutely delicious!
18. Everyone's locker was cleaned out.
19. The nurses and doctors are meeting in the conference room.
20. The sun sets at eight.

B. Make the subject and verb agree.

Number your paper 1–10. Choose the correct form of the verb for each sentence.

1. The binding on these books (is, are) imitation leather.
2. Where (were, was) you when I called?
3. One of the seniors (was, were) waiting.
4. Those two seventh-graders (does, do) well in the orchestra.
5. Each of the players (has, have) a number.
6. One of the pages (were, was) in color.
7. (Was, Were) you very tired on Saturday?
8. The lights of the city (was, were) visible below.
9. Several starlings (were, was) eating the cherries.
10. The number of boys and girls (was, were) about equal.

C. Use the right verb with a compound subject.

Number your paper 1–10. Write the correct form of the verb for each sentence.

1. Chris and her sister (ride, rides) their bikes to school.
2. Neither Kay nor the others (was, were) able to come.
3. (Haven't, Hasn't) Wendy or the others finished the project either?
4. Dr. Keifer and her assistants (is, are) in the clinic.
5. The book on the desk and the one on the shelf (is, are) Joe's.
6. The wheat fields and that rainbow (is, are) beautiful.
7. Either Jim or his friends (is, are) delivering papers.
8. Mike and the Simpsons (is, are) old friends.
9. Neither the tap shoes nor the ballet slippers (is, are) big enough.
10. (Is, Are) the barnacles and mussels still on the beach?

D. Use the right verb in inverted sentences.

Number your paper 1–10. Write the correct form of the verb for each sentence.

1. Here and there (rises, rise) the smoke of a campfire.
2. After graduation (comes, come) the party.
3. Overhead (hover, hovers) a long-tailed kite.
4. Between the passengers (squeeze, squeezes) Raul with his guitar case.
5. Suddenly, as if from the waves, (appear, appears) the sun.
6. Near the farm turn-off (is, are) a stone bridge.
7. Above the rec room entrance (dangle, dangles) an air-conditioning vent.
8. Late in the season (come, comes) the real tests.
9. In front of the house (is, are) three pillars.
10. On the lawn of the city hall (stand, stands) two Civil War cannons.

E. Use the correct verb with *there.*

Choose the correct form from the two in parentheses.

1. There (was, were) photographs from the musical on the bulletin board.
2. (Is, Are) there any stamps for these letters?
3. There (was, were) not another boat in sight.
4. (Is, Are) there any good movies on TV tonight?
5. There (is, are) felt-tipped pens in that cupboard.
6. (Is, Are) there any evidence other than that?
7. There (was, were) no leather belts with branding marks.
8. There (is, are) still hope.
9. (Weren't, Wasn't) there another pair of shoes in the closet?
10. There (is, are) almost half an hour before curtain time.

Section 10

Capitalization

The use of capital letters is called **capitalization.** When you use a capital letter at the beginning of a word, you *capitalize* the word.

Capital letters are used to make reading easier. They call attention to the beginnings of sentences and to certain special words.

Proper Nouns and Adjectives

Capitalize proper nouns and proper adjectives.

A **proper noun** is the name of a particular person, place, or thing.

> Elizabeth   Sweden   Congress

A **common noun** is the name of a whole class of persons, places, or things. It is not capitalized.

> boy   girl   town

A **proper adjective** is an adjective formed from a proper noun.

> Swedish   Congressional

Names of Persons

Capitalize the names of persons and also the initials or abbreviations that stand for those names.

> Melinda R. Eaton   Lauren A. Banfield   William J. Franklin, Jr.

Capitalize titles used with names of persons and abbreviations standing for those titles.

> Doctor Maria A. Sandquist   Dr. Maria A. Sandquist

Do not capitalize titles that are used as common nouns.

> One of our police captains is Captain Daniel Jeffries.
> The presiding officer was President Mary Gomez.
> She will be president again next year.

Capitalize titles of people and groups whose rank is very important.

Titles of important people, such as those of the President and Vice-President of the United States, are capitalized even though these titles are used without proper names.

The Vice-President presides over the sessions of the Senate.
The Queen attended the opening of Parliament.

Family Relationships

Capitalize such words as *mother, father, aunt,* and *uncle* when these words are used as names.

Hello, Mother. Is Dad home yet?

These words are not used as names when they are preceded by a possessive or by such words as *a* or *the.*

I talked with my mother about it.

The Pronoun I

Capitalize the pronoun *I*.

Did you get the postcard that I sent?

The Deity

Capitalize all words referring to the Deity, to the Holy Family and to religious scriptures.

God	the Bible	the Torah
the Father	the Gospel	the Talmud
the Lord	Allah	the Koran

Exercises   Use capital letters correctly.

A. Number your paper 1–10. Copy the following sentences. Change small letters to capital letters wherever necessary.

1. My favorite aunt is aunt rose.

2. She is my father's sister.

3. Four players in the Baseball Hall of Fame are ernie banks, jackie robinson, sandy koufax, and mickey mantle.

4. Do you know the prince of monaco's last name?

5. We made french onion soup in home economics class.

6. My sister linda is personnel director.

7. The president of the united states was there.

8. My mother said, "Ask dad if he brought the camera."

9. Muslims study the koran; jews study the torah.

10. Two well-known women in the game of golf are babe didrikson zaharias and patty berg.

B. Number your paper 1–10. Copy the following sentences. Change small letters to capital letters wherever necessary. Also change the capital letters to small letters wherever necessary.

1. It was president jimmy carter who spoke at general anderson's retirement.

2. On monday i had an appointment with the dentist.

3. The names on the door were dr. natalie j. sanders and martin able, jr.

4. Cheryl was elected President of our club; Darnell, the Treasurer.

5. Last spring, we saw margaret court, virginia wade, and chris evert play in several tennis tournaments.

6. Edmund p. hillary climbed the highest mountain in the world.

7. The queen of england made him a knight.

8. Once he was a british beekeeper.

9. Christopher columbus sailed under the spanish flag.

10. The coast was explored by portuguese sailors.

Geographical Names

In a geographical name, capitalize the first letter of each word except articles and prepositions.

The article *the* appearing before a geographical name is not part of the geographical name and is therefore not capitalized.

Continents: North America, South America, Asia

Bodies of water: the Indian Ocean, Lake Superior, the Jordan River, Cape Cod Bay, the Caspian Sea

Land forms: the Pyrenees, the Sinai Peninsula, the Grand Canyon, the Syrian Desert

Political units: Delaware, the District of Columbia, the British Isles, the Commonwealth of Massachusetts, the West Indies, San Francisco

Public areas: Gettysburg National Park, Fort Niagara, Mount Rushmore, Statue of Liberty

Roads and highways: Central Avenue, Route 447, Garden State Parkway, Van Buren Avenue, the Ohio Turnpike, State Street

Directions and Sections

Capitalize names of sections of the country but not of directions of the compass.

Cotton was king in the South.
Cities in the Southwest are flourishing.
It is just north of Paris.
They flew east through the storm.
She lives on the north side of the street.
The lake is west of our cottage.
The hurricane moved northward.

Capitalize proper adjectives derived from names of sections of the country. Do not capitalize adjectives derived from words indicating direction.

an **E**astern school	a **s**outherly course
a **W**estern concept	an **e**astern route

Exercises   Using capital letters correctly.

A. Number your paper 1–10. Find the words in the following phrases that should be capitalized. Write the words after the proper number, using the necessary capital letters.

1. a street in paris, france
2. berthoud pass over the rockies
3. pike's peak near colorado springs
4. the pacific coast beaches
5. one block north of first avenue
6. near the catskill mountains
7. near the gulf of mexico
8. represents the seventh congressional district
9. the transamerica pyramid in san francisco
10. the great plains of the west

B. Follow the directions for Exercise A.

1. We drove from toronto to detroit on the macdonald-cartier freeway.
2. We saw buffalo at custer national monument.
3. In the carolinas we found out about southern hospitality.
4. The southernmost continent is antarctica.
5. Colonel Powell explored the grand canyon of the colorado.
6. The gateway arch in st. louis, missouri, is 630 feet high.
7. A toll bridge extends over the straits of mackinac.
8. The arlington memorial bridge extends across the potomac river to the lincoln memorial.

9. Our new neighbors come from southeast asia.

10. Is the united nations building on fifth avenue in new york city?

Names of Organizations and Institutions

Capitalize the names of organizations and institutions.

General Motors Corporation   Stacy Memorial Hospital
Nichols Junior High School   Laya and Franklin, Inc.

Do not capitalize such words as *school, college, church,* and *hospital* when they are not used as names.

the emergency entrance at the hospital
the basketball team of our school

Names of Events, Documents, and Periods of Time

Capitalize the names of historical events, documents, and periods of time.

Industrial Revolution   Bill of Rights
World War II   Middle Ages

Months, Days, and Holidays

Capitalize the names of months, days, and holidays.

February   Wednesday   Labor Day
April   Sunday   New Year's Day

Exercises   **Use capital letters correctly.**

A. Number your paper 1–10. Copy each of the following groups of words. Wherever necessary, change small letters to capitals or capitals to small letters.

1. the month of march
2. veterans day, november 11
3. Eisenhower high school
4. the Battle of Bunker Hill
5. fire prevention Week
6. Industries and Colleges
7. Louisiana state university
8. the house of representatives
9. a Weekend in june
10. the civil war

B. Number your paper 1–10. Find the words that should be capitalized in the following sentences. Copy each sentence, using the necessary capital letters.

1. The fourth thursday in november is thanksgiving day.

2. In our anthology, *Black Roots,* we read selections by maya angelou and anne moody.

3. The emancipation proclamation was written during the civil war.

4. The middletown team will play washington high school.

5. In new orleans, mardi gras is celebrated with parades and many festivities.

6. The first ten amendments to the constitution of the united states are called the bill of rights.

7. We saw the chicago bears play the new york jets at soldier field in chicago.

8. One of the largest companies is xerox corporation.

9. Our class will visit the museum in april.

10. The period of the 1930's in the united states was known as the great depression.

Languages, Races, Nationalities, Religions

Capitalize the names of languages, races, nationalities, and religions, and also adjectives derived from them.

Irish linen   German band   French language
Italian heritage   Lutheranism   African art

Ships, Trains, Airplanes, Automobiles

Capitalize the names of ships, trains, airplanes, and automobiles.

> **U.S.S.** *Constitution*   *Concorde*
> *Wabash Cannonball*   Firebird

Abbreviations

You know that an **abbreviation** is a shortened form of a word. You also know that abbreviations of proper nouns and proper adjectives are capitalized.

Capitalize the abbreviations *B.C.* and *A.D.*

> Julius Caesar was born in the year 100 **B.C.**
> Christopher Columbus landed on San Salvador in **A.D.** 1492

Capitalize the abbreviations *A.M.* and *P.M.*

> The bus leaves at 8:05 **A.M.** and returns at 5:30 **P.M.**

Exercises   **Use capital letters correctly.**

A. Number your paper 1–10. Copy each of the following groups of words. Wherever necessary, change small letters to capitals.

1. the new african nations
2. a scottish writer
3. a lutheran minister
4. bought a new ford
5. the spanish language
6. 2:30 p.m.
7. 10:00 a.m.
8. the year 40 b.c.
9. a.d. 300
10. the s.s. *france*

B. Number your paper 1–10. Copy each of the following sentences. Wherever necessary, change small letters to capitals.

1. We will sail on the s.s. *queen elizabeth* the first weekend in may.

2. Mother will complete her master's degree at purdue university next august.

3. The buddhist religion originated in india.

4. Banking hours are from 8:30 a.m. to 5:00 p.m.

5. We rode the amtrak from kansas city to albuquerque.

6. Every tuesday and thursday the german band plays polkas.

7. My sister can speak spanish, but she cannot write it.

8. Although illinois is called the land of lincoln, abraham lincoln was born in kentucky.

9. This roman emperor gave his name to the month of august.

10. The datsun is a japanese automobile.

First Words

Sentences

Capitalize the first word of every sentence.

My sister plays basketball. **S**he is the captain of the team.

Poetry

Capitalize the first word in most lines of poetry.

> **A** word is dead
> **W**hen it is said,
>   **S**ome say.
> **I** say it just
> **B**egins to live
>   **T**hat day.

        —Emily Dickinson

Sometimes, especially in modern poetry, the lines of a poem do not always begin with a capital letter.

Quotations

Capitalize the first word of a direct quotation.

When you use a **quotation,** you use the words of a speaker or writer. If you give the *exact* words of the speaker or writer, you are giving a **direct quotation.** If you change the words of the speaker or writer to your own words, you are giving an **indirect quotation.** Be sure that you can tell the difference between the two kinds.

Here are two examples of a direct quotation:

"Close the window, please," Ms. Smith said to Jerry.
Sarah said, "My parents bought a new car."

Here are two examples of an indirect quotation:

Ms. Smith asked Jerry to close the window.
Sarah said that her parents had bought a new car.

Notice that an indirect quotation does *not* begin with a capital letter.

Sometimes a direct quotation is interrupted by explanatory words like *she said.* Here is an example

"Well," she said, "you may be right."

Notice that the second part of this kind of direct quotation does not begin with a capital letter.

When a direct quotation is interrupted in this way, it is called a **divided quotation.**

If the second part of a divided quotation starts a new sentence, the second part must begin with a capital letter, like any other new sentence.

"I don't know," he said. "You may be right."
"We met Ellen," said Jane. "She was with her father."

Exercises   Use capital letters correctly.

A. Number your paper 1–10. Find the words in the following sentences that should be capitalized. Write the words after the proper number, using the necessary capital letters

1. the doors open early. no one can enter after 2 p.m.
2. "hi," said bill. "we won. are mom and dad home?"
3. thanksgiving is always the fourth thursday in november.
4. a harvest mouse goes scampering by
   with silver claws and a silver eye.
5. sailing is a favorite sport for visitors to cape cod.
6. uganda, kenya, and chad are nations in africa.
7. hope is the thing with feathers
   that perches in the soul,
   and sings the tune without the words,
   and never stops at all.
8. "you are late," said b. j. pate.
9. "there's no school tomorrow," said heather. "it's veterans day."
10. what's that old saying about "a month of sundays"?

B. Follow the directions for Exercise A.

1. call disc o. dan. ask him to play your favorite song.
2. "nurse," said dr. dee, "hold this while i get some alcohol."
3. grand canyon is a national park. It is in northwestern arizona.
4. you can see the colorado river from toroweap point.
5. some havasupai indians live at the foot of the gorge.
6. many years ago mother shipton made rhymes about the future.
7. for every parcel i stoop down to seize,
   i lose some other off my arms and knees.
8. what do the shopkeepers want? they want more parking.

9. barton industries, inc., is constructing a new plant near chicago.

10. it was many and many a year ago,
    in a kingdom by the sea,
  that a maiden there lived whom you may know
    by the name of annabel lee;

Letters

Capitalize the first word, words like *Sir* and *Madam,* and the name of the person addressed in the greeting of a letter.

    Dear Sir: Dear Mrs. Cooper:
    Dear Mr. Herrara: Dear Ms. Ashley.

In the complimentary close, capitalize the first word only.

    Sincerely yours,   Yours very truly,

Outlines

Capitalize the first word of each line of an outline.

    II. Things to be considered
       A. Breed
          1. Kinds of dogs
          2. Uses of dogs
       B. Training

Titles

Capitalize the first word and all important words in the titles of books, poems, short stories, articles, newspapers, magazines, plays, motion pictures, works of art, and musical compositions.

The words *a, an,* and *the* (called **articles**) are not capitalized unless they come at the beginning of a title. Conjunctions and prepositions (such as *and* and *of*) are not capitalized either, except at the beginning of a title.

Book: *The Fellowship of the Rings*
Poem: "The Road Not Taken"
Short story: "The Lottery"
Article: "Space Age Grand Tour"
Newspaper: *The Wall Street Journal*
Magazine: *Natural History*
Play: *Fiddler on the Roof*
Motion picture: *Star Wars*
Work of art: *Sunflowers* (by Van Gogh)
Musical composition: Handel's *Messiah*

Exercises   Use capital letters correctly.

A. Number your paper 1–10. Copy each of the following phrases, using the correct capital letters.

1. a *daily news* subscription
2. II. poetry
   A. british
      1. "sea fever"
      2. "my last duchess"
   B. american
3. a *reader's digest* article
4. the painting, *blue boy*
5. *rocky*, the award-winning film
6. sincerely yours,
7. Read "sailing the skies of summer"
8. the cast of *our town*
9. an early novel, *The deerslayer*
10. dear ms. martin

B. Number your paper 1–10. Find the words in the following sentences that should be capitalized. Write the words after the proper numbers, using the necessary capital letters.

1. dear mrs. gomez: Your subscription to *national geographic* ends today.

2. They sang "the sounds of silence" for an encore.

3. The *bathers by a river* is in the Art Institute.

4. Our copy of *the detroit free press* ended up on the porch roof.

5. During christmas vacation, we saw *the nutcracker suite* at the arie crown theater.

6. Read "builders for a golden age" in *american heritage*.

7. Mother and Dad went to see *the wiz* in Chicago.

8. I. short stories

    A. american

        1. "the night the ghost got in"

        2. "the outcasts of poker flat"

    B. british

9. Mother reads *the wall street journal*.

10. dear sir:

    have you read *the daily times* lately?

Additional Exercises

Capitalization

A. Use capital letters correctly.

Copy the following sentences. Change small letters to capital letters wherever necessary.

1. My mother and my father enjoy playing cards with mr. and mrs. olsen.
2. My favorite poet of all time is emily dickinson.
3. There is a great french pastry shop just down the street.
4. Did i tell you i saw loretta lynn in concert last weekend?
5. The three all-time home run hitters are hank aaron, babe ruth, and willie mays.
6. The president sent the vice-president on a fact-finding mission to africa.
7. We asked mother if we could invite lou and amy for dinner.
8. In some religions god is called jehovah.
9. The king of sweden is married to a german woman.
10. Janelle and I gave a demonstration speech on japanese origami.

B. Use capital letters correctly.

Number your paper 1–10. Find the words in the following sentences that should be capitalized. Write the correct form of each word beside the proper number on your paper.

1. The bermuda triangle is an area in the atlantic ocean where many boats and airplanes have vanished.

2. Did you say that greenleaf avenue is four blocks north of maple street?

3. Part of the soviet union is in europe, and part is in asia.

4. The drive east from naples, florida, to fort lauderdale will take you through big cypress swamp.

5. The mississippi river forms a natural border between illinois and iowa.

6. Many people still think of cowboys and indians when you mention the west.

7. The atacama desert in chile is one of the driest spots on earth.

8. Gettysburg national park is only about forty-five kilometers south of the pennsylvania turnpike.

9. Lake ontario flows into the saint lawrence river.

10. Much of the world's oil comes from the middle east.

C. Use capital letters correctly.

Number your paper 1–10. Find the words that should be capitalized in the following sentences. Copy each sentence, using the necessary capital letters.

1. Last year my birthday was on a wednesday.

2. Didn't sharon buy that dress at carol lewis and company?

3. I thought that lincoln junior high school was in skokie, illinois.

4. Mike will be in calumet hospital until next monday.

5. In our school everyone dresses up on april fool's day.

6. Mrs. laur is an executive at the stannix corporation.

7. O. j. simpson endorses hertz, incorporated.

8. Fresh vegetables are usually not expensive in july and august.

9. I always buy candy for my parents on valentine's day.

10. When my sister graduates from high school, she wants to go to ohio state university.

D. Use capital letters correctly.

Number your paper 1–10. Find the words in the following sentences that should be capitalized. Write these words after the proper number, using capital letters correctly.

1. Marsha's plane leaves Tucson at 11:55 a.m. and arrives in Denver at 2:05 p.m.
2. Was there really a ship called *h.m.s. bounty?*
3. Ann likes most kinds of food, but her favorite is italian.
4. The kentucky derby is held every may at churchill downs in louisville, kentucky.
5. Everyone in Elena's family speaks both spanish and english.
6. Frank converted his chevy van into a camper.
7. Steve Goodman wrote a song about a train called *the city of new orleans.*
8. The traditional date for the founding of Rome is 753 b.c.
9. The last Roman emperor, Romulus Augustulus, ruled until a.d. 476.
10. The three major races are caucasian, negro, and mongolian.

E. Use capital letters correctly.

Number your paper 1–10. Find the words in the following sentences that should be capitalized. Write the words after the proper numbers, using the necessary capital letters.

1. mary jane has two sisters. they both live in connecticut.
2. "well, i can't wait until thursday," ms. garvey said. "i need that drill by monday at the latest."
3. we saw the soccer match between the new york cosmos and the fort lauderdale strikers.
4. "raul, will you deliver this package?" asked mrs. jefferson. "it must get there today."

5. franklin d. roosevelt was born in hyde park, new york.

6. "are you going to answer that phone," dr. fields asked her assistant, "or shall i do it?"

7. My aunt and uncle took andrea and beth to the astrodome to see the houston astros play the atlanta braves.

8. "is it may or june that has thirty-one days?" brian asked.

9. tony bought that old ford. why did he do it? that's a good question.

10. the world is weary of the past,
    oh, might it die or rest at last!

F. Use capital letters correctly.

Number your paper 1–10. Find the words in the following sentences that should be capitalized. Write the words after the proper numbers, using necessary capital letters.

1. Charlene and Debbie went to see *jaws* three times.

2. Did you read "making perfect pancakes" in last Sunday's *gazette*?

3. Mother's favorite song is "twilight time."

4. yours truly,

5. The rand junior high girls' basketball team beat miner junior high in the play-offs last friday.

6. One of america's most famous women athletes was babe didrikson.

7. Many people think that *guernica* is picasso's greatest painting.

8. I. american authors and works

    A. laura ingalls wilder

        1. *little house on the prairie*

        2. *the first four years*

9. Everyone in our family enjoyed *star wars*.

10. dear neighbor:

    have you missed finding *newsweek* in your mailbox every week?

Section 11

Punctuation

Punctuation is the use of commas, periods, semicolons, and other marks in writing. The marks used are called **punctuation marks.**

Good punctuation will help your readers understand what they read. It will show them where to pause or stop. It will tell them whether they are reading a statement, an exclamation, or a question.

End Marks

The punctuation marks that show where a sentence ends are called **end marks.**

There are three very important end marks: (1) the **period;** (2) the **question mark;** (3) the **exclamation point** (or **exclamation mark).**

The Period

Use a period at the end of a declarative sentence.

A **declarative sentence** is a sentence that makes a statement. It is the kind of sentence you use when you want to tell something.

My sister plays the piano.

A declarative sentence is often shortened to one or two words; for example, in answering a question.

Where are you going to put the ladder?
Over there. (*I am going to put it over there.*)

Use a period at the end of an imperative sentence.

An **imperative sentence** is a sentence that requests or tells someone to do something.

Please open the window.

If the imperative sentence also expresses excitement or emotion, an exclamation point is used after it.

Look out!

Use a period at the end of an indirect question.

An *indirect question* is the part of a statement that tells what someone asked, but that does not give the exact words of the person who asked the question.

Judy asked *whether the movie was worth seeing.*

Now compare the above indirect question with a *direct question:*

Judy asked, "Is the movie worth seeing?"

A direct question gives the exact words of the person who asked the question. It is always followed by a question mark, as in the above example.

Use a period after an abbreviation or after an initial.

An **abbreviation** is a shortened form of a word.

mm. *(millimeter)*	km. *(kilometer)*
in. *(inch or inches)*	Dr. *(Doctor)*
Sept. *(September)*	Tues. *(Tuesday)*

A name is often shortened to its first letter, which is called an **initial.**

O. J. Simpson *(Orenthal James Simpson)*
Susan B. Anthony *(Susan Brownell Anthony)*

Sometimes an abbreviation is made up of two or more parts, each part standing for one or more words. A period is then used after each part.

B. C. *(Before Christ)*   S. Dak. *(South Dakota)*

Periods are omitted in some abbreviations. If you are not sure whether an abbreviation should be written with or without periods, look up the abbreviation in your dictionary.

FM *(frequency modulation)*
mph *(miles per hour)*
UN *(United Nations)*

Use a period after each number or letter that shows a division of an outline or that precedes an item in a list.

(An Outline)	(A List)
I. Trees	1. meat
A. Shade trees	2. potatoes
1. Elms	3. ice cream

The Question Mark

Use a question mark at the end of an interrogative sentence.

An **interrogative sentence** is a sentence that asks a question.

Has anyone seen my dog?

The above sentence gives the exact words of the person who asked the question. It is called a *direct question.* A question mark is used only with a direct question.

Do not use a question mark with an indirect question. Instead, use a period.

An *indirect question* is the part of a statement that tells what someone asked, without giving the exact words.

Kelly asked *whether anyone had seen her dog.*

The Exclamation Point

Use an exclamation point at the end of an exclamatory sentence.

An **exclamatory sentence** is a sentence that expresses strong feeling.

What a terrific game that was!

An exclamation point is also used at the end of an imperative sentence that expresses excitement or emotion.

Hurry up!

Most imperative sentences, however, should be followed by a period.

Please shut the door.

Use an exclamation point after an interjection or after any other exclamatory expression.

An **interjection** is a word or group of words used to express strong feeling. It is one of the eight parts of speech. Words often used as other parts of speech may become interjections when they express strong feeling.

Oh! How beautiful!
Wow! What an exciting movie!

Avoid using the exclamation point too frequently. Use it only when you are sure it is needed.

Exercises   Use periods, questions marks, and exclamation points correctly.

A. Copy the following sentences. Supply the missing punctuation.

1. Was Mr J E Edwards in Buffalo, N Y, on June 19, 1978
2. Look out That shelf is falling
3. Mr and Mrs T A Stock, Miss Sarah Temple, and Dr G B Torker spoke at the board meeting
4. How did the cat get into the birdcage
5. Write to J B Lippincott Co, publishers of the book
6. We listened to news broadcasts at 6:00 P M and at 7:30 A M
7. Ms Sue M Horton teaches swimming at the Y M C A
8. Help This carton is too heavy for me
9. On the card was printed "Dr Stephanie James, D D S"
10. How peaceful it is here Is it always this way

B. Copy the following sentences. Supply the missing punctuation.

1. Did Mrs Bryant call Dr Loras about the appointment
2. How dare you say that
3. Wow That was an exciting race
4. Please let me see that book Is it yours
5. Pete asked me whether I had seen Dr M J Thomas
6. She lives at 1720 Pennsylvania Ave, Washington D C
7. My plane left Boston, Mass, at 11:45 A M and arrived in St Louis, Mo, at 2:15 P M
8. Do Mr and Mrs F L Schaefer live here
9. This map of Fresno, Calif, is drawn on a scale of 1 in to ¼ mi, isn't it
10. Sue asked Mrs Cassini if she knew Ms Williamson

C. Write eight original sentences. In the first five sentences, show five different uses of the period. In the sixth sentence, show the use of the question mark. In the last two sentences, show two different uses of the exclamation point. Be prepared to give the reason for each end mark used.

The Comma

When you speak, you do not say everything at the same rate. You pause, to show that there is a break in your thought. You put words into groups, pausing at the end of the group. You use the pause to help your listeners understand which words go together.

In writing, the comma is used to show which words go together. Commas also show your readers where to pause. If they read right on without pausing, they will be confused.

The Comma To Avoid Confusion

Some sentences can be very confusing if commas are not used in them. Here are two examples of such sentences:

> In the morning mail is delivered.
> After eating my dad takes a nap.

Now notice how much clearer a sentence is when a comma is used:

> In the morning, mail is delivered.
> After eating, my dad takes a nap.

Use a comma whenever the reader might otherwise be confused.

Exercise   Use a comma to avoid confusion.

Copy each of the following sentences. Use a comma to make the meaning clear.

1. I have the potato salad and the hamburgers are right there in the refrigerator.
2. Before coloring her little sister put all her other toys away.
3. When the climbers reached the top coats were necessary.
4. No matter what I do not want another milk shake.
5. By the time she woke up the neighborhood was very quiet.
6. Circling the airplane approached the field.
7. When we entered the room was empty.
8. After they finished the table was cleared.
9. Sue ordered hot chocolate ice cream, and cake.
10. While painting my sister accidentally broke a window.

Commas in a Series

Use a comma after every item in a series except the last.

In writing, a series consists of three or more items of the same kind. These items may be nouns, verbs, modifiers, phrases, or other parts of the sentence.

A comma is placed after every item in a series except the last. Note these examples:

1. We *packed, ate,* and *left* for home.
   (The three items in this series are verbs.)

2. *Tom, Mary, Eve,* and *Ray* won prizes.
   (The four items in this series are nouns.)

3. The arms of the machine moved *up and down, in and out,* and *back and forth.*
   (The items in this series are the groups of adverbs *up and down, in and out,* and *back and forth.*)

4. We could not decide whether to ride *to the old mill, to the beach,* or *over Sunset Hill.*
   (The items in this series are the phrases *to the old mill, to the beach,* and *over Sunset Hill.*)

5. It was getting dark, a wind blew down from the mountain, and Henry began to wonder where he was.
   (The items in this series are sentences.)

Use commas after the adverbs *first, second, third,* and so on.

We had three reasons: first, we weren't interested in fishing; second, we had no transportation; third, we had other things to do.

When two or more adjectives precede a noun, use a comma after each adjective except the last one.

It was a bright, brisk, invigorating day.

226

Sometimes two adjectives are used together to express a single idea made up of two closely related thoughts. Adjectives used in this way are not usually separated by a comma.

A *little old* man knocked at the door.
A *big red* truck pulled into the driveway.

When you say the two sentences above, notice that you do not pause between the adjectives.

Exercises   Use commas correctly to separate items.

A. Copy the following sentences. Add commas where they are needed.

1. These three girls were with us: Michelle Richards Martha Rose and Joanne Cary.

2. In his pockets Terry had a bent penny a pencil stub about a yard of string a comb and two rubber bands.

3. Mrs. Harrison ordered the ginger ale and cola checked on the supply of paper plates and cups and called the farmer to get permission for us to picnic.

4. Here are the kinds of sandwiches we had: peanut butter and jelly tomato and bacon ham and cheese and egg salad.

5. Last summer Ted helped with the haying fed the chickens went after the cows and hoed the garden.

6. Do three things: first get the book from the library; second make an outline; third write the report.

7. The three pairs were Bill and José Jim and Manny and Bob and Carl.

8. Please check the addresses of these persons: Ms. Sondra Jackson Dr. Joyce L. Reiner and Mr. and Mrs. George Abel.

9. That was a long hard train ride.

10. I saw them slide scramble and tumble down the slope.

B. Copy the following sentences. Add commas where they are needed.

1. That evening we unloaded the car set up the tent climbed into our sleeping bags and went to sleep.

2. In the morning the sun rose over the hills the birds were singing in the trees and fish jumped in the lake.

3. You may go to the swimming area on the nature trail or into town.

4. Karen Jack and Juanita went swimming; and my mother my father and I went to the store.

5. For supper we had hot dogs buns pickles and baked beans.

6. About midnight I woke up. First there was a loud crash outside; second the dog barked; third things rustled on the table.

7. When I looked out, the garbage can was overturned and two curious black-masked raccoons were on the picnic table.

8. Slowly quietly and thoroughly they investigated the table.

9. They nibbled the cookie argued over an apple and turned up their noses at a piece of pickle someone had dropped.

10. Dad said, "At least it wasn't a bobcat a skunk or a big bear."

The Comma after Introductory Words

Use a comma to separate an introductory word or group of words from the rest of the sentence.

Yes, Paula is my sister.
Climbing down the tree, I ripped my pocket on a snag.

The comma may be omitted if there would be little pause in speaking.

At last the plane landed.

Commas with Interrupters

Use commas to set off words or groups of words that interrupt the flow of thought in a sentence.

This bike, however, is in better physical condition.
The answer, I suppose, will never be known.

Exercises **Use commas to set off words correctly.**

A. Copy the following sentences and add commas where necessary.

1. The Assembly Committee as I said earlier will meet on Thursday.
2. No I haven't seen that movie.
3. Janet's absence is excusable I am certain.
4. The Safety Committee of course needs good equipment.
5. The test results I suppose will be posted tomorrow.
6. However Jan prefers to work on her own.
7. The library Bill had said was closed.
8. Several of the hikers nevertheless made the trip in an hour.
9. This paper for example has no watermark.
10. After all Maria is a college senior.

B. Copy the following sentences and add commas where necessary. One sentence does not need any commas.

1. Pat I hope will make a better shortstop than Chris.
2. No you may not stay at Ellen's for dinner.
3. In slalom skiing on the other hand you use only one ski.
4. Mary has a Siamese cat I think.
5. Did you hear by the way that there was a sellout crowd at the game last night?
6. Running to third I tripped and sprained my ankle.

7. Maybe Sue will join us.

8. Finally the last marathon runner entered the Olympic Stadium.

9. Yes the game has been postponed.

10. While vacationing in Montreal Allison and I met many French-speaking people.

Commas with Nouns of Direct Address

Use commas to set off nouns of direct address.

When you are speaking to someone, you like to use that person's name. When you do, you are using the **noun of direct address.**

> Call me tonight, Jane, if you can.

In the above sentence, *Jane* is the noun of direct address. It names the person whom the speaker is addressing (speaking to).

If commas are omitted with nouns of direct address, the sentence may confuse the reader. Here is an example of such a confusing sentence:

> Help me bake Jon and you may have some cookies.

Commas with Appositives

Use commas to set off most appositives.

Appositives are words placed immediately after other words to make those other words clearer or more definite. Most appositives are nouns. Nouns used as appositives are called **nouns in apposition.** In the following sentence, *co-captains* is a noun in apposition (an appositive).

> Karen and Maria, our co-captains, accepted the trophy for our team.
> Our science teacher, Miss Bell, will not be back next year.

When an appositive is used with modifiers, the whole group of words is set off with commas.

Joe, the boy in the blue shirt, is Dave's cousin.

When the noun in apposition is a first name, it is not usually set off by commas.

This is my friend Tony.

Exercises Use commas with nouns of direct address and with appositives.

A. Copy the following sentences. Add commas wherever necessary. After each sentence, write your reason for using commas in it.

1. Mother have you met Mr. Gillespie our music teacher?
2. Ms. Mantoya this is my father Mr. Brown.
3. Mr. Ingram our English teacher is coming now Dad.
4. Dad this is Mr. Ingram our English teacher.
5. Miss Jenkins this is Cynthia my sister.
6. Mrs. Harmon I'd like you to meet my sister Jovita.
7. Mary this is my classmate Tanya Jefferson.
8. Ms. Swisher our math teacher is from Alaska.
9. Well folks dinner will be ready any minute now.
10. José this is my brother Larry.

B. Rewrite the following pairs of sentences. Combine each pair into a single sentence by using a noun in apposition.

Example: Mrs. Douglas is mayor of our town. She will speak next.

Mrs. Douglas, mayor of our town, will speak next.

1. The fastest runner is Penny Torrens. She is on the track team.

2. We have a favorite horse. Her name is Daisy Belle.

3. The author is Mark Twain. He knew a lot about people.

4. The girl in the tan sweater is Paula. She likes to go camping.

5. There was only one hit against Tate. It was a single.

6. Karen is on the swimming team. She is my classmate.

7. The second largest city in the United States is Chicago. It was founded in 1803.

8. Our pitcher is Bill Phillips. He injured his arm.

9. Miss Parsons is our music teacher. She plays the piano.

10. One of my favorite books is *The Miracle Worker*. It's a play about Helen Keller and Annie Sullivan.

Commas with Quotations

Use commas to set off the explanatory words of a direct quotation.

Remember that when you use a quotation you are giving the words of a speaker or writer. You are said to be *quoting* the words of the speaker or writer. If you give the *exact* words, you are giving a **direct quotation.** Usually you include explanatory words of your own, like *Joyce said, Peggy answered,* or *Bill asked.*

Jeff said, "Mother and I are going to the store."

In the above sentence, the explanatory words come *before* the quotation. A comma is then placed after the last explanatory word.

Now look at this quotation:

"Let's visit the zoo," said Joe.

In the above sentence, the explanatory words come *after* the quotation. A comma is then placed after the last word of the quotation, as you can see.

Sometimes the quotation is separated into two parts.

"If it rains," he said, "it'll probably be just a shower."

The above sentence is an example of what is called a *divided quotation*. It is called "divided" because it is made up of two parts that are separated by the explanatory words. A comma is used after the last word of the first part. Another comma is used after the last explanatory word.

The quotations you have just looked at are all direct quotations. A quotation can be either *direct* or *indirect*. In an **indirect quotation** you change the words of a speaker or writer to your own words. No commas are used.

Ms. Mooney said *that she enjoyed visiting our class.*

Exercise   Use commas with direct quotations.

Number your paper 1–10. In the following sentences, find the words after which commas must be used. Write the words and add the commas. Also write the word after each comma that you add. If a sentence needs no commas, write the word *Correct.*

Example: Patricia said "I'm glad to see you, Jane."
    1. said, "I'm

1. Liz asked "Won't your mother let you have a dog?"
2. "But London Bridge is no longer in London" Art said.
3. Jim said "Everyone has gone to the beach today."
4. Dr. Gonzales said that Sandy had broken her arm.
5. "Did you know" asked Angie "that Alpha Centauri is the nearest star?"
6. "I like the climate of Seattle best of all" answered Tom.
7. Denise asked "Have you ever flown in a helicopter?"
8. "I can fix that faucet in ten minutes" Mary boasted.
9. Ken asked if we could drop him off first.
10. "I believe" shouted the announcer "that we have a winner!"

The Comma in a Compound Sentence

You will remember that a **compound sentence** consists of two simple sentences joined together.

Use a comma before the conjunction that joins the two simple sentences in a compound sentence.

Chris got back from his trip,̸ and now he's sleeping.

The comma is not necessary in very short compound sentences when the parts are joined by *and*.

We were thirsty and we were hungry.

However, always use a comma before *but* or *or*.

We were thirsty,̸ but we weren't hungry.

Do not confuse a compound sentence with a sentence that has only a compound predicate. The two parts of a compound predicate are *not* joined by commas.

We can stop here or go on to Toronto.

If a compound predicate has more than two parts, the parts are joined by commas.

We came early,̸ worked hard,̸ and left late.

Exercises   Use commas correctly.

A. Number your paper 1–10. Decide where the commas should be placed. Write the word before the comma. Write the comma and the conjunction that follows. Two sentences have compound predicates and need no commas. Write the word *Correct* for those sentences.

Example: Our library is small but it has a good selection of reference books.

small, but

1. I'd like to go to the show but I have too much work to do.

2. The picture was excellent but I didn't enjoy waiting in line.

3. We stopped on the side of the road and ate our lunch.

4. On the moon the temperature rises to over 200° in the daytime but it drops far below zero at night.

5. There was an annoying noise in the car but we could not locate the cause.

6. You can have two large containers or use three small ones.

7. Can you stay for dinner or are you leaving early?

8. The coach drew a diagram and the players studied it hard.

9. We raked the leaves into neat piles but the wind blew them away.

10. Ellen played the piano and Sue performed a Mexican folk dance.

B. Follow the directions for Exercise A.

1. I don't really want to go but I will if you come with me.

2. The mail carrier delivered two small packages and he asked me to sign for them.

3. The book wasn't very long but she couldn't finish it.

4. Is a meter shorter than a yard or is it the other way around?

5. We went to the State Fair yesterday and spent the entire day there.

6. Are you in a hurry or can you stop for some ice cream?

7. At first she couldn't dance at all but now she's pretty good.

8. He flew to San Francisco and took a bus from there.

9. Nancy brought the sandwiches and cole slaw but she forgot the lemonade.

10. These jeans are too long and they don't fit at the waist.

Commas in Dates

Use commas to set off the parts of dates from each other.

Thursday, November 9, 1978

If a date is used in a sentence, place a comma after the last part of the date.

February 20, 1962, was the day on which the first American orbited the earth.

Commas in Locations and Addresses

Use commas between the name of a city or town and the name of its state or country.

Des Moines, Iowa

Use commas to separate the parts of an address.

1943 Meech Road, Williamston, Michigan 48895

If an address is used in a sentence, place a comma after the last part of the address.

From Omaha, Nebraska, we drove to Wichita, Kansas.
Please send the order to 125 West Lincoln Highway, DeKalb, Illinois 60115, as requested.

Commas in Letter Parts

Use a comma after the greeting of a friendly letter and after the complimentary close of any letter.

Dear Dana,   Sincerely yours,

Exercises   Use commas correctly.

A. Copy the following sentences. Add commas where they are needed.

1. The first Boston Marathon was held on April 19 1897.

2. Are you talking about Kansas City Missouri or Kansas City Kansas?

3. Sherlock Holmes lived at 221B Baker Street London.

4. Send your reply to Campbell and Surprenant, Inc. 135 South LaSalle Street Chicago Illinois 60603.

5. He was born on April 3 1963 so he's an Aries.

6. Donna's new address is 4652 Orchard Street Oakland California.

7. We're going to the museum on Thursday May 5.

8. Does this address say Gary Indiana or Cary Illinois?

9. My older brother hasn't had many birthdays because he was born on February 29 1960.

10. Someday my address will be 1600 Pennsylvania Avenue Washington D. C.

B. Follow the directions for Exercise A.

1. My cousin and I were both born on September 4 1962.

2. Why is 10 Downing Street London famous?

3. Eleanor Roosevelt was born on October 11 1884 and died on November 7 1962.

4. Where were you on Friday June 24 1977?

5. Reno Nevada is farther west than Los Angeles California.

6. Saturday July 26 is Kathryn's birthday party.

7. The best hot dogs are at Petey's 110 Washington Street Elm Forest.

8. Address your letters to the *Chicago Sun-Times* 401 North Wabash Avenue Chicago Illinois 60611.

9. We lived at 130 Rand Road Austin Texas from May 1 1973 to April 30 1977.

10. The only historical date I can remember is July 4 1776.

The Semicolon

Use a semicolon to join the parts of a compound sentence when no coordinating conjunction is used.

Mother threw the coat away; it was worn out.

The Colon

Use a colon after the greeting of a business letter.

Dear Sir or Madam: Gentlemen:

Use a colon between numerals indicating hours and minutes.

9:30 A.M.

Use a colon to introduce a list of items.

We need the following items: paintbrushes, tubes of paint, a palette, and canvas.

Exercise   Use semicolons and colons correctly.

Copy the word before and after the missing punctuation mark and add the correct punctuation mark.

1. Mary Ann is my sister Dan is my twin brother.
2. The last vote was counted Jane was elected.
3. Class will be held at 2 15 P.M. in the music room.
4. The pupils with the highest marks are as follows Michael Karnatz, Susan O'Brien, and Janet Newcombe.
5. Here is what Jack wants a compass, a pencil, and ink.
6. The time of the game has been changed from 1 00 P.M. to 2 00 P.M.

7. Sally decided against the 10-speed bike she's going to get a 3-speed instead.

8. My parents grow a lot of vegetables in their garden peas, lettuce, beets, carrots, and sweet corn.

9. Sheila is going to New York this summer she's never been there before.

10. Which of the following flavors is your favorite boysenberry cheesecake, fudge brownie, or rocky road?

The Hyphen

Use a hyphen to separate the parts of a word at the end of a line.

> My father gets extra pay when he has to work over-
> time at the office.

Use a hyphen in compound numbers from twenty-one through ninety-nine.

> thirty-two seconds   forty-three pencils

Use a hyphen in fractions used as modifiers.

> We hope to have a *three-fourths* majority.
> (*Three-fourths* modifies *majority*.)

Use a hyphen or hyphens in such compound nouns as *great-aunt* and *commander-in-chief*.

Use a hyphen or hyphens between words that make up a compound adjective used before a noun.

> We have an up-to-date encyclopedia.
> *But:* Our encyclopedia is up to date.

> I rode my ten-speed bike to school.
> That VW has a four-cylinder engine.

Exercise   Use hyphens correctly.

Copy the words in each sentence that need hyphens and add them.

1. Marilyn's sister in law worked as a policewoman before she became a lawyer.

2. The trip back to Bob's took forty five minutes.

3. Today only, felt tip pens are reduced from eighty nine cents to fifty nine cents.

4. A two thirds majority vote by Congress is needed to override the President's veto.

5. Sonja's great grandparents came here from Norway in 1892.

6. I hope those money hungry, cattle rustling outlaws meet up with The Kid.

7. Eileen's mother bought her a peach colored blouse and a lime green jumper.

8. An eight cylinder engine has more power, but a six cylinder engine will burn less gas.

9. The Mason Dixon line, which divides the North and South, was surveyed by Charles Mason and Jeremiah Dixon.

10. The President is also commander in chief of the armed forces.

The Apostrophe

To form the possessive of a singular noun, add an apostrophe and an s.

girl + **'s** = girl's   man + **'s** = man's
boy + **'s** = boy's   Charles + **'s** = Charles's

To form the possessive of a plural noun that does not end in s, add an apostrophe and an s.

women + **'s** = women's   mice + **'s** = mice's

240

To form the possessive of a plural noun that ends in s, add only an apostrophe.

friends + ' = friends'   countries + ' = countries'

Exercises   **Form the possessives of nouns correctly.**

A. On a piece of paper, write the possessive form of the following nouns.

1. doctor	11. computer
2. stewardess	12. conductor
3. producer	13. artist
4. elephant	14. librarian
5. Les	15. reporter
6. electrician	16. horse
7. Ms. Prentiss	17. actress
8. Randy	18. counselor
9. employee	19. Mrs. Thomas
10. architect	20. principal

B. On a piece of paper, write the plural form of each of the following nouns. After the plural form, write the plural possessive for each noun.

1. family	11. teacher
2. student	12. bookkeeper
3. county	13. salesperson
4. nurse	14. company
5. woman	15. dentist
6. optometrist	16. man
7. astronaut	17. accountant
8. city	18. journalist
9. lawyer	19. orthodontist
10. paramedic	20. carpenter

Use an apostrophe in a contraction.

Writing contractions is not at all mysterious if you understand that the apostrophe simply replaces one or more omitted letters:

we are → we're	where is → where's
she is → she's	they are → they're
here is → here's	cannot → can't
there is → there's	could not → couldn't
I would → I'd	will not → won't
we will → we'll	was not → wasn't
they will → they'll	would not → wouldn't

Look out, too, for *it's* and *its*. Remember:

It's (with an apostrophe) always means *it is* or *it has*.
Its (without the apostrophe) is the possessive of *it*.

Example: *It's* time for the bird to have *its* bath.

Remember, too, that no apostrophe is used with the possessive pronouns *ours, yours, his, hers, theirs*.

Example: These magazines are *ours*.
Those on the table are *theirs*.

Look out for *who's* and *whose*. Remember:

Who's (with an apostrophe) means *who is* or *who has*.
Whose (without the apostrophe) is the possessive of *who*.

Examples: *Who's* going with you to the movie?
Whose house is that?

Two other contractions that you should watch are *you're* and *they're*. *You're* means *you are*. Do not confuse it with the possessive pronoun *your*. *They're* means *they are*. Do not confuse it with the possessive pronoun *their*.

Examples: *You're* now in *your* own classroom.
They're visiting *their* aunt.

Use an apostrophe to form the plurals of letters, figures, and words used as words.

Children used to be told to mind their *p's* and *q's*.
Carol should form her *3's* and *7's* more carefully.
Pam's story was full of *but's*.

Exercises **Use apostrophes correctly.**

A. Copy these sentences, inserting apostrophes where they are needed.

1. Jim cant go because hes helping his parents.
2. Its late. Havent you finished yet?
3. Were going to keep working till weve finished.
4. Ill turn on Carls desk lamp. Wont that help?
5. Thats fine. Well work much faster now.
6. Wheres the paint for the puppets faces?
7. Its on the garage shelf. Its Mrs. Steins paint. Dont waste it.
8. My puppet wont sit up. Its back isnt stiff enough.
9. Heres the book you wanted. Its been checked out until now.
10. Wheres the paste? Im ready. Lets go.

B. Look at each pair of words in parentheses. Choose the word that belongs in the sentence.Write it on your paper.

1. (*Wasn't, Wasnt*) Mr. Lopez (*they're, their*) teacher last year?
2. (*Who's, Whose*) going with you to the concert? I hope (*you're, your*) able to find someone.
3. Which poster is (*her's, hers*)?
4. (*It's, Its*) hard to believe that the car has lost (*it's its*) muffler already.

5. (*Here's, Heres*) the pump for (*you're, your*) bicycle tire.

6. (*We'll, Well*) all be happy if it (*doesn't, doesnt*) rain.

7. (*You're, Your*) the one (*who's, whose*) going to Mexico, aren't you?

8. Kathy and Peg are going to the play, but they (*don't, dont*) have (*they're, their*) tickets yet.

9. Mrs. LaRette (*doesn't, doesnt*) know (*who's, whose*) bike is in the driveway.

10. (*They're, Their*) team has had much more practice than (*our's, ours*).

Quotation Marks

Use quotation marks at the beginning and at the end of a direct quotation.

Quotation marks [" "] consist of two pairs of small marks that resemble apostrophes. They tell a reader that the exact words of another speaker or writer are being given.

Matt said, "I'm going to wash the family car."

Quotation marks are *not* used with indirect quotations:

Matt said *that he was going to wash the family car.*

Sometimes a direct quotation is divided into two or more parts by explanatory words. In such a case, each part of the quotation is enclosed in quotation marks.

"If that team wins," Patty whispered, "I'll be surprised."

Remember that the second part of a divided quotation begins with a small letter unless it is a proper noun or unless it starts a new sentence.

"If you're ready," said Paul, "we can leave now."

"I saw Mr. Prichard," said Amy. "He was in the supermarket."

The first part of a divided quotation is followed by a comma that is placed *inside* the quotation marks.

"When you wash the car," Dick's father said, "use a soft cloth."

Explanatory words in a divided quotation are followed by either a comma or a period *outside* the quotation marks. A comma is used after the explanatory words if the second part of the quotation does not begin a new sentence. A period is used after the explanatory words if the second part of the quotation is a new sentence.

"Help me set the table," said Mother, "and then call your sister."
"I've finished my homework," Dan said. "It was easy."

Explanatory words at the beginning of a sentence are followed by a comma *outside* the quotation marks. The period at the end of the sentence is placed *inside* the quotation marks.

My uncle answered, "I'll send you a postcard."

Explanatory words at the end of a sentence are followed by a period. The quoted words at the beginning of the sentence are followed by a comma *inside* the quotation marks.

"I'll send you a postcard," my uncle answered.

Exercise   Use quotation marks correctly.

Write each of the following sentences three ways as a direct quotation.

Example: Of course you can go.

1. He said, "Of course you can go."
2. "Of course," he said, "you can go."
3. "Of course you can go," he said.

1. If you like, we will stay.
2. At least you like potatoes.
3. Well, there's another way to do it.
4. At noon the pool will open.
5. Aunt Mary is going to visit us.

Place question marks and exclamation points inside quotation marks if they belong to the quotation itself.

Mother said to Tim, "Have you finished the dishes?"
"Look out!" Dad shouted.

Place question marks and exclamation points outside quotation marks if they do not belong to the quotation.

Did Rachel say, "Meet me in the library"?
The teacher said, "Class will be dismissed an hour earlier"!

Exercises   **Use quotation marks correctly.**

A.   Copy the following sentences. Punctuate them correctly with quotation marks, end marks, and commas.

1. Did you notice Inspector Blaine asked anything peculiar about the suspect

2. Just that he wore a khaki trench coat and a hat that hid his face I replied

3. I reminded the Inspector that I had caught only a glimpse of the mysterious person as he raced by me

4. Are you certain that he was tall and limped as he ran Blaine asked

5. Correct I answered I also believe he favored his left side

6. Oh by the way I added he was carrying a small suitcase, too

7. Would you mind coming down to the station and making a statement Blaine asked

8. I told him that I wouldn't mind, but that I preferred to keep my name out of the newspapers

9. No need to worry he remarked as he opened the squad car door for me

10. I thanked him for his courtesy and discretion and got in

B. Write each of the following sentences as a direct quotation.

Example: Next week I start my new job.

1. "Next week," Sally said, "I start my new job."

or

2. Sally said, "Next week I start my new job."

or

3. "Next week I start my new job," Sally said.

1. Last night I had a terrible dream.
2. Walk three blocks and turn right.
3. Certainly you can go to the movies.
4. Thank goodness my glasses aren't broken.
5. The shirts are dirty, but the slacks are clean.
6. By the way, that clock is ten minutes fast.
7. Next summer our whole family is driving to California.
8. Perhaps poodles are smarter, but I still prefer collies.
9. Green apples give me a stomachache.
10. All it takes to open that paint can is a screwdriver.

You may wonder how to use quotation marks when you are quoting *two or more sentences of a single speaker*. Notice how the following quotation is punctuated.

"Can the repairman come tomorrow?" asked Jean over the telephone. "Mother needs to use the washing machine. She can't use it at all now."

Only one set of quotation marks would be needed if the example read as follows:

Over the telephone Jean said, "Can the repairman come to-morrow? Mother needs to use the washing machine. She can't use it at all now."

In writing *dialogue* (conversation), begin a new paragraph every time the speaker changes:

"Mr. Scott invited the family to his camp for the after-noon," said Jean. "He told Father to stop and blow his horn."

"Well," said Barbara, "what happened?"

"Father stopped the car, blew his horn, and then stalled the motor. We had to walk up the hill."

Exercise   Punctuate conversations correctly.

Rewrite the following conversation. Make correct para-graph divisions and use the right punctuation.

Ms Marlow was waiting for the children to take their seats Everyone was crowded around Billy Everyone please sit down said Ms Marlow Billy has a black eye cried Eric What happened Billy asked Ms Marlow I poked myself in the eye with my elbow answered Billy smiling That's impossible Billy No it isn't Ms Marlow I stood on a chair giggled Billy

Additional Exercises

Punctuation

A. Use periods, question marks, and exclamation points correctly.

Copy the following sentences. Supply the missing punctuation.

1. Dr Peggy S Nilsen, M D , introduced Gov Brown to the audience
2. Are you sure that Sarah has a driver's license
3. Get off that roof before you fall and get hurt
4. Send the coupon to Ms Lauren May, 619 N Lewis Rd, St Cloud, Minn, by the first of June.
5. Do you think John can get seven people in that tiny car
6. P J asked if she could borrow my bicycle
7. Wow What an easy test that turned out to be
8. Don't open your eyes until I count to three
9. Pam asked which car got better mileage
10. King Tutankhamun's tomb remained untouched from 1352 B C until A D 1922, when Howard Carter found a secret entrance

B. Use a comma to avoid confusion.

Copy each of the following sentences. Use a comma to make the meaning clear.

1. In the field mice had burrowed under the grass.
2. With this ice cream would taste very good.

3. After painting Kathy went cycling.
4. Outside the playing field was in chaos.
5. Coming past the students noticed the bulletin board.
6. Once before the stage curtain had stuck halfway up.
7. To Mary Pat gave a beautiful bracelet.
8. When you are eating your hands should be clean.
9. Because they hurried the class made mistakes.
10. Inside the theater was dimly lighted.

C. Use commas correctly to separate items.

Copy the following sentences. Add commas where they are necessary.

1. Laura Sally Lynn and Tad are going to the soccer match.
2. After dinner, we cut the lawn trimmed the bushes and weeded the garden.
3. Penny plays tennis racquetball and ping pong very well.
4. During the school play, Ellen Trisha and I were in charge of changing the scenery handling the costumes and directing the make-up crew.
5. This summer we are driving to Colorado Utah and Wyoming.
6. Please do these three things for me: first mail this package at the post office; second return the books to the library; and third pick up the cleaning.
7. Ken Stabler Fran Tarkenton and Ken Anderson have been leading quarterbacks in professional football.
8. Would you like to go to the movies with Amy José and me?
9. We really enjoyed seeing Chris Evert Billie Jean King and Margaret Court play tennis.
10. Jim cleaned up the kitchen Miki vacuumed the living room and dining room and I went to the grocery store.

D. Use commas to set off words correctly.

Copy the following sentences and add commas where necessary.

1. About midnight however I woke up.
2. Sitting quietly the children listened to the storyteller.
3. We'll get back we hope in time for the performance.
4. This book for example is one of the best novels I have read.
5. The Chicago River by an act of man flows backward.
6. You realize of course that the plans must be canceled.
7. Barking furiously the dog ran to the window.
8. If it rains however the picnic will be canceled.
9. The announcements I think have already been read over the intercom.
10. These athletes by vote of the sports writers were named to the All-City Team.

E. Use commas with appositives.

Rewrite the following pairs of sentences. Combine each pair into a single sentence by using a noun in apposition.

1. Mrs. Eaton is my science teacher. She is from Australia.
2. The girl in the blue sweatshirt is Karen. She is the fastest swimmer on the team.
3. *Rumble Fish* is an exciting book. It was written by S. E. Hinton.
4. One of the speakers at our banquet was Bruce Jenner. He was the decathlon winner in the Olympics.
5. Our optometrist is Dr. Stewart. She has an office in the plaza.
6. Ms. Hogan is our P. E. teacher. She coaches the girls' track and field team.

7. Rod Carew is an outstanding baseball player. He plays first base for the Minnesota Twins.

8. "Welcome Back, Kotter" is my favorite TV show. It will be starting a new season in the fall.

9. The movie I saw was *Star Wars*. It was one of the most exciting and creative science fiction films I have seen.

10. Dorothy Hamill performs with the Ice Capades. She is an Olympic gold medal winner.

F. Use commas with direct quotations.

Number your paper 1–10. In the following sentences, find the words after which commas must be used. Write the words and add the commas. Also write the word after each comma that you add. If a sentence needs no commas, write the word *Correct*.

1. Lori said "Do you want to use my backpack?"
2. My mother said that she would drive us to the concert.
3. Jill said "Here is the door to the stage."
4. "I'll show you how to use the drill press" Ms. Olsen said.
5. "You must finish your homework first" Dad answered.
6. "If you'd like to borrow my bike" said Kay "you may use it this weekend."
7. Linda said that she'd water all of the plants.
8. "Do you plan" Bill said "to go to the movie?"
9. Danny said that he liked this kind of chair.
10. "Of course" she said "you can come with us."

G. Use commas correctly in compound sentences.

Number your paper 1–10. Decide where the commas should be placed. Write the word before the comma. Write the comma and the conjunction that follows. Two sentences have compound predicates and need no commas.

1. We went sailing on Saturday but the bad weather on Sunday kept us at home.

2. We have studied the metric system in math and in home economics we use only metrics in our measurements.

3. Will you be going anywhere during spring vacation or will you be staying home?

4. After the hockey game, we stopped at Burger King and ate dinner.

5. We saw the movie *Sounder* in my English class but I enjoyed reading the book even more.

6. The state gymnastics meet was held at Prospect High School but we were unable to get tickets.

7. The Smithsonian Institution in Washington, D. C., is a fabulous place to see but it would take days to see it all.

8. My sister and I enjoyed walking the Freedom Trail in Boston but our favorite tour was at the United Nations in New York.

9. We sponsored a car wash and raised enough money for a field trip.

10. Our science class built a mini-greenhouse and we grew many plants and flowers throughout the year.

H. Use commas correctly in dates and addresses.

Copy the following sentences and add commas where they are needed.

1. The new law will go into effect on January 1 1979.

2. Mail your reservation to Camp Twilight 1515 North Powderhorn Road Bessemer Michigan 49911.

3. Should this letter be sent to Evanston Illinois or Evanston Wyoming?

4. Beth was born on November 26 1976 in Wheeling Illinois.

5. We went to Hershey Pennsylvania and Bethesda Maryland to visit our relatives.

6. Luanne and Carrie visited their grandparents in Orlando Florida and then flew to Atlanta Georgia to see their sister.

7. My brother goes to Knox College in Galesburg Illinois and my sister goes to Michigan State University in East Lansing Michigan.

8. The tour to Mexico will leave December 26 1979 and will return January 3 1980.

9. Because my parents worked for the government, we have lived in Tokyo Japan and Anchorage Alaska.

10. On October 28 1886 the Statue of Liberty was dedicated as a national monument.

I. Use semicolons and colons correctly.

Copy the word before and after the missing punctuation mark and add the correct punctuation mark.

1. The following students will please report to the office Meg Francis, Steve Jonas, and Pam Mead.

2. Patti goes to the dentist tonight Peter will go on Saturday.

3. Call me before 230 P. M. tomorrow.

4. We need these items poster board, magic markers, and spray paint.

5. Please call these players and tell them practice has been canceled Joan, Katie, Pat, and Karen.

6. We went to the movies they went roller skating.

7. The mail should arrive between 1230 P. M. and 115 P. M.

8. When the alarm sounded at 6 45 A. M., I was not ready to face the day.

9. Be sure to bring these materials to sewing class tomorrow your pattern, material, thread, scissors, and a zipper.

10. The bus leaves promptly at 330 P. M.

J. Use hyphens correctly.

Copy the words that need hyphens and add the hyphens.

1. A three fifths majority is needed to win this election.
2. We won four fifths of all the votes cast.
3. My sister's four cylinder Mustang gets great gas mileage.
4. My brother in law is a medical technologist.
5. Jason found that he had only thirty two cents left.
6. My great grandparents are from Germany.
7. My parents have their own ten speed bicycles.
8. She's a little known artist, but her work is very good.
9. Jenny was ninety nine percent sure that the plan would work.
10. Is today the twenty third or the twenty fourth?

K. Form the plurals and possessives of nouns correctly.

On a piece of paper, write the plural form of each of the following nouns. After the plural form, write the plural possessive for each noun.

1. prince
2. chairperson
3. woman
4. actress
5. manager
6. editor
7. engineer
8. party
9. typist
10. technologist
11. secretary
12. mechanic
13. staff
14. studio
15. plumber
16. parent
17. family
18. pilot
19. teller
20. designer

L. Use apostrophes correctly.

Copy the following sentences, inserting apostrophes where they are needed.

1. Theres a new rock group in town tonight. Lets go to their concert.

2. Leslies bike was stolen, so shell have to walk to school tomorrow.

3. My mothers not home yet. Ill bet she had to work late.

4. The 1960s were exciting, but I dont think Id want to live through them again.

5. Whos going to walk the dog? Its not my turn.

6. Hed better be careful with that plant. Its Ms. Jamess favorite.

7. Theyll leave us alone if were quiet.

8. I cant tell your *es* and *is* apart.

9. Wont you tell me whats wrong? Youre so quiet.

10. Ill go if theyre going, too. Itll be fun.

M. Use quotation marks correctly.

Copy and punctuate the following sentences.

1. Where can we get some kite string asked Paula

2. We have a garden in the back yard said Jane

3. Ellen asked Does it always rain so much here

4. Wow exclaimed Joe That helicopter ride was exciting

5. It's three o'clock said Mrs. Barrett We'd better start home.

6. Meg said John and Amy this is Mr. and Mrs. Holliday.

7. The airport and its runways are closed repeated the radio announcer.

8. If we don't panic said Marcia calmly we'll find our way out.

9. Did you ask Alan if he wanted to come along asked Chris

10. Bret said that she was an excellent teacher Roberta added

N. Punctuate conversations correctly.

Rewrite the following conversation. Make correct paragraph divisions and use correct capitalization and punctuation.

I feel marvelous exclaimed Mr. Zim to his wife as he fastened his seatbelt I can't believe that I have been afraid to fly all these years just sit back and relax said Mrs. Zim as she fastened her own seatbelt soon we will be in Hawaii after a while Mr. Zim excitedly remarked how silly I have been there's nothing to it this is the smoothest ride I have ever experienced I feel as safe and secure as I do on the ground no wonder replied Mrs. Zim as she looked out her window we haven't left it yet.

Section 12

Spelling

Being a good speller doesn't just happen. It takes practice, and you have to learn a few simple rules. If you do have trouble spelling, you may be relieved to know that generations of students have shared the same difficulty. Those students have had to learn to overcome their weaknesses. You can, too.

Although there is no simple way to teach you how to spell, there are several methods you can use to attack your spelling problems. These methods of attack are discussed in this chapter.

It is important to have good spelling skills. You will use these skills when you write reports for school. You will use them when you write friendly letters and business letters, and you will use them when you fill out a job application. If you care what others think of you, you will need to be able to spell words correctly.

A General Method of Attack on Spelling

1. Find out what your personal spelling demons are and conquer them. Go over your old composition papers and make a list of the words you misspelled on them. Keep this list and master the words on it.

2. Pronounce words carefully. It may be that you misspell words because you don't pronounce them carefully. For example, if you write *probly* for *probably*, you are no doubt mispronouncing the word.

3. Get into the habit of seeing the letters in a word. Many people have never really looked at the word *similar*. Otherwise, why do they write it *similiar?*

Take a good look at new words, or difficult words. You'll remember them better. Copy the correct spelling several times.

4. Think up a memory device for difficult words. Here are some devices that have worked for other people. They may help you, either to spell these words or to make up your own memory devices.

> **acq**uaint (*cq*) To get **acq**uainted, I will *seek you*.
> princi**pal** (*pal*) The princi**pal** is my *pal*.
> princi**ple** (*ple*) Follow this princi**ple**, please.
> bus**i**ness (*i*) I was involved in big bus**i**ness.

5. Proofread everything you write. In order to learn how to spell, you must learn to examine critically everything you write.

To proofread a piece of writing, you must read it slowly, word for word. Otherwise, your eyes may play tricks on you and let you skip over misspelled words.

6. Learn the few important spelling rules given in this chapter.

A Method of Attack on Particular Words

1. **Look at the word and say it to yourself.** Be sure you pronounce it correctly. If it has more than one syllable, say it again, one syllable at a time. Look at each syllable as you say it.

2. **Look at the letters and say each one.** If the word has more than one syllable, divide the word into syllables when you say the letters.

3. **Write the word without looking at your book or list.**

4. **Now look at your book or list and see whether you spelled the word correctly.** If you did, write it again and compare it with the correct form again. Do this once more.

5. **If you made a mistake, note exactly what it was.** Then repeat 3 and 4 above until you have written the word correctly three times.

Rules for Spelling

The Final silent e

When a suffix beginning with a vowel is added to a word ending in a silent e, the e is usually dropped.

relate + ion = relation   believe + ing = believing
amaze + ing = amazing   create + ive = creative
fame + ous = famous   continue + ing = continuing

When a suffix beginning with a consonant is added to a word ending in a silent e, the e is usually retained.

hope + ful = hopeful   waste + ful = wasteful
state + ment = statement   move + ment = movement
noise + less = noiseless   wide + ly = widely

The following words are exceptions:

truly   argument   judgment   ninth   wholly

Words Ending in y

When a suffix is added to a word ending in y preceded by a consonant, the y is usually changed to i.

easy + ly = easily   happy + ness = happiness
sixty + eth = sixtieth   clumsy + ly = clumsily
city + es = cities   marry + age = marriage

Note the following exception: When -ing is added, the y does not change:

hurry + ing = hurrying   worry + ing = worrying
study + ing = studying   copy + ing = copying

When a suffix is added to a word ending in y preceded by a vowel, the y usually does not change.

enjoy + ed = enjoyed   play + ing = playing
employ + er = employer   destroy + er = destroyer

Exercises **Words and their suffixes.**

A. Find the misspelled words in these sentences and spell them correctly.

1. Our class is competeing in the state science fair.
2. The magician's performance was truely amazeing.
3. My brother and I had an argument about rakeing the leaves.
4. The nurse placed the baby carfully on her shoulder.
5. By the seventh inning, the game was hopless for our team.
6. The troop leaders are arrangeing chairs for tonight's scout meeting.
7. The dareing circus performers walked easyly across the tightrope.
8. My grandparents were gratful for the pictures we sent them.
9. The chef's createion looked terrific but tasted awful.
10. It was truly exciteing to meet the actors and actresses backstage.

B. Add the suffixes as shown and write the new word.

1. silly + ness
2. messy + est
3. twenty + eth
4. marry + ing
5. crazy + ly
6. relay + ed
7. spray + ing
8. beauty + ful
9. glory + ous
10. hasty + ly
11. play + ful
12. supply + ing
13. employ + ment
14. fly + er
15. lazy + er
16. dirty + est
17. fancy + ful
18. study + ous
19. enjoy + able
20. pretty + er

The Addition of Prefixes

When a prefix is added to a word, the spelling of the word remains the same.

mis + spell = misspell   mis + pronounce = mispronounce
il + legal = illegal   im + perfect = imperfect
im + mobile = immobile   dis + approve = disapprove
pre + record = prerecord   ir + regular = irregular

The Suffixes -*ness* and -*ly*

When the suffix -*ly* is added to a word ending in *l*, both *l*'s are retained. When -*ness* is added to a word ending in *n*, both *n*'s are retained.

actual + ly = actually   thin + ness = thinness
real + ly = really   even + ness = evenness

Exercise **Words with prefixes and suffixes.**

Find the misspelled words in these sentences and spell them correctly.

1. The owner is disatisfied with the people who live upstairs.
2. We received a thoughtfuly written thank-you note.
3. In English class we are learning about iregular verbs.
4. The uneveness of our sidewalk makes skateboarding dangerous.
5. We were practicaly finished eating when it began to rain.
6. Our car is parked legally, but yours is in an ilegal space.
7. My ceramic vase is slightly mishapen.
8. Scrooge's meaness was replaced by kindness and charity.
9. Dr. Martin's handwriting is almost ilegible.
10. I mispelled two words in my essay because I misspronounced them.

Words with the "Seed" Sound

Only one English word ends in *sede: supersede.*
Three words end in *ceed: exceed, proceed, succeed.*
All other words ending in the sound of *seed* are spelled *cede:*

concede   precede   recede   secede

Words with *ie* and *ei*

When the sound is long *e* (*ē*), the word is spelled *ie* except after *c.*

I Before E

believe   shield   yield   fierce
niece   brief   field   pier

Except After C

receive   ceiling   perceive   deceit
conceive   conceit   receipt

The following words are exceptions:

either   weird   species
neither   seize   leisure

Exercise   Words with the "Seed" Sound and Words with *ie* and *ei*

Find the misspelled words in these sentences and spell them correctly.

1. Bicycle riders should yeild the right of way to pedestrians.

2. The Student Council will procede with its plans for a dance.

3. I lost the reciept for the hockey equipment I rented.

4. My mother's salary excedes that of many people in her office.

5. There are wads of paper on the cieling of the gym locker room.

6. The doctor gave me a prescription to releive my pain.

7. Niether Missouri nor Kentucky seceded from the the Union during the Civil War.

8. My aunt bakes special cookies for all her neices and nephews.

9. The playing feild was too wet for the game to proceed.

10. The candidate did conceed the victory to her opponent.

Doubling the Final Consonant

Words of one syllable, ending in one consonant preceded by one vowel, double the final consonant before adding -ing, -ed, or -er.

bat + ed = batted   bed + ing = bedding
get + ing = getting   grab + ed = grabbed
big + er = bigger   slim + er = slimmer

put + ing = putting
run + er = runner
run + ing = running

The following words do not double the final consonant because *two* vowels precede the final consonant:

treat + ing = treating   loot + ed = looted
feel + ing = feeling   near + er = nearer

Exercise **Doubling the Final Consonant**

Add the suffixes as shown and write the new word.

1. dig + ing   5. pair + ed
2. fear + ing   6. win + er
3. fat + er   7. split + ing
4. slap + ed   8. drop + ed

9. roar + ed 15. dim + er
10. let + ing 16. slug + er
11. hop + ing 17. swim + ing
12. bat + er 18. trap + ed
13. creep + ing 19. scream + ing
14. wrap + ed 20. pat + ing

Words Often Confused

accept means to agree to something or to receive something willingly.

except means to exclude or omit. As a preposition, *except* means "but" or "excluding."

> Kay did *accept* the Hansens' invitation to go camping with them.
> The seventh grade will be *excepted* from locker inspection this week.
> Everyone *except* the team and the cheerleaders will sit in the bleachers.

all ready expresses a complete readiness or preparedness.

already means previously or before.

> The pilots and their crew were *all ready* for the landing.
> We had *already* made arrangements to take the early train.

capital means excellent, most serious, or most important.

capitol is a building in which a state legislature meets.

the Capitol is the building in Washington, D. C., in which the United States Congress meets.

> The thief had previously been arrested for a *capital* offense.
> The committee held a special meeting at the *capitol* building.
> We visited the *Capitol* in Washington, D. C., last summer.

des′ert means a wilderness or dry, sandy region with sparse, scrubby vegetation.

de·sert′ means to abandon.

dessert (note the change in spelling) is a sweet, such as cake or pie, served at the end of a meal.

> The Mojave *Desert* is part of the Great American Desert in southern California.
> When we ran out of fuel, we *deserted* our car to find a gas station.
> Jon and Sue baked a strawberry pie for *dessert*.

hear means to listen to, or take notice of.

here means in this place.

> Because of poor acoustics, we couldn't *hear* the speaker.
> We finally arrived *here* in Seattle after a flight delay in Denver.

its is a word that indicates ownership.

it's is a contraction for *it is* or *it has*.

> The city lost *its* power during the thunderstorm.
> *It's* almost noon and I haven't finished my work.

lead (lēd) means to go first.

led (lĕd) is the past tense of *lead*.

lead (lĕd) is a heavy, silvery-blue metal.

> A circus wagon pulled by Clydesdale horses will *lead* the parade.
> This wagon has *led* the parade for many years.
> *Lead* is one of the heaviest metals, yet it melts at a very low temperature.

lose means to mislay or suffer the loss of something.

loose means free or not fastened.

Our car began to *lose* some of its power as we reached the summit of Pike's Peak.

The hinges on the back gate are quite *loose*.

past refers to that which has ended or gone by.

passed is the past tense of *pass* and means went by.

Our *past* experience with that team has taught us to use a different defense.

We *passed* through the Grand Tetons on our vacation last summer.

piece refers to a section or part of something.

peace means calm or quiet and freedom from disagreements or quarrels.

We cut the lumber into several smaller *pieces* in order to build the bookshelves.

There was a certain *peace* as I sat and watched the sunrise.

plane is a flat, level surface or a carpenter's tool.

plain means clearly understood, simple, or ordinary. It can also refer to an expanse of land.

In geometry, we learned how to measure many kinds of *planes*.

In shop, we used a *plane* to smooth and level the boards.

Driving through Kansas, you see farms scattered across the *plains*.

principal describes something of chief or central importance. It also refers to the head of an elementary or high school.

principle is a basic truth, standard, or rule of behavior.

The *principal* cities of France include Paris, Marseilles, Lyons, and Nice.

The *principal* of our school presented the awards at the assembly.

We will study the *principles* of democracy in our American government class.

quiet refers to no noise or to something rather peaceful or motionless.

quite means really or truly, and it can also refer to a considerable degree or extent.

> Everyone was absolutely *quiet* during the graduation ceremony.
> We were *quite* sure that the school bus would be late.

stationary means fixed or unmoving.

stationery refers to paper and envelopes used for writing letters.

> The new digital scoreboard will be *stationary* in the large gym.
> Two students in my art class designed the school *stationery*.

there means in that place.

their means belonging to them.

they're is a contraction for *they are*.

> Please put the groceries over *there* on the counter.
> In 1803, the explorers Lewis and Clark led *their* expedition to the western United States.
> Sue and Pam are skiing and *they're* going snowmobiling, too.

to means toward, or in the direction of.

too means also or very.

two is the number 2.

> We all went *to* the zoo last weekend.
> It was much *too* cold to go cross-country skiing.
> *Two* television stations carried the President's speech.

weather refers to atmospheric conditions such as temperature or cloudiness.

whether helps to express choice or alternative.

> Daily *weather* reports are studied by meteorologists.
> *Whether* we call or write for reservations, we must do it soon.

whose is the possessive form of *who*.

who's is a contraction for *who is* or *who has*.

> Do you know *whose* bicycle is chained to the parking meter?
> *Who's* going to volunteer to help at the children's Christmas party?

your is the possessive form of *you*.

you're is a contraction of *you are*.

> Please take *your* books back to the library today.
> *You're* going there right after school, aren't you?

Exercises   Words Often Confused

A. Choose the right word from the words in parentheses.

1. All of the players (accept, except) the goalie were involved in the argument.

2. The refreshments are (all ready, already) for the parent-teacher meeting.

3. Be sure to check your paper for the correct use of (capital, capitol) letters.

4. This is no time to (desert, dessert) our baseball team!

5. We ran out of gas while crossing the (desert, dessert).

6. The weather (hear, here) has been extremely cold.

7. (It's, Its) hard to remember certain dates in American history.

8. Our puppy wags (it's, its) tail as soon as I enter the room.

9. Theodore Roosevelt (lead, led) the charge up San Juan Hill.

10. A drum majorette will (lead, led) the marching band.

11. The latch on the door is (lose, loose) and needs to be fixed.

12. Every winter I (lose, loose) at least two pairs of gloves.

13. This (past, passed) year I had a special tutor to help me in math.

14. Three summers have (past, passed) since I went away to camp.

15. Loretta has (already, all ready) decided that she wants to be a veterinarian.

B. Choose the right word from the words in parentheses.

1. The Treaty of Versailles established (piece, peace).

2. Would you like to try a (piece, peace) of pecan pie?

3. The carpenter used a (plane, plain) to even the top of the door.

4. We studied the (principles, principals) of government in social studies.

5. The (principle, principal) actors took their bows.

6. I am (quiet, quite) nervous about going to high school.

7. I received a letter from the mayor on her official (stationery, stationary).

8. Our neighbors never let (their, there) cat out at night.

9. (They're, There) widening Main Street to provide more parking places.

10. That movie was (to, too) funny for words.

11. If the (weather, whether) permits, we will have a picnic.

12. The police officer wondered (whose, who's) fingerprints were on the door.

13. (Whose, Who's) making all that noise?

14. Call us when (your, you're) ready.

15. The coach says (your, you're) the best hitter on the team.

Index

Sources of Quoted Materials

Illustrations

83 84 85 86 87 / 9 8 7 6 5 4 3 2 1